The Port of
Medieval
London

The Port of
Medieval London

Gustav Milne

TEMPUS

First published 2003

PUBLISHED IN THE UNITED KINGDOM BY:
Tempus Publishing Ltd
The Mill, Brimscombe Port
Stroud, Gloucestershire GL5 2QG

PUBLISHED IN THE UNITED STATES OF AMERICA BY:
Tempus Publishing Inc.
420 Wando Park Boulevard
Mount Pleasant, SC 29464

British Library Cataloguing in Publication Data.
A catalogue record for this book is available from the British Library.

ISBN 0 7524 2544 7

Typesetting and origination by Tempus Publishing.
Printed in Great Britain by Midway Colour Print, Wiltshire.

CONTENTS

ACKNOWLEDGEMENTS

A book that claims to summarise a thirty-year excavation programme must inevitably pay homage to a veritable army of archaeologists and historians whose work in muddy trenches, laboratories or libraries provided the source material upon which I have drawn so heavily. There is simply not space to name them all – the following brief list of archaeologists from the Museum of London stands as a record of the particular debt owed to the field teams led by Julian Ayre, Dick Bluer, Trevor Brigham, Bob Cowie, Geoff Egan, Peter Ellis, Charlotte Harding, Chris Harrison, Dick Malt, Peter Marsden, Bill McCann, Louise Miller, Steve Roskams, John Schofield, Ken Steedman, Jo Stevenson, Bruce Watson and Robin Wroe-Brown, not forgetting Tim Tatton-Brown who introduced me to waterfront excavations fully thirty years ago. The unstinting weekend labours of the City of London Archaeological Society on those Thames-side sites is also warmly recognised.

The research of specialists such as Lynn Blackmore, Geoff Egan, Damian Goodburn, Clive Orton, Jane Liddel, Alison Locker, Jacqui Pearce, Frances Pritchard and Alan Vince has been extensively utilised, as has the documentary research produced by the Centre for Metropolitan History and by the London Record Society. The Museum's Archaeological Archive team, including John Shepherd and Cath Maloney, also provided valuable information while the debt to scholars from previous generations who worked on the records held by the Corporation of London remains undiminished.

Of the illustrations produced specifically for this book, most were expertly prepared by Jenny Stripe, with some by Kitty Brandon, while the elegant reconstructions of the port were by Chris Unwin, based on work initially produced for Andy Topping now of the new Museum in Docklands. Help with the photographic images was supplied by Ken Walton (UCL) and Andy Chopping (MoLAS). As the credits in the captions show, the Museum of London supplied the lion's share of the images, with others provided by the Ashmolean Museum, the British Library, Guildhall Library, the Thames Archaeological Survey and the Museum of London Archaeology Service. I am most grateful to all those bodies, and to the London Archaeological Research Facility for its support of the project.

Research for the book was ably assisted by Melody Nazworth (Cumberland College), useful references were provided by Helen Clark (UCL), Nathalie Cohen (Thames Archaeological Survey), Damian Goodburn (Museum of London), and Maryanne Kowaleski (Fordham University), while inspiration and support was also provided by colleagues and inquisitive students at University College London. Insightful comments on a draft of the text were kindly provided by John Clark for the Museum of London and particularly by Tony Dyson. I have tried to incorporate their most helpful suggestions whenever possible, but omissions, misinterpretations and inaccuracies remain my responsibility. Finally, the patience of the publishers, Peter Kemmis Betty and Emma Parkin, is gratefully recognised.

I hope this book reflects some of the largely untapped potential that the Herculean labours of London's waterfront archaeologists have recorded. It is intended as an introduction to a new study of the City's medieval maritime archaeology. If, therefore, it encourages the writing of a better book, or even a series of such studies, then that will more than justify pumping out all that water, digging up all that peat, drawing all those timbers and washing all those finds.

1

PROLOGUE

The Thames was the cause

The significance of the river to the medieval city is unambiguously stated in the fifteenth-century *Liber Albus* (Riley 1861), which declares that London was founded 'in the year from the beginning of the world 4032 . . . of which foundation, building and construction, the Thames was the cause'. Although latter-day archaeologists might dispute the dating, none would question the overriding importance of the river to the development, prosperity and independence of the city. Londoners long claimed governance of both the town and the Thames. It was during the later medieval period that this town grew to be the largest in the land. Certainly by the thirteenth century it had established itself as the principal port in the kingdom, head and shoulders above its rivals. Its success was founded in no small part on its position on the tidal Thames (**1**), the broad river that could carry ships from the North Sea up to London on an incoming tide, and return them to the estuary as it ebbed. When the Elizabethan antiquary John Stow described the City's location, he commented: 'if it were removed more to the west it should lose the benefit of the ebbing and flowing, and if it were seated more towards the east, it should be nearer to danger of the enemy' (Wheatley 1956, 486). He also added that London's inland location helped it to service a wide hinterland, benefiting much of 'the inner parts of the realm', and provided 'good air' when compared with that in the marshy lower estuary.

This new study is not just about the harbour which John Stow would have known as a child in the early sixteenth century, or the Plantagenet port in which one Geoffrey Chaucer worked as controller of customs in the late fourteenth century, but how it developed from its beach-market origins in the seventh century into the New World of the Tudor era. What did the harbour upon which the wealth of the capital depended look like? How did it change as the town, its merchants and their ships changed during that long period? This book addresses some of these questions, presenting a new study of the maritime archaeology and topography of the medieval harbour that sustained London for close on a thousand years.

The workings of the medieval harbour have not always received the attention they deserve. In Joseph Broodbank's *History of the Port of London*, published in 1921 to celebrate the opening of the Port of London Authority's new head quarters on Tower Hill, the pre-Elizabethan period merits a mere 48 of the 512-page survey. More recent studies of the port undertaken by economic historians have been able to make wider use of such documentary

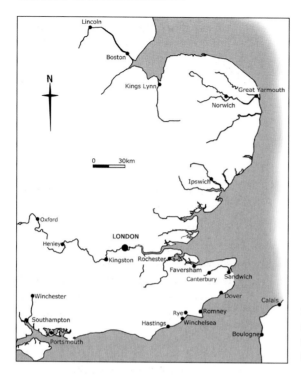

1 *The port of London, set at the head of the Thames estuary, shown in relation to other medieval ports and towns referred to in the text.* J. Stripe, London ARF

data as has survived. These include contemporary accounts that, written in the patois of the port, open a window on a world in which manufactured goods and raw material were counted and costed, listed and loaded, bought and sold. There is an unintentional poetry about the petty customs accounts returned by the likes of Chaucer and his successors as they recorded:

> a dry vat with 11,000 grey skins, 1 straw of wax weight 10 quintals; 2 hogsheads with 600 lampreys; 2 lasts of herring; 3 sacks of hemp; 16 quarters of wheat; 1 firkin of green ginger; 160 goads of cotton russet, 3 cloves of wool, 1 maund with 2 rolls of Osnabruck, 17 barrels of Corinth raisins, 1 hogshead with 23 dozen spurs, 6 dog stones, 4 vats of Cologne woad, 6 tuns, 1 pipe and 5 roods of wine, 308 cases of sugar (of which 30 are powdered); 1 chest with 32 diverse histories; 6 gross of spectacle cases; 10 dozen puppets; 2 chess boards and a feather bed (Cobb 1990).

To that rich vein can be added the results of a 30-year programme of extensive excavations on the London waterfront. Here on a wide range of well-preserved waterlogged sites, the changing face of the ancient harbour has been revealed in the most remarkable detail. This evidence is of great significance in its own right, but also provides a fresh perspective that allows the documentary data related to the development of the port to be reviewed and reassessed. The resulting picture is a vivid reconstruction of the working port of London, that dynamic engine of the medieval economy. The topographical history of waterfront development, from an uncluttered open foreshore to an intensively-developed set of wharves and warehouses, mirrors the City's progress from beach market to merchant port. The physical evidence of this crucial economic and social change has now been plotted with precision by archaeologists recording the long pattern of waterfront encroachment.

A conflict of agencies

Although we now know that the Plantagenet port was hailed as 'the Chief of the Realm', its path to pre-eminence was neither straightforward nor pre-ordained. London was not always the royal and commercial capital; before the bridge was built in c.1000, it was not always the nodal focus of communications in south-east England; it was not always set below the tidal head of the Thames. There was a time when Winchester was the English 'capital', and when English kings were buried in France in preference to Westminster, and when Boston ranked as the nation's premier port. There was even a time when the Thames was not tidal in London's reach and when there was no bridge below Oxford. Indeed, the scale of London's ultimate success as a port was as unforeseen in the tenth century as it was unimagined in the seventh.

The agents and agencies that shaped its history were as much in conflict as in conjunction. London suffered many fires, enemy invasion and occupation, civil wars, debilitating famines and plagues the occurrence of which were often unpredicted, the results unpredictable. The crown was not always at one with the town: the City was not always able to determine its own governance or its own fate. Initially at least, the sweep and cycles of wider European history had more influence on the port than it had on them. The relationship of London to its changing hinterlands, to other English ports, to alien merchants and moneylenders, was not consistent. There were tensions between the city's oligarchy and other elements of the citizenry, between waterfront property owners, tenants and commoners, between private wharves and public access. Even the Thames itself was by no means a pliant or passive agent: it could (and did) flood, swamping the wharves and sweeping away the bridge on more than one occasion. There were major structural and technical challenges to resolve before the harbour could service the port in the manner to which it needed to become accustomed.

A new study

The story of London's port reflects this chaotic genesis. For the purposes of this book then, our 1,000-year study will be presented through five thematic studies set alongside eight chronological chapters reflecting the more readily-identifiable major changes. Indeed, our book is best seen not as an examination of just one long-lived port, but of *ports* in the plural, so profound were some of the changes experienced. Our first phase covers the period from *c*.600 to 900 (chapter 3), when the Saxon port of Lundenwic lay to the west of the abandoned site of Roman Londinium. The settlement and its harbour were dramatically shifted eastwards, back inside the Roman town walls in *c*.AD 900, in part at least a response to the Viking raids, as described in the second phase (chapter 4). The third phase is marked by the construction of the first medieval timber bridge over London's river in *c*.AD 1000, a significant event marking another eastwards shift in the harbour's focus in a period which sees London fall first to Danish and then Norman overlords (chapter 5). The fourth phase sees the transition from a beach market to a merchant port, a major development that closes the Saxon story and opens the new chapter on the later medieval merchant port (chapter 6). The bridge is one of the key factors in the port's development, and its reconstruction in stone between 1176 and 1209 clearly reflects further changes described in the study of the thirteenth-century port (chapters 7 & 8). The Hundred Years War and the terrible visitation of the Black Death in the mid-fourteenth century changed the trajectory of the medieval port, town and nation, as chapter 10 shows. The fifteenth century was, in the main, one of gradual recovery in spite of political upheaval and dynastic change (chapter 12). Aspects of the fishing industry (chapter 9), harbour construction (chapter 11) and shipbuilding (chapter 13) are also examined, but are treated thematically rather than strictly chronologically.

Our study ends with the Reformation and the Dissolution of London's monastic houses from 1520 to 1540, events which signal a profound break with the late medieval attitude to religion and a sudden redistribution of land and wealth. This final phase also saw the gradual opening up of the New World, as well as a reform of the customs and of the port itself. Early Elizabethan London, with its new markets, new ship types and new brick-built customs house, represents a port which owed its success as much to the firm foundation upon which it was built as to the novel opportunities it so keenly exploited. Thus the port reorganisation and surveys of 1558/9, at a time when tobacco had just been introduced to Europe, will be taken as the end-date for our study.

A number of inter-relating themes are therefore considered in this volume: archaeological, topographical, economic, environmental, nautical and artefactual. The results of those considerations are presented broadly chronologically and viewed alongside summaries of some of the principal published sources for London's medieval history. The result hopes to provide an integrated view of the material history of the harbour, set in its social and topographical context.

Today, little survives on London's riverside walkway to remind City workers, tourists or even archaeologists of the harbour that served the medieval town. However, there is a tangible memorial to the Plantagenet port in the wealth of port-related place-names such as the Vintry, Garlickhithe, Timberhithe, Wool Quay, Galley Quay, the Ropery, Hay Wharf, Salt Wharf, Fish Street Hill or Friday Street. This book is a rediscovered history of those half-forgotten names.

2

ARCHAEOLOGY
OF A MEDIEVAL PORT

The chronology of discovery

Where was London's medieval harbour? Sections of the medieval waterfront walling can still be seen at Westminster and on Tower beach, but the last fragment of the medieval waterfront to remain visible at foreshore level in the City itself, the footings of the fifteenth-century riverwall at Baynard's Castle, succumbed to the pressures of commercial redevelopment in 1890 (MacMichael 1890, 173). By then a complex of multi-storey warehouses on a series of privately-owned wharves dominated the working waterfront. Nevertheless, for those with eyes to see, the excavations for the associated building foundations and new sewers provided further opportunities to observe elements of the medieval port. In 1848 Sir William Tite reported that:

> . . . there is abundant evidence of the care and skill anciently employed for the substantial support of the haven, and even for the gaining of ground from the river in the construction of quays; thus strengthening the view already expressed, that the commercial convenience of the City as a port was always regarded as an object of the first importance.

He had been able to deduce that nearly all the land south of Upper and Lower Thames Street (the road which runs parallel to, but some 100m north of the River) 'had been gained from the river by a series of strong embankments' (Tite 1848, xxiii-xxiv). For example, work on the new Custom House site at Wool Quay between 1813 and 1817 revealed 'three distinct lines of wooden embankment' as well as a river wall faced with Purbeck stone (Laing 1818, 5-6), while the insertion of a sewer in Water Lane, to the west of the City, exposed a post and plank revetment in 1849 (RCHM 1928, 148). In 1890 it was even reported that the remains of a 'mysterious ship' has been seen below the floor of the new Pilkingtons warehouse (MacMichael 1890, 174).

It was therefore clear that there had been substantial encroachment on the London waterfront, but it was not known precisely when, how or why that process began. However, in 1905 F. Hilton-Price recorded a feature which he thought was a medieval river wall midway between Thames Street and the modern riverfront. He also made the astute observation that very few Roman artefacts were recovered north of that alignment, and none at all south of it, while the lack of finds of a date later than the end of the sixteenth century suggested that the site must have been built over by that time. During the building of Adelaide Place in 1921 a substantial section of the northern-most arch of the medieval stone bridge was revealed, and in 1937 the eastern end of cutwater of the second pier was exposed when New Fresh Wharf was under construction. Both those sites were set well behind the modern river wall, demonstrating that the waterfront had been advanced riverwards since 1176 (Watson et al. 2001, 170). In the early 1960s, Roman river gravels had been identified at Dowgate by the Guildhall Museum, while borehole data had been studied and the natural river bank had finally been located at the foot of Lambeth Hill by Professor Grimes (Grimes 1968, 57-64).

Thus it could be suggested that virtually all the land south of Thames Street had been won from the river during the post-Roman period. Part of the lost port could now be located: it lay beneath the Victorian warehouses occupying a vast area some 2km east-west by 100m north-south. The excavation of the early sixteenth-century river frontage on the Whitehall palace site well to the west of the City in 1938-9 and again in 1950 demonstrated how deeply stratified and how well-preserved such waterfront sites could be (Thurley 1999). The question in 1960 was would the City archaeologists have sufficient resources and time to conduct the deep and detailed excavations necessary to record their ancient harbour?

The answer was, at first, a resounding 'no'. The City had suffered terrible bomb damage during the Blitz of 1940-1; now it needed to rebuild itself and get back to business. In 1969, the provision for archaeology in the nation's capital was at an all time low: one fully-stretched archaeological officer and an all too rapidly increasing programme of large scale redevelopment. The digging of the deep foundations for the new buildings destroyed the archaeological remains, usually without being recorded and often without even being seen. One of the major projects conducted at the time was the construction of a new river wall on the western part of the City waterfront, between Blackfriars and Trig Lane (**colour plates 1** & **2**). A Roman ship had been discovered and hastily recorded in 1962 during the first phase of this development (a rare and important discovery), clearly demonstrating the archaeological potential of the London waterfront (Marsden 1994). However, there was no adequate monitoring of the river wall project, as it progressed eastwards.

All this stands in stark contrast to the position in other European countries. In Germany, when a late medieval wreck was discovered in the River Weser in 1962, all the timbers were carefully retrieved and conserved: the reconstructed *Cog* is now proudly on display in the maritime museum in

2 *The wreck of a late medieval river barge recorded within a cofferdam during the rebuilding of the waterfront near Trig Stairs in 1970.* Blackfriars III, Museum of London

Bremerhaven. In Denmark in the same period, no fewer than five medieval wrecks were excavated, lifted and conserved: these were then displayed in the award-winning Viking Ship museum in Roskilde, officially opened by King Frederik IX on 20 June 1969 (Olsen *et al.* 1995, 42).

Just five days later on the London waterfront, there was a rather different response when another vessel was rudely exposed by the mechanical excavators on 25 June. It was left to a group of dedicated volunteers to record the remains as best they could before the vessel was broken up. Later analysis showed that it was a river barge, carrying a cargo of bricks for the rebuilding of London after the Great Fire of 1666. The lessons had still not been learned by 25 November the following year, when the mechanical grab ripped up part of a late medieval barge near Trig Stairs (**2**). Just three days (and no funding) were made available to record the vessel. The following week, on 1 December yet another medieval wreck was encountered: Peter Marsden records that 'unfortunately there was no time to excavate and little time to clean and record this new find' (Marsden 1996, 105). It was simply sketched, photographed and discarded. The history of the harbour deserved better than this: there was no political will and no public campaign to match the one that so dramatically saved the medieval Newport Ship in Wales in 2002.

But attitudes were slowly changing. The lead came from the south bank, where the Southwark and Lambeth Archaeological Excavation Committee mounted a series of rescue excavations on the Toppings Wharf from 1970-2 (Sheldon 1974). This work recorded Roman occupation levels on part of the site but also clear evidence of later flooding and erosion together with later medieval waterfront features including part of a timber jetty. As this work was drawing to a close in 1972, a major rescue excavation was mounted by the Guildhall Museum team on the Baynard's Castle site, at the western end of the City waterfront (**colour plate 3**). The well-preserved façade of a late-medieval building together with deeply stratified waterlogged deposits of medieval date were recovered in what was intended to be a five-month excavation. Then the work schedule was dramatically curtailed to just one month. On the final weekend, the Easter bank holiday, the last desperate salvage excavations were recorded in full view of the public and the national press. The resulting furore led to questions in the House of Commons as well as within the Corporation of London. One consequence was that a full-time professional archaeological unit was set up in the City in December 1973. The new team would adopt much of the agenda set out by Martin Biddle in his influential *Future of London's Past*. This report, much affected by the Baynard's Castle affair, declared that:

> . . . the history of the waterfront is critical for all periods of London's archaeology . . . here lie the wharves and jetties . . . and even the wrecks of ships and their cargoes. The depth of the archaeological deposits along the waterfront is considerable, and they are still remarkably undamaged by comparison with other areas of the City . . . the waterlogged nature of the deposits still surviving will have a major contribution to make to a knowledge of London's trade connexions at home and abroad, her manufactures, and the details of her daily life in the medieval period (Biddle 1973 4.14; 4.51).

These prophetic statements in no way overstate the case; that urban waterfront sites were richly endowed was already clear from work in Bergen (Norway), an influential report on which had been published as long ago as 1959 (Herteig 1959). The universality of well-preserved waterfront encroachment was duly confirmed by projects in England at Plymouth (1963-9) and King's Lynn (1964) for example (Milne & Hobley 1981). Indeed, while the *Future of London's Past* was in the press in the summer of 1973, the Guildhall Museum mounted another waterfront excavation, this time on the site of the Old Custom House, close by the Tower. Having watched the work at Baynard's Castle the previous year, this time I decided to join in. We found the well-preserved remains of a Roman quay, medieval timber-faced wharves standing 2m tall, half a ship and the foundations of the Customs house where one Geoffrey Chaucer served as

Customs controller in the late fourteenth century (Tatton-Brown 1974). I gave up the day job and decided to become an archaeologist.

The new unit, the Museum of London's Department of Urban Archaeology, made the study of the waterfront a priority, not least because much of that zone was suddenly ripe for redevelopment. The waterfront warehouses which had once been such a feature of the working port were rendered obsolete with the adoption of containerisation and the consequent progressive closure of the enclosed docks downstream. Between 1967 and 1981 all the docks were closed from St Katharine's by the Tower to the Royals as far as Beckton. The only docks to survive were at Tilbury, some 25 miles east of the City. It was rather ironic that the dramatic collapse of London as a port (it had once been the largest in the world) provided the unique archaeological opportunity to uncover the full history of the ancient harbour.

In the first 10 years of its hectic life, the Museum's archaeological unit mounted major medieval excavations at sites near Billingsgate and Swan Lane, either side of the medieval bridgehead, and at Trig Lane, Baynard Castle and Puddle Dock sites, at the western end of the waterfront (**colour plates 3 & 4**). When the first phase of the City's rescue archaeology programme ended

3 *The depth of the waterfront stratigraphy is shown here on the Trig Lane site in 1976, where the rear elevation of a superbly preserved mid-fourteenth century riverfront revetment is being recorded. Note the ever-present pump, without which work could simply not progress.* TL 74 Museum of London

with the Billingsgate excavations in 1983, much had been achieved. Many embankments, timber-faced revetments and masonry river walls had been recorded and dated from the eleventh to the fifteenth century, and tonnes of artefacts retrieved. The work had emphatically confirmed the suggestion that the land south of Thames Street had been won from the river in the medieval period (4). A firm chronology for that process of encroachment had been established, using a combination of coin and artefact analysis with the seductive precision of tree-ring dating, or dendrochronology, a technique first introduced to London archaeology in 1973.

But for the archaeologists working on the north bank, two very large questions remained unanswered. Roman quay structures had also been found, but the earliest significant activity on the medieval waterfront could be dated no earlier than the eleventh century; so what had happened to the medieval harbour from AD 500 to 1000? The second problem concerned the bridge; at what date was the first medieval bridge built over the Thames: and where was it? The work was by no means over.

The last question was resolved by excavations on the opposite bank of the Thames, on the Fennings Wharf site in 1983-4, where archaeologists uncovered the abutment of the late twelfth-century stone bridge. Beneath that, evidence for earlier timber bridges was uncovered and subsequently dated back to the early eleventh century (Watson *et al.* 2001). The first questions was resolved

4 *Controlled excavation of a sequence of medieval riverfront encroachments, looking south-west: the fifteenth-century masonry river wall (top) replaced two phases of fourteenth-century timber-faced wharves on the Trig Lane excavations.* Museum of London

5 *Archaeological investigations on the waterfront were often a combination of detailed controlled excavations in some areas, alongside extensive 'watching briefs'. Here the archaeologists watch briefly as the machine bucket removes a twelfth-century wharf timber in 1989*

partially be excavations outside the City in Covent Garden in 1985, which showed that the mid-Saxon town of Lundenwic was established there from AD 600 to 900 (Cowie & Whythead 1989). This was a seismic shift in our understanding of London's development, and opened up a whole new chapter in its archaeological history. Relocation of the settlement accounted for much of the hiatus identified by the work on the City waterfront, but it still left a full century or so unaccounted for, since the Saxons seemed to have left Lundenwic to return to the safety of the old Roman City walls in *c.*AD 900.

The final part of the equation was resolved by the second phase of the City waterfront programme. The last unexcavated section, from Queenhithe to Dowgate, came up for redevelopment from 1988 onwards, and the Museum teams (later known as MoLAS, the Museum of London Archaeology Service, following major reorganisation in 1991), were able to mount another series of major excavations over that period. The work was funded by the developers themselves, which meant that the archaeologists all too often worked alongside the piling rigs and mechanical excavators as the building works progressed (**5**). The results were remarkable, every bit as dramatic as the first phase. Crucially, it was now possible to show that the earliest Saxon waterfront development in the City was not in the area of the later bridgehead (where reason seemed to dictate it should be) but here in the west, in the wards of Queenhithe and Vintry (see **7**).

Meanwhile, beyond the City wall, excavations had sampled the late seventh-century riverfront embankment south of Covent Garden in 1988, while later medieval waterfront sites had been excavated in advance of massive redevelopment projects in Southwark, where the fine Thames-side town-houses belonging to Edward II, Falstoff and the Bishop of Winchester had all been investigated over a ten-year period (Bluer 1993). Later Medieval water-front development associated with the area south of the Strand and west of Fleet had also been studied, with the recent work of Pre-Construct Archaeology on the Whitefriars and Arundel House sites (Proctor 2000).

The enlarging of London (6 & 7)

A building lease for Pakeman's Wharf dated to 1384 records that one Richard Wilson would 'enlarge [the said wharf] Thameswards . . . on his own proper costs' (Salzman 1952, 464). Archaeology has shown that he was not alone in his desire to encroach upon the river. One of the more spectacular features of the medieval waterfront programme was the discovery of so many well-preserved timber or masonry riverfront revetments, as our long list of excava-tions shows. These structures, dating particularly from the twelfth to the fifteenth century, often survived to a height of 2m or so on the north bank, marking stages in the seemingly continuous process of riverward encroachment that was such a pronounced feature of the topographical development of the area between Thames Street and the river. Each new re-facing of the water-front would be erected on the foreshore to the south of the previous frontage,

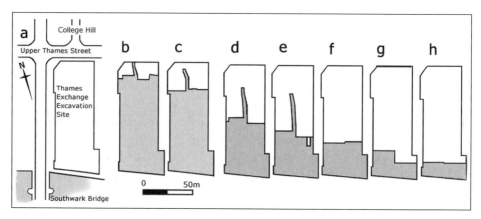

6 *A medieval riverside encroachment sequence, recorded on properties either side of College Hill (Thames Exchange excavations (TEX88) at Three Cranes Wharf). Note the infilling of the inlet in the thirteenth century.* J. Stripe, LARF
KEY A: site location in relation to modern streets; B: late tenth century; C: late eleventh century; D: late twelfth century; E: early thirteenth century; F: mid-thirteenth century; G: late thirteenth century; H: early fourteenth century

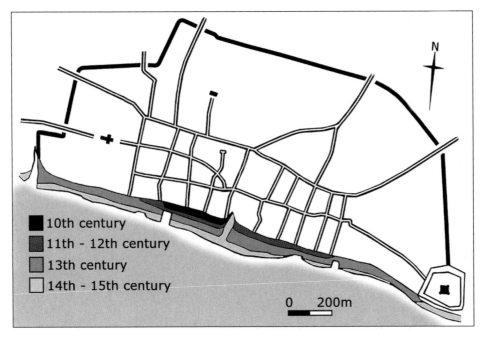

7 *The chronology of medieval riverside encroachment, in relation to the early medieval City street grid and location of St Paul's, Guildhall and the Tower. The earliest waterfront embankments are of tenth-century date, discovered in the Queenhithe/Vintry area, and not in the vicinity of the later bridge.* J. Stripe, LARF

and then the area behind it would be filled up with dumps of contemporary refuse, including much organic material. The distinctive aroma of that peat-based material remains one of the abiding memories of all waterfront archaeologists. Those levels would sometimes be sealed by occupation surfaces, although the footings of later basements often truncated the archaeological horizon at the point. On the riverwards side, sandy foreshore deposits would then accumulate up against the face of the riverfront revetment forming the level onto which the next phase of encroachment would be built. These four components, the underlying foreshores, the revetments themselves, the dumped deposits behind them, and the surfaces above them, form the four principal elements in the stratigraphic sequence encountered on most waterfront sites in the City. Thus, rather than the oldest deposits always being at the lowest levels on the site, the earliest deposits on the waterfront are found in the landward end of the excavation, with the latest at the riverward side.

The *extent* of the width of the zone of reclaimed land in the City, up to 100m in some areas, demonstrates that the process of encroachment was a major topographical development: medieval London was significantly larger at the end of the period than at the beginning. The *chronology* has been established for the north bank, with the earliest extensions recorded in the Queenhithe, Vintry and Dowgate area in the tenth century with the construction of timber, clay and rubble embankments. Following the construction of the first medieval bridge by *c.*1000, those upriver structures were extended southwards while new embankments were raised, extending eastwards from the Dowgate waterfront. Immediately downstream of the new bridge, embankments were constructed in the Billingsgate area. The twelfth century saw riverwards extensions (often retained by stave-built revetments) in all these areas as well as developments to the west, beyond Fish Wharf. In the thirteenth and early fourteenth century, elaborately timber-framed post-and-plank revetments retained major encroachments across the length of the City waterfront, extending west beyond Baynard's Castle and east as far as Custom House.

Much of the land in the City had thus been won by the fifteenth to sixteenth centuries, although there was some further localised extension associated with the rebuilding of the quayside after the Great Fire of 1666. In the main, the largest increments seem to have been won in the thirteenth and fourteenth centuries, with rather more modest developments in the preceding and succeeding periods. That period also seems to have marked a major phase of land reclamation on the southern shore, with its markedly different island topography. Here embankments were raised (Bankside), marshes drained and revetted landfill deposits extended riverwards as Southwark's medieval waterfront was also transformed. The attempted constriction of the Thames between two advancing banks had a severe effect on the hydrology of the river, causing increased erosion, for example. The archaeological studies of several waterfront sites suggest that this problem was particularly noticeable on the inside of the great meander upon which London sits; as the City advanced, so Southwark suffered.

Harbour inventory

The last thirty years has therefore witnessed a major series of major waterfront developments in the historic City and on the Southwark shore often preceded or accompanied by archaeological investigations. Most of the major projects are shown on figure **8** and are summarised below. It should be stressed that while some of the entries record relatively small-scale work, others encapsulate seriously large excavations. In sum, London has acquired (half by accident half by design) the largest medieval harbour investigation in Europe, a fact sometimes obscured by the episodic and protracted nature of the excavation programme.

Westminster
Excavations in 1963 recorded the moated Jewel Tower, built in 1365. Although not on the River Thames itself, the masonry facing of the moat itself is an example of medieval riverfront walling which remains visible to this day (Green 1976).

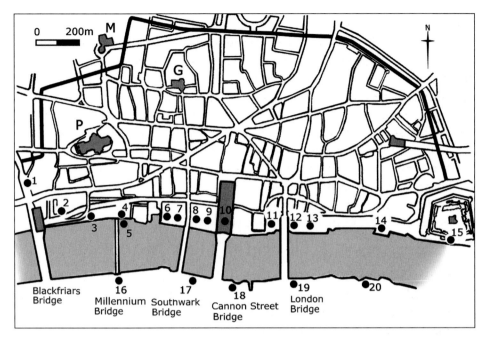

8 *Much of London's medieval harbour has now been excavated and destroyed in advance of modern redevelopment. The numbers on this map mark the locations of some major archaeological investigations in the City and Southwark.* J. Stripe, London ARF
KEY 1: Confluence of River Fleet; 2: Puddle Dock; 3: Baynard's Castle; 4: Trig Lane; 5: Trig Stairs; 6: Queenhithe; 7: Vintry; 8: Three Cranes Wharf; 9: Dowgate, confluence of Walbrook; 10: Steelyard; 11: Swan Lane; 12: London Bridge (N); 13: Billingsgate; 14: Old Custom House; 15: Tower Wharf & Watergate; 16: Millennium Bridge (S); 17: Bankside; 18: Winchester Palace; 19: London Bridge (S), Fennings Wharf; 20: Fastolf's Place & the Rosary

Whitehall

Some of the earliest waterfront excavations in London were conducted in 1938-9 and then recommenced after the war in 1950 on the Thames frontage associated with the royal palace at Whitehall: well-preserved remains of the masonry riverwall built between 1514 and 1546 were recorded (Thurley 1999).

Strand (**13**) *18-20 York Buildings (YKB88)*

A small-scale but highly significant excavation in 1988 exposed a section of a mid-Saxon brushwood and rubble embankment overlying foreshore deposits. The trees from which the associated planks and piles were cut had been felled *c*.AD 670-690 (Cowie 1992).

Arundel House (**13**) *ADL97*

Excavations and observations in 1997-8 recorded traces of mid-Saxon foreshore features; thirteenth- to fourteenth-century timber waterfront structures; late fourteenth-century masonry river wall (Proctor 2000).

21

Whitefriars
Excavation in 1999 between Tudor St and Tallis St on a site developed by the Carmelites (Whitefriars) recorded several phases of thirteenth- to fourteenth-century encroachment, incorporating timber revetments and subsequently masonry river walls.

River Fleet (**8** no. 1)

WEST BANK:
a) Old City of London Boy's School BOY86
Excavations in 1986-7 at the south-western edge of the Fleet-Thames conflu-ence located traces of an embankment on the western side of the River Fleet, overlain by reclamation deposits marking a 50m southward advance of the Thames frontage associated with a mid-fourteenth-century masonry river wall.
b) Bridewell Palace BRI78/ Tudor Street TUD78
Excavations and observations beneath the foundations of the early sixteenth-century Bridewell Palace recorded part of fourteenth- and fifteenth-century piled revetments and a masonry river wall on the western edge of the River Fleet. The latest timber revetment incorporated fragments of a clinker built boat (Gadd & Dyson 1981)

EAST BANK:
a) Fleet Valley Project PWB88
One of the largest single excavation projects ever conducted in the City concerned the excavation of an area some 500m north-south by 20m east-west along the eastern edge of New Bridge Street, incorporating much of the eastern bank of the Fleet river. Features of particular note relating to the history of the medieval port include the remains of a mid-eleventh-century timber bridge over the Fleet; the construction of the masonry-walled Fleet prison on an island in the river in the1080s, the late twelfth-century reclama-tion of a large bankside area upon which a tidal mill was established; fragments of twelfth-century boat timbers; a sequence of reclamation deposits on the east bank, not to mention the very substantial remains of the riverside defensive wall, built in AD 1280-1320 (McCann 1993).
b) New Bridge Street NBS84
Controlled excavation in 1984 recorded medieval encroachment on east bank of the Fleet truncated by the 1280-1320 City wall extension.
c) Queen Victoria Street QVS85
Controlled excavation in 1985 recorded the late thirteenth to early fourteenth-century masonry river wall facing the Thames, with evidence for river stair.

Puddle Dock (**8** no. 2) *Mermaid Theatre THE79*
Controlled excavation in 1979 recorded the timber baseplates of a thirteenth-

century revetment marking the first phase of medieval waterfront encroachment at the western end of the City waterfront.

Baynard's Castle (**8** no. 3) *BC72/ BC75/ BYD81*
A protracted programme of excavations and observations from 1972-6, with further work in 1981, exposed the well-preserved footings of the palatial fifteenth-century riverside town house called Baynard's Castle together with the masonry-faced inlet known as the East Watergate on its western side. The earliest medieval encroachment on the site incorporated timber revetment structures dating to the thirteenth century, erected after the late Roman river side wall had been levelled following its collapse in or by the twelfth century.

Trig Lane (**4** & **8** no. 4) *Trig Lane TL74/ Sunlight Wharf SUN86/ Millennium Bridge City MBC98*
Controlled excavation of large site on west side of Trig Lane 1974-6 (Milne & Milne 1982) with extended observations of adjacent area in 1986 (Hunting 1988), followed by excavation of adjacent property to west (along Boss Alley) prior to construction of the Millennium Bridge (Ayre & Wroe-Brown 2002). A long sequence of medieval encroachments over at least four contiguous properties were traced from the twelfth to the fifteenth century. A series of timber revetments including part of a fishmonger's wharf, and two later medieval masonry river walls were recorded, together with the remains of riverstairs, the foundations of waterfront buildings and some clinker boat fragments.

Trig Stairs (**8** no. 5)
The wrecks of two late medieval clinker-built river barges were uncovered and hastily recorded during the construction of the new riverside walkway in 1970 close to Trig Stairs (Marsden 1996).

Queenhithe (**8** no. 6, **9** & **colour plate 5**) *Bull Wharf BLL79, BUF90; Upper Thames Street UPT90*
Excavations and observations on adjacent properties in 1979 and 1990-95 recorded two mid-Saxon burials in the foreshore overlying the Roman quay, and a long sequence of later waterfront activity commencing (significantly) in the late ninth century. The series of clay and timber embankments and later timber-faced revetments (incorporating reused ship timbers) marked the phases of development that gave rise to the present form of the Queenhithe inlet.

Vintry (**8** no. 7) *Vintry VRY89*
Excavations and observations revealed a complex pattern of waterfront utilising Saxon wood and clay embankments, replaced by a sequence of timber-revetted encroachments either side of an inlet. The site lay on the western side of the area known as the Vintry, the Anglo-Norman wine-importing quarter, and

9 *Excavating the timber facing of a Saxon waterfront embankment on the Queenhithe site.* BUF 90
MoLAS

footings related to medieval warehouses and buildings associated with Vintner's
Hall were also recorded. Notable finds included reused late Saxon ship and
house timbers.

Three Cranes (**8** no. 8) *Thames Exchange TEX88*
Excavations and observations in 1988-90 investigated a series Saxon and later
medieval waterfront encroachments within the easternmost area of the Vintry.
The brushwood and rubble embankments dated to the tenth century, associated with many reused ship timbers. The later timber-faced revetments ranged
from the eleventh to the fourteenth century, and incorporated part of a
twelfth-century wine wharf, including a jetty and the foundations of a
warehouse building (Milne 1992).

Dowgate (**8** no. 9) *Public Cleansing Depot PCD59*
A late Saxon waterfront embankment was observed in 1959 during building
works. It comprised layers of brushwood and silt and was sealed by thirteenth-century reclamation dumps retained by a front-braced timber
revetment. The masonry foundations of a building thought to be part of a
large fifteenth-century waterfront latrine (Whittington's Longhouse) were
also recorded.

Steelyard (**8** no. 10) *Cannon Street Station UTA87*
Limited excavation of reclamation deposits beneath the masonry footings of the late twelfth-century Hanseatic Guildhall (later known as the Steelyard) exposed Saxon brushwood and clay embankments, a stave wall of possible twelfth-century date and a late medieval masonry river wall 10m north of the present frontage.

Swan Lane (**8** no. 11) *Seal House SH74/ Swan Lane SWA81*
Controlled excavations and observations over these two adjacent sites in 1974 and 1981-2 recorded evidence of a long series of medieval riverfront encroachments dating back to the eleventh century. Timber revetments were superseded by masonry river walls by the late fourteenth to fifteenth century. A noticeable feature of the overlying medieval occupation levels was the remains of a thirteenth-century dyehouse.

London Bridge (north side) (**8** no. 12) *Adelaide Place & New Fresh Wharf*
A substantial section of the first arch from the medieval stone bridge was exposed during the construction of Adelaide Place in 1921, while the eastern end of the cutwater for the second pier was revealed in 1937 during the New Fresh Wharf redevelopment (Watson *et al.* 2000).

Billingsgate (**8** no. 13) *New Fresh Wharf NFW74 FRE78 / St Magnus SM75/ Billingsgate Lorry Park BIG82 BWB83*
A long series of controlled excavations and observations on three adjacent properties in 1973-6 and 1982-3 revealed a long sequence of medieval waterfront encroachment, commencing in the early eleventh century with a series of brushwood and clay embankments laid out over the remains of the late Roman timber quay (Steedman 1992). Subsequent advances in the twelfth to fifteenth centuries were also recorded, in addition to the footings of a long series of masonry waterfront buildings, including warehouses, domestic structures and part of the riverside church of St Botolph. Timbers recovered from the riverfront revetments included reused fragments from houses and boats.

Custom House (**8** no. 14) *CUS73*
During construction of the new Custom House in 1813-7 three lines of wooden embankments and a later masonry river wall were observed. Excavations and observations in 1973 on the adjacent property recorded waterfront encroachments retained by timber revetments overlying the remains of a Roman quay. The medieval structural sequence commenced in the thirteenth century, and including part of a timber-framed jetty, a substantial fragment of a clinker-built boat and the masonry foundations of the late fourteenth-century Custom House (Tatton-Brown 1974).

Tower of London (**8** no. 15)
Major waterfront features still surviving here include a thirteenth-century watergate (Wakefield Tower), a fourteenth-century watergate (Traitors Gate) and the fourteenth-century masonry-faced quay of Tower Wharf itself.

Millennium Bridge (**8** no. 16) *Bankside Power Station 1948; Millennium Bridge MFB98*
During the construction of the power station (now Tate Modern) in 1948, parts of two clinker-built boats were found, at least one of which was probably late medieval in date. Excavations in 1998-9 recorded a sequence of twelfth- to fifteenth-century riverfront revetments and associated features, in addition to a later sequence of encroachment structures. These included fragments from a sixteenth-century 'western barge' (Ayre & Wroe-Brown 2002).

Bankside (**8** no. 17) *5-15 Bankside & 37-46 Bankside BS81/ BKS81/ 5BS87*
Excavations and observation in 1981 and 1987 on sites to the east recorded a fourteenth-century timber revetment incorporating clinker-boat planking and a later fourteenth-century masonry wall as well as clinker-boat planks from vessels of fourteenth- and late fifteenth-century date.

Winchester Palace (**8** no. 18)
During the major excavation programme in 1983-4 that investigated Winchester Palace, built for the Bishop in the mid-thirteenth century, three phases of the associated Thames frontage were recorded. The first two incorporated timber revetments, of which the second was dated to the mid-fourteenth century, and this was superseded by a fifteenth-century masonry river wall.

London Bridge (south side) (**8** no. 19)
Toppings Wharf & Sun Wharf TW70 TW84 Fennings Wharf FW83
Excavations on this site close to London Bridge in 1972-4 and demonstrated that the south bank of the Thames had been scoured by a major flood, perhaps the event documented in October 1294. Subsequent developments included an inlet with fourteenth- and fifteenth-century timber features and the remains of a possible jetty (Sheldon 1974). Excavations and observations in 1983-4 recorded an impressive section of the landward abutment of the masonry London Bridge (constructed 1176-1209), surviving largely intact up to the level of the base of the arch vaulting. Dendrochronological samples taken from the wooden piles used in the foundations were from trees felled in 1185-7. Also recorded were the substantial remains of a timber box-work structure that had been rebuilt three times, thought to represent part of an earlier timber bridge, from which timbers from trees felled some time after AD 970 were derived. Other finds on this important site included fragments of ship timbers (Watson *et al.* 2001).

10 *Archaeologists start work on a new trench on a massive waterfront site in Southwark*

Fastolf's Place and the Rosary (**8** no. 20 & **10**)
Abbots Lane, Morgans Lane, Gun & Shot Wharf, MORE London Bridge
A mammoth programme of excavations and observations was conducted periodically from 1986 to 1999 over this vast waterfront site. Two large moated
Thames-side enclosures were recorded: the Rosary, a residence built for
Edward II in 1325, and Fastolf's Place, built for Sir John Fastolf in 1443. Some
earlier waterfront features were recorded in addition to revetments incorporating sections of reused clinker-built boats, as well as fishponds and part of a
tidal watermill (Bluer 1993)

Rotherhithe
Excavations in 1986-7 investigated the mid-fourteenth-century moated
riverside residence built for Edward III between 1353-1377, 1km from the
City, with a tower at its north-west which presumably led to a bridge over the
moat, thence to a wharf on the Thames (Norton 1988).

The publication programme has not kept pace with the excavations, and
consequently by no means all of the results of this huge project are in print.
This is hardly surprising given the scale of the undertaking and considering
that sites elsewhere in London, such as the Roman harbour at Regis House,
the No. 1 Poultry project, the Guildhall amphitheatre site and the extensive
cemetery site at Spitalfields were also vying for attention. Nevertheless there

are several detailed waterfront reports published (e.g. Ayre & Wroe-Brown 2002; Milne & Milne 1982, Milne 1992; Proctor 2002; Steedman *et al.* 1992), monographs on the boat and ship fragments (Marsden 1994, 1996) and another on the bridge (Watson *et al.* 2001), as well as an internationally acclaimed series of volumes on the well-preserved assemblages of artefacts from those sites (1987–1998); these are listed in the bibliography. As for the rest of the site reports, until such time as that huge body of work can be brought to the press, this more modest volume provides a summary of the wealth of information created by the last 30 years of excavation and research on the medieval London waterfront.

3

MART OF MANY NATIONS

Lundenwic, the Saxon port

Much has been written on the port of Roman London, following a series of major excavations in the City beginning in 1973. In addition to the books, articles and reports, there is even a model of the harbour on permanent display in the Museum of London. The mid-Saxon port is less well-known, but lasted almost as long as its more famous ancestor. There have been very limited archaeological investigations on the mid-Saxon waterfront, while our understanding of the town itself – its extent, its form, its chronology, its dynamic – is still rudimentary but developing fast. What follows is therefore a report of work in progress on the emporium that flourished from AD 600 to 900. Given the pace and continuous nature of archaeological research and excavation in the London area, it is to be hoped that this summary of the port of Lundenwic will be substantially revised and extended in the near future. This chapter will therefore serve as an introduction to some of the methodologies, themes and approaches used by archaeologists seeking to establish the nature of an ancient port, rather than a detailed account of London's mid-Saxon harbour. It will also stand as a stark reminder of the crucial importance of external agencies in the shaping of London's history.

The broad outlines of the political context in which this new port grew up can be suggested by consideration of the scanty documentary records surviving in Bede's eighth-century account of the *Ecclesiastical History of the English Nation* (Stevens 1970) and in the later Saxon compilation known as the *Anglo-Saxon Chronicle* (Garmonsway 1972), together with incidental references in sundry charters and law codes (Whitelock 1955). There is a documentary reference to Roman *Londinium*, retrospectively dated to the mid-fifth century, that refers to the turmoil that followed the barbarian Saxon incursions and invasions. The entry in the *Anglo-Saxon Chronicle* for *c*.456 records that warriors led by Hengist and Aesc fought against the Britons, perhaps in a battle near Crayford, where some 4,000 were killed. The rest of the Britons fled from Kent to London 'in great terror'. What actually happened next is not mentioned. However, the archaeological evidence suggests that the City walls do not seem to have saved them, since the settlement was subsequently abandoned for a century or so.

The next relevant documentary reference was compiled in the early eighth century by the Venerable Bede, a monk working in a Northumbrian monastery. He describes the ordination of Bishop Mellitus over a century earlier in 604, who was to preach in the province of the East Saxons (Essex) which was 'divided from Kent by the River Thames, and borders on the Eastern Sea. Their metropolis is London which is situated on the banks of the river, and is the mart of many nations resorting to it by land and sea'. He adds that Ethelbert, the King of Kent, 'built the church of St Paul in London' (Stevens 1970, 68-9). The acceptance of Christianity was initially too novel a departure for the heathen English, as London drove out the bishop in 616. It would be some forty years before the minster church was re-established. Other buildings are mentioned in decrees of 685 made by Hlothere and Eadric, two later Kentish kings: 'if a man of Kent buys property in London, he is to have two or three honest *ceorls* or the King's town reeve as witness' and the deal was to be concluded 'at the King's hall in that town' (Whitelock 1955, 360).

The economic and social context for the development of this mid-Saxon port still requires further archaeological research. A more detailed study is required of the nature and chronology of the demise of Londinium related to the pattern of the Germanic, Saxon settlement that subsequently developed in the Thames valley. It seems that there were a number of fifth- and sixth-century hamlets by the cemeteries recorded at Greenwich, Hanwell, Mitcham and Croydon for example. But was Lundenwic developed in the seventh century as a regional administrative centre, a temporary, periodic market, or was it, to begin with, just another fishing and farming settlement? The sitting of the minster church of St Paul's there in 604 certainly suggests the former, since most of that generation of 'missionary' churches were located specifically to take advantage of a pre-existing social, economic and political network. Proximity to the local king or sub-king's base (*villa regalis*) provided not only protection but ready access to the treasury as well as the region's established route ways.

The all too brief incidental documentary references describe a town transformed in the seventh century, but where was it? The answer was one of the most remarkable discoveries of the late twentieth century, for the lost Saxon town did not lie directly over the abandoned Roman site of Londinium as many had imagined, but was in a quite separate location to the west of the deserted walled site (Haynes 2000, 175-205). The Saxon settlement had been established in the area we now know as Covent Garden. This missing chapter in the capital's history was only revealed in 1985, following excavations on the Jubilee Market site on the southern edge of the main piazza. Work elsewhere in the area has begun to define the limits of the town, which stretched from Shorts Gardens to the Thames, and from Trafalgar Square to the Royal Opera House. There were also outlying farms, such as the one found beneath the Treasury in Downing Street, between the main settlement and the ancient church of St Peter's on Thorney Island. This was known as the 'West Minster'.

The new town that succeeded Londinium therefore had a new site, a new language and a new culture: it even had a new name, Lundenwic, of which the 'wic' element means 'market' town or 'emporium'. It is possible that the settlement incorporated a mixture of farmers and small holders, together with craftworkers dealing in bone, antler, metal or cloth as well as fishermen and traders on the riverbank. How marked such distinctions were in the mid-Saxon period is a moot point: it was, of course, quite possible for someone to be a fisherman, farmer *and* trader, depending on the time of year, the opportunities to hand and how hungry your children were. There was also the small matter of your obligation to your lord: for Lundenwic, that would be a variety of kings or sub-kings of Kent, Essex, Wessex or Mercia, depending on the changes in the political and military landscape.

In keeping with contemporary practice in northern Europe, transactions of riverbourne trade would have taken place on the waterfront, actually from boats pulled up on the foreshore (**11**). Initially, at least, the system needs no shops, stalls or warehouses and no major cargo-handling facilities. It has its origins primarily in the need for a simple neighbourhood exchange centre, rather than solely upon long-distance trade networks. The location of other such market locations may be suggested from the place name element 'wic' at Hampton Wick, Twickenham, Greenwich or Woolwich, for example. A variety of small boats laden with local produce would be commonplace, a riverside version of a street market, in an age when more people owned small

11 *Mid-Saxon beach market at Lundenwic.* Artist's reconstruction by Chris Unwin

boats than kept a horse and cart. This type of market was common throughout northern Europe, and acted as a focus for both local and long-distance trade, barter and exchange.

The specific location of the beach market would be clearly defined, just as any street market is. The officially-recognised site was known by the term *ripa emptoralis* (trading shore). A grant of land in Surrey made by King Frithuwald in 672 mentions that the estate was on the south bank of the Thames opposite 'the port of London where ships come to land', which is the earliest surviving unambiguous reference to the port and to the beach market there (Dyson 1980). Naturally, a toll could be charged on the boats moored there – *navium stationes*, the equivalent of paying rent for a market stall. Tolls would be collected for whoever owned the rights for that particular site, usually the king. The actual collection of tolls was the responsibility of the port-reeves, officials who are already mentioned in the plural in a document dated to 734-5. This particular instance refers to a special concession granted by King Athebald of Mercia for vessels owned by a bishop: 'the remission of all dues on two ships, which are exacted by the tax-gatherers in the port of London' (Brooke 1975, 367-8).

That charter relates to the long period when Lundenwic was under the control of Mercia; since that kingdom was centred on the midlands, a harbour on the tidal Thames would be a major asset. A letter written in 796 to Offa, King of Mercia, from the Emperor Charlemagne refers to the traffic and trade between England and continental Europe in this period, and comments on the need for protecting English pilgrims and merchants travelling abroad: '. . . let [the pilgrims] travel in peace without any trouble. Nevertheless if any are found among them not in the service of religion, but in the pursuit of gain, let them pay the established duties at the proper places. We also will that merchants shall have lawful protection in our kingdom according to our command: and if they are in any place unjustly aggrieved, let them apply to us or our judges, and we shall take care that ample justice be done to them' (Haddan & Stubbs 1871, 496-8).

Artefacts, traffic and trade (colour plate 6)

Study of such documentary matter that has survived has therefore built a broad framework upon which a general chronology of the Saxon port can be built. But can this be extended by consideration of the material evidence, recovered from the recent excavation programme? Regardless of whether medieval archaeological sites are waterlogged or desiccated, urban, ecclesiastical, royal or rural, pottery is likely to be the most common artefact recovered. Other materials may have decayed, rusted or been burnt, but even broken pottery is remarkably robust. As is now standard practice, once the sources and kiln sites have been identified and dated, then sherds of that particular ware can be used to suggest a date-range for the layers or buildings they were associated with during excavation. But use as a dating medium is only one aspect of medieval ceramic studies. Pottery was widely used throughout the medieval period, sometimes traded in its own right, sometimes brought in as containers of more valuable cargoes, sometimes simply serving as the cooking pots or storage jars used by the sailors or merchants themselves. Whatever its initial function, the presence of non-local pottery in Lundenwic for example, demonstrates contact and traffic of some sort (though not necessarily direct) with other areas of England or other ports in Europe. In the absence of other data, or as a comple-ment to them, study of the pottery recovered from medieval London can therefore do more than simply assist in furnishing a chronology for the port's gradual development. As Lynn Blackmore (1999) and others have shown, the close dating allied with the accurate provenancing of the pottery is very instructive. Once it is known precisely both where and when a particular type of pottery was produced, then useful general pictures can be painted showing not just the extent of the town's immediate economic hinterland, but also how the port's external trade network developed. Such pictures are of great impor-tance especially when viewed comparatively and particularly in the absence of detailed written records such as customs accounts.

Study of the pottery from the settlement has already identified two distinct phases in the port's development, the first suggesting rather limited horizons, the second a significant expansion. From 630 to 750, for example, the most common English pottery found in Lundenwic is a chaff-tempered ware made locally, possibly in the Essex area. This suggests a relatively modest hinterland for the first phase of the port's development. Presumably most of its grain, meat, fuel, wool, hay and timber supplies were derived from the immediate locale, which implies a community in which farming in all its forms was still a prime concern. Next to no imported pottery is associated with this phase, although the presence of freshwater and marine fish species shows that at least some river and coastal traffic was accommodated there. Indeed the town already had a mint by the mid-seventh century, since gold coins known as *thrymsas* bearing the name *Londiniv*, *Londenvs* or similar have been found in Kent and also in Hampshire and Wiltshire. The silver coins known as primary *sceatta* series B may also have been minted in London, and have a rather wider distribution, extending from south-west France to western Jutland (Hobley & Hodges 1988, fig 44).

Significantly, a rather wider range of pottery is found in the later levels at Lundenwic. This represents the much wider regional and national roles played by the port in the late eighth and ninth centuries that presumably developed with the size of its population. The important link to the east coast trade network is represented by the Ipswich ware, the ubiquitous sandy grey wheel-thrown pottery imported in quantity from East Anglia. This is found alongside shell-tempered pottery from the Woolwich or Greenwich area of Kent as well as small quantities of material from the Mercian midlands.

This noticeable increase in the size of its English hinterland is mirrored by evidence for increasing contact with contemporary emporia such as Dorestad in the Netherlands and Quentovic, in the Pas de Calais. Thus the presence of North French Reduced ware and Rhenish Buff wares from the later seventh century onwards suggests that, after a generation or so, Lundenwic had established itself sufficiently to attract the attention of traders from ports such as Dorestad, one of the great centres of Frisian merchants engaged in the carriage of quernstones, wine and various luxury goods. In return, Lundenwic may have been exporting wool or cloth, as it most certainly did in the later medieval period. What is clear is that excavations in all parts of the settlement have produced plenty of evidence of clothworking, in the form of spindle whorls, bone thread pickers, a linen smoother, a carding comb and many loomweights (**colour plate 6**) – including some 500 from the Royal Opera House excavations alone – as well as the bones of sheep in quantity.

This suggestion of an expansion in trade from the later seventh century onwards is supported by the coin evidence. The silver coinage referred to as 'primary phase' *sceattas* was minted in Lundenwic, but in AD 730 a new phase of coins bearing the legend *d(e) Lundinia* first appears. By the late eighth century, silver pennies had become the common currency, and London minted pennies for the Mercian kings such as Offa (757-96), and Coenwulf (796-821). The 55 *sceattas* so far recorded from Lundenwic represent a respectable cash economy and include at least two Frisian coins (MoL 2000, 187). In Alfred's time, hard currency issued from the king's treasury was used to pay four particular sections of society. First there was the church which took the lion's share, then came the bodyguard of soldiers and thanes (but not of course the rank and file of the common militia). The wages of particular craftsmen or other royal workers were also met directly from the treasury, unlike most other royal officials and shire reeves who were recompensed by taking a proportion of the taxes they collected. The final use of the freshly-minted coin was for gifts and providing hospitality for visitors to the court (Whitelock 1972, 66-7). From those principal sources, the silver then circulated through the market system in exchange for metals, salt, slaves, imported produce and so forth, ultimately returning to the treasury as rent, fines or taxes. Alongside the hard currency was an extensive system of food rents, renders, tithes and obligations involving payments in kind and in labour; over time these too would be commuted into cash as the medieval economy developed.

The trading contacts that developed in Lundenwic were maintained and extended in the eighth century and beyond, as the recovery of Reliefbandamphora, fine Badorf, Tating and North French white and buff wares shows. The actual amount, or more accurately, the proportion of continental imported pottery, is also of significance here: in Lundenwic, some 12 per cent of the ceramic material is imported, a similar figure to that from Hamwic, the forerunner of Southampton, but apparently less than the 20 per cent figure currently quoted for Eoforwic, the mid-Saxon emporium near York (Blackmore 1999). This summary of the changing trading contacts enjoyed by Lundenwic can be enhanced by consideration of other artefacts: lava quernstone from Niedermendig in Germany and schist honestones from Norway have also been found by the excavation team. There is, in addition, an incidental documentary reference to another trade, the slave trade, in 679. Following a battle between two warring Saxon kingdoms near the River Trent, a youth was captured by the Mercians. He was then bound 'and sold at Lundenwic to a Frisian' (Stevens 1970, 200) whose merchants were controlling the cross-channel trade at the time.

The form of the settlement itself shows evidence of expansion and change, as exemplified by the results of the recent Royal Opera House site (Malcolm & Bowsher 2003), the largest controlled excavation investigated in Lundenwic. Here two large enclosures either side of a well-maintained metalled road had been laid out over a seventh-century cemetery, clear evidence for the northwards expansion of Lundenwic by c.AD 670. However, the internal layout of the buildings within these enclosures did not take on a characteristically 'urban' character until the later eighth century, the age of Offa. Only then did a dense development of contiguous buildings set gable-end onto the street appear. If that sequence is typical of Lundenwic as a whole, then the population clearly doubled or trebled during the later seventh and eighth centuries, implying that the income from rentals and trade also increased markedly.

Harbour excavations at Dorestad and London

Lundenwic was developing at the same time as a handful of other port towns such as Hamwich, the forerunner of Southampton on the south coast, and Ipswich on the east coast. In addition to those emporia, it now seems that there were a number of more modest market centres set in riverine or inland locations, sites that have produced significant numbers of coins, demonstrating their market function (Ulmschnieder 2000). To this regional and national network can be added the international ports, such as Quentovic near Calais and Dorestad, near the mouth of the Rhine, both of which have been subject to archaeological investigations. At Dorestad in the Netherlands, for example, a large area of what may be interpreted as the Frisian merchant quarter on the Hoog Straat site was excavated in 1970-5 and promptly published in 1980. Here was a 50ha harbour site on a silted-up tributary of the Rhine. Pile lines representing the wooden revetments retaining the earthern fill of fifteen contiguous jetties or causeways were recorded, extending from the dry land over the foreshore of the ancient river bed. Each was between 6 and 8m wide and up to 1m tall, and had been progressively extended riverwards by up to some 200m between c.AD 675 and 875. The wattlework which retained the

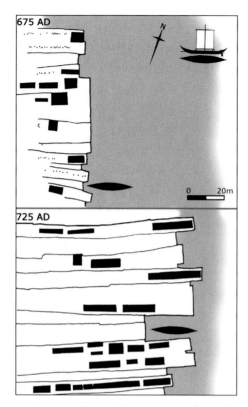

12 *The Frisian port of Dorestad, Netherlands: interpretive plans showing the extensive waterfront encroachment next to the Rhine, between the seventh and eighth centuries, based on the Hoog Straat excavations. The inset diagram is of the contemporary Sutton Hoo ship drawn to the same scale.* After Van Es 1980, J. Stripe, LARF

infilled 'jetties' was usually of ash, but rather more substantial oak piles were also recorded, and these could be interpreted as the foundations of waterfront buildings (**12**). A remarkably clear picture of mid-Saxon waterfront topography emerges from this excavation, with access way and buildings set just above the high tide mark directly overlooking the open foreshore where the beach market would have operated. Over 70 coins were recovered, some minted at Dorestad, but with others from Strasbourg, Cologne, Tours, Meaux, Narbonne, Milan and Venice, representing something of the extent of the port's trading activities, a considerably more impressive range of mints than the contemporary Lundenwic assemblage. Maritime artefacts included many clenched nails, representing small, medium and large clinker-built ships, iron boat hooks and a range of ship-building tools including axes, adzes and spoon bits (Van Es & Verwers 1980).

John Clark (pers. comm.) has translated an important reference to St Boniface arriving in Lundenwic 'where there is a market for the sale of goods' to take the ship back to 'Dorstet' in 716 and to journey to 'Cuentawich' in 718 (Levison 1905), implying clear connections between these north European ports. However, the evidence for waterfront activity in Lundenwic cannot, as yet, begin to match that of Dorestad. There have been few archaeological investigations of the waterfront between the Strand and the Thames. Foreshore deposits or features were briefly observed under Charring Cross station in 1987 and at 12 Buckingham Street the following year and then a decade later under Arundel House (**13**). Nevertheless the most substantial study remains that at York Buildings in 1988, just behind the Victoria Embankment (Cowie 1992). The base of the excavated trenches revealed sandy foreshore deposits over 100m landwards of the present day course of the Thames. A low brushwood and rubble embankment had been laid over the foreshore, retained by a pile and plank revetment: the feature was traced for a distance of some 3.8m. The oak planks were sampled for dendrochronological analysis, and it was shown that they had been cut from trees felled between AD 670 and 690. The brushwood mat was up to 0.2m thick, with its upper surface at +0.8m above OD (Ordnance Datum = present sea-level). This modest excavation therefore established the line of the seventh-century waterfront, the level of the contemporary river, and demonstrated that the harbour was already undergoing substantial modifications in the precise period that Frithuwald's charter of 672 first mentions the phrase the 'port of London where ships come to land' (Whitelock 1955, 440).

Boats and ships

At least two types of vessels would have been seen in the London beach market: dugout boats, (fashioned from hollowed out trunks) representing a common method of transport for inland waterways, and the larger planked boats, propelled by oar or sail, for estuary, coast or cross-channel work. Archaeological evidence for both types has been recovered from cemetery sites in East Anglia, at Snape and at Sutton Hoo, for example. The dugout tradition is long-lived, reaching right back into prehistory and continuing into the thirteenth or fourteenth century in England. Such vessels would be made and used by families living on the banks of the Thames and its tributaries. The boats would be shallow-draft vessels 2 to 4m in length, propelled by paddle or pole, and could carry two or three people or a modest cargo to and from market. The remains of such a dugout have been found at Walthamstow, for example, and two samples from it have been dated to AD 675-680, and 650-685 (Marsden 1996, 222). It would thus seem to be contemporary with the mid-Saxon port of London.

The plank-built boats represent a rather different socio-economic group. The outline of the vessel recorded in Mound One at the royal cemetery in Sutton Hoo (Suffolk) in 1939 will serve as an example of such seventh-century craft (Delgado 1997, 411-3); it was some 27m long, a beam of 4.4m and a depth amidships of 1.22m. She was built from nine strakes of overlapping oak planks on each side, held together with iron nails clenched over diamond-shaped roves or washers. (A similar-sized clench nail was found in a mid-Saxon pit in Maiden Lane, Lundenwic). There were 26 internal frames or ribs set just under 1m apart in the Sutton Hoo ship. There were positions for up to 40

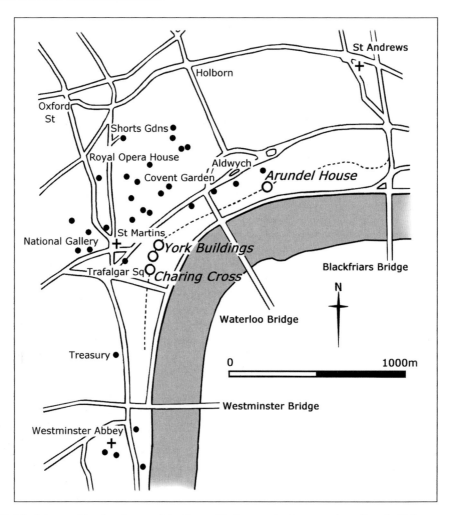

13 *The lost port of Lundenwic: map of the Covent Garden area showing approximate line of mid-Saxon river bank (dashed), with sites of investigations of contemporary foreshore features shown as open circles. Black dots mark position of other discoveries of mid-Saxon material from the Lundenwic settlement.*
J. Stripe, LARF

rowers (20 per side) and evidence was observed of claw-shaped tholes upon which the oars would pivot on the uppermost plank edge. A steering oar or rudder was mounted on the starboard (steer-board) stern quarter. The lines of the ship, her flat bottom with round bilges and her leaf-shaped plan suggested to Edwin Gifford that it could also have been propelled by a mast and sail. He subsequently constructed a replica along those lines in 1993, and observed that she performed well with a single square sail. Mid-Saxon shipbuilders could therefore build large sea-going shallow-draft craft that could be easily adapted for sailing or rowing, or for trading or raiding.

Maritime resources

Large stake-built fish traps of mid-Saxon date have been recorded from various sites in the inter-tidal zone, and include three large examples from the Blackwater estuary in Essex. The weir from the Nass at Tollesbury had walls a mere 120m long, the pile-built structure at Sales Point, Bradwell-on-Sea, was up to 340m long, while the Collins Creek, Tollesbury fish trap, the largest in the county, was 2,550m east-west by 700m north-south (Strachan 1997). Clearly fishing was a serious concern in mid-Saxon England, and merited a substantial investment of industry and resources. Presumably fish caught by the falling tide in traps as large as these were being husbanded on a scale to provide food in prodigious quantities, some of which may well have been transhipped to Lundenwic.

The Thames Archaeological Survey, working on the London foreshore with the Richmond Archaeological Society and the Wandsworth Historical Society, have recorded two early Anglo-Saxon fish-traps at Barn Elms and Putney and three mid-Saxon examples (Cohen forthcoming), at Chelsea (**colour plate 8**), Isleworth and again at Barn Elms. The best-preserved traps are at Chelsea (dated to AD 730-900) and Isleworth (dated to AD 650-890). Both were constructed with roundwood piles up to 0.13m in diameter (presumably to support hurdlework) set in a V-shape configuration with a long 'neck' in which the fish were trapped. The 33 piles of the Isleworth trap form the remains of a trap facing downstream, and thus may have been used to catch fish such as salmon. The Chelsea trap is by far the larger of the two, for which some 84 posts have been recorded between 0.3m and -2m OD in this area of rapid erosion. Since it faces upstream it must have been designed to ensnare creatures such as very large quantities of eels swimming downstream (Salisbury 1991, 76). It is worth recalling that, in the assemblages of fishbones recovered from the excavations at Lundenwic, eel was numerically the most significant, with pike and roach representing other freshwater species.

There was also clear evidence for the townsfolk's consumption of marine species such as cod, haddock, herring, whiting, bass, plaice and flounder as well as shellfish such as oyster from the estuary. The Royal Opera House site even produced a vertebra from a longfin pilot whale. Such a thriving coastal and inshore fishing industry was not just of importance for the diet of the Saxons. Fishermen would have provided the craft, contacts and the seamanship required to conduct traffic and trade in other commodities if the fishing was poor or the price was right: the development of ports and of long-distance trade often moves in tandem with the development of a strong fishing industry in this period. It seems that Lundenwic was no exception to that rule.

The Thames was not just a crucial transport highway and a provider of drinking water and fish in abundance, but it was also a source of power, as is shown by the discovery of mid-Saxon watermills at Old Windsor (Berks) and more recently at Ebbsfleet (Kent) in advance of the Channel Tunnel Rail Link. It would seem reasonable to assume that Lundenwic too may have benefited from the new technology of the horizontal watermill, since there would have been several suitable sites close to the town, near the Fleet or the Tyburn for example.

The sacking of Lundenwic

There are records of fire, that scourge of ancient cities, attacking Lundenwic in 764 and 798: presumably those events were (more or less) accidental disasters, but far worse was to follow. In 801, 841 and 852 the town's prosperity attracted the unwelcome attentions of Viking raiders, who sacked the settlement amidst 'great slaughter' (Garmonsway 1972). This was a period when much of Europe was threatened by violent punitive attacks by Scandinavian raiders, destroying lives, towns and trade; the London mint went out of production from 851 for over a decade. In 871-2 the Host returned with a vengeance yet again, taking up occupation in the port. Hoards of coins, such as silver pennies found near Middle Temple or the Northumbrian *stycas* from the Royal Opera House excavation, had been buried in desperation by Londoners in anticipation of such attacks. They are a poignant reminder of those savage times since it seems that no Saxons survived to recover them.

Although other interpretations are possible, these raids might provide the context for some rather unusual mid-Saxon burials found well to the east of the Lundenwic settlement. Two skeletons were recorded in an isolated location in an excavation at Rangoon Street, within the old Roman city walls. They were a male and female, buried with their heads to the north. Even more unusual were two other burials, this time actually on the Saxon foreshore, near Queenhithe. Both were females, buried some 5m apart. One had clearly met a violent death, as the marks on her skull showed. But she had then been carefully laid out on a bed of reeds between two marker piles driven into the foreshore at her head and between her knees. After that she had been covered in a blanket of bark, a sample of which provided a date of AD 670-880. A mound of gravel had been raised over the burial, forming a feature that would have been visible at low tide by anybody moving along the river (Wroe-Brown 1999).

It was not until 878 that the tide turned, when Alfred, King of Wessex, led the fight back. The *Anglo Saxon Chronicle* records that 'he fought a tremendous battle against the entire and serried pagan army, and overthrew the pagans with a great carnage'. He then moved on to recover London from the Danes. The plans that the great warlord then put into action in the last decade of that hard-fought century had a profound and lasting effect on the subsequent history of the harbour, the town and the nation. The battered and defenceless old 'wic' (*Aldwych*) had to be abandoned. If London was to have a future, it would have to be moved to a more defensible location.

4

THE MOVING OF LONDON

Tenth-century new town

The once-prosperous port of Lundenwic was abandoned in or by the late ninth century in favour of a more readily defensible location: the old walled site of Londinium was selected. It would have to serve not just as a port but as a frontier fortress, for it lay just to the west of the River Lea. This was the boundary of that part of England still under English Law and that under the Danelaw, an area stretching from East Anglia to Northumberland. As the old century closed, the English began to gradually drive forwards to retake the Danish lands. Secure bases were essential for this major military initiative, and a series of defended towns were established to serve that purpose, the so-called 'burghal hidage towns'. The role of the new London as a fortress is clearly shown in 894, for example. It is recorded that King Alfred marched to London and in company with the citizens, arrived at Benfleet, having heard that a large (Danish) army had assembled there. A severe battle was fought with the pagans, but the Christians put them to flight, demolished their earth-works, carried their wives and children to London, sunk some of their ships, and burned others, transporting some to London and some to Rochester (Garmonsway 1972). There is apparently a remarkable archaeological concor-dance with that event, for during the construction of the railway bridge over Benfleet Creek in the mid-nineteenth century, the remains of charred ships were uncovered and 'in and about them lay great quantities of human skeletons' (Spurrell 1885, 294).

In King Athelstan's time (924-39) the re-conquest was well underway, and London's role extended to include more mercantile affairs in addition to its military obligations. Athelstan's II Law reminded all town dwellers that their defences had to be repaired annually, but also that such defended settlements were to be developed as centres of trade: 'all buying is to be within a town'; this was to ensure its proper regulation. There was also to be but one coinage over the entire King's dominion and 'no-one is to mint money except in a town'. The port of London was already leading the field here, being awarded no fewer than eight moneyers to Rochester's seven, Winchester's six and Southampton's two, whilst most boroughs had but one (Whitelock 1955, 384). The implication is clearly that London anticipated eight times more cash transactions than most others towns and four times more than the important south-coast harbour of Southampton. Its increasing importance is mentioned again in Edgar's Law code (959-67) when it was decreed that the nation should observe 'one standard of measurement and one standard weight . . . as is observed in London and Winchester' (Whitelock 1955, 397).

The site developed as the new town of Lundenburh in the late ninth and early tenth centuries was surrounded by the repaired walls of *Londinium* on both the landward and riverward sides (**14**). Few traces of the Roman settlement survived within the circuit to constrain development. The marsh, or moor (as in Moorgate), to the north of the city provided a further line of defence on that side, while the wide mouth of River Fleet defined the western boundary, now marked by Farringdon Road and Blackfriars Bridge. To the south, the waters of the Thames lapped up against the foot of the Roman riverside wall at high tide. The archaeological evidence now suggests that the initial area of proposed settlement was confined to the zone bordered by what is now Cheapside to the north, St Paul's to the west, Billingsgate to the east and the River wall to the south. This settlement core was crossed by some ten parallel north-south streets subdividing the area into broadly regular insulae. There were five such blocks either side of the Walbrook valley, formed by the stream that once disgorged into the Thames close to the site of present-day Cannon Street Station. The principal east-west landward route at this stage

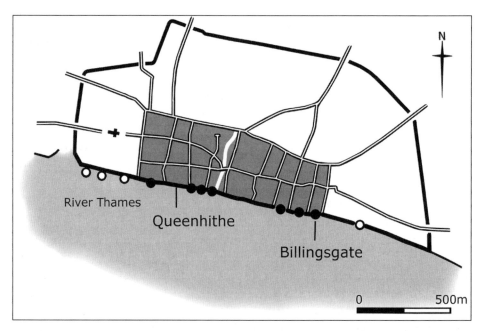

14 *Lundenburh: plan of the tenth-century port, showing occupied area (tinted) enclosed within old Roman city wall. Black dots indicate waterfront excavations where Saxon waterfront embankments have been recorded; the open dots indicate waterfront excavations where encroachment did not begin until the twelfth or thirteenth century. J. Stripe, LARF*

15 *A tenth-century wattle work structure on the Saxon foreshore under excavation.* TEX 88 Museum of London

probably ran along the line of Ludgate-Eastcheap, the road which led directly westwards along the Strand to Aldwych/Lundenwic, and thence to Westminster. As for the north-south streets, the majority of these probably terminated in the south at a gate or gap in the riverside wall, giving access to the common foreshore and the Thames.

Thus the securely-walled settlement incorporated three elements: a settlement core surrounded by a large open area suitable for the mustering of troops or refugees (or markets in times of peace) and finally the minster church of St Paul's. This was a town that met Alfred's concept of society, a conjunction of men who work, men who fight, and men who pray, as cited in his translation of Boethius' *Consolation of Philosophy*.

But what of the harbour? Two late ninth-century charters concerning the grant of land around Queenhithe provide an indication. Study of these remarkable documents (Dyson 1978; 1990) has shown that a beach market had already been established there, the proceeds from which were to go to the Bishop of Worcester. In addition the same bishop as well as the archbishop of Canterbury both had mooring rights there, clear evidence that a beach market had not only been established as a primary concern for the new town, but that its value was already fully recognised by the leading dignitaries of the day.

Archaeology has confirmed that picture. There was still no bridge at this stage and consequently river traffic could thus pass upstream and downstream unimpeded. The most recent archaeological evidence shows that the main

16 *Lost on the London waterfront: a silver penny from the reign of Alfred the Great (871-899) showing the London monogram.*
Museum of London

focus of mercantile activity was not in the centre of the waterfront but set well to the west. The zone extended from the mouth of the Walbrook stream to Queenhithe, originally known as Aethelred's Hithe, after the eponymous ealdorman who played a key role in the successful resettlement of the port. The government of London was entrusted to that warrior by Alfred, whose daughter Aethelred subsequently married. Initially the harbour was no more than the open foreshore, and consequently few substantial structures could be anticipated by the archaeological team. At the Thames Exchange site, for example, the earliest foreshore features excavated there were a half-collapsed series of light wattle fences (**15**). To the west near Queenhithe, the archaeologists on the Bull Wharf site uncovered two trestle structures that may initially have supported gang planks for a walkway over the foreshore. The timbers came from a tree felled some time after AD 880 according to the dendrochronological analysis. There was also a low gravel embankment to the east, and dendrochronological samples from associated timbers from that structure have provided a felling date of AD 890. This all seems suspiciously resonant of the famous date of AD 886, when it is recorded that King Alfred 'after all the burning of cities and slaughter of people, rebuilt London in a splendid manner' (Thorpe 1841). Three coins were also recovered from the foreshore there, all of which had been minted in London, complete with the London monogram (**16**). These particular coins are usually regarded as a propaganda issue, commemorating Alfred's triumphal taking of the City. The Bull Wharf excavation of that the ninth- to early tenth-century foreshore site therefore neatly encapsulates the modest but auspicious moment when the new port was born (Wroe-Brown 1999).

All the port's activities were thus focused on the area of open foreshore between the riverside wall and the Thames. However, the beach was only exposed at low tide, and was inundated twice daily. To increase the viability of the harbour, artificial embankments were built principally to provide a larger area of level, dry land between the wall and the water. A secondary use was that these embankments may have helped protect the base of the riverside wall from erosion by the river. Most of the embankments recorded seemed to comprise a thick raft of brushwood at the base, within which silt would be trapped and over which clay was dumped and surfaced with gravel or other materials (**colour plate 5**). One such mid-tenth-century embankment was recorded on the Thames Exchange site. Its riverward face of this embankment was initially retained by low planked revetments supported by piles driven into the foreshore. In the late tenth century the next revetment extended the water-front some 5m southwards (**17**). Another line of earthfast piles was set out, each one some 0.4m apart and over 2m long. At least eight runs of cleft oak boards (split with wedges, not sawn) were set against the landward side of the piles, but without any nails or pegs. The ends of the planks were cut with notches, and these interlocked with similar notches cut in the planking for the east face of the revetment, joining in the southeast corner. The revetment stood some 1.5m above the contemporary foreshore, and mixed dumped deposits had been thrown in behind the planking onto which a horizontal brace was laid, locked onto the head of the corner pile. The brace was sealed by more dumped material, which was sealed by a cobbled surface laid at 0.09m OD. Dendrochronological samples were taken from this and a related structure, and their study showed that the timbers had been taken from trees felled around AD 970. Traces of a building which was broadly contemporary with the

17 *Tenth-century timber revetment from a Saxon waterfront embankment at Three Cranes Wharf.* TEX 88
Museum of London

revetment were examined some 9m to the north. In this manner the open foreshore was transformed into an artificial embankment standing proud of (most) high tides.

The tenth-century embankments were not continuous, since there were deliberate gaps left between sections. The structures have been interpreted variously as flood-dykes or as platforms for beaching boats, while some have seen the gaps as 'docks' designed to accommodate shipping (e.g. Steedman *et al*. 1992, 119). When viewed alongside later waterfront structures, what is known about contemporary vessel construction, and many years working on the Thames foreshore in all weathers, a rather different interpretation is possible. The Saxon embankments were built between the still-standing Roman riverside wall and the Thames in a period when shallow-draft ships were designed to be beached (as the Bayeux Tapestry elegantly demonstrates), and did *not* require elaborate jetties, wharves or dockside facilities. The prime purpose of the brushwood and clay embankments must have been to provide an area of dry land for Londoners wishing to gain access to the river, or to any vessels moored or drawn up there, whatever the state of the tide. Without such embankments, easy access to the river would only be possible at low tide. Such a situation was more than a minor inconvenience; it rendered the old site of Londinium totally impractical as a port for as long as the riverside wall survived. Indeed, the noticeable lack of dry ground between the wall and the water at high tide must have been one of the deciding factors in the selection of the Strand foreshore as the focus for the mid-Saxon settlement, as discussed in the previous chapter. The construction of the new ground to the south of the riverside wall in the late Saxon period therefore combined the much needed waterfront access demanded by the port with the security provided by the Roman masonry.

In the tenth century, this man-made bank was confined to the western end of the waterfront, from Queenhithe to the confluence with the Walbrook. It served as the focus for the beach markets where imported produce might be purchased from the vessels bringing cargoes in, and goods from London sold or exchanged. It was also an area used by fishermen and boatbuilders, and where the citizens could gain access at any state of the tide for water for washing or for drinking, or for their animals. However, there were few permanent structures here (as compared to the dense urban development of the later medieval waterfront) as the riverside embankment would be abandoned during times of siege when the Londoners retreated behind the safety of the defensive walls. The riverward end of each of the main north-south lanes that comprised London's primary street grid often coincided with a gap in the embankment and a gate cut through the riverside wall. This was where Londoners or their livestock could get directly to the river or the foreshore at low tide or, alternatively, up onto the embankment at high tide. Initially these embankments and landing places were regarded as common facilities and a wide range of activities were conducted there: drawing of water, washing, watering horses, loading ships, accessing the beach market.

As time progressed, some of these *hithes* took on particular functions, sometimes to the exclusion of others, restricting access (e.g. private wharf) or controlling access (e.g. public markets), whilst others remained 'common', with unrestricted access. This protracted development from a once common, open waterfront embankment to a subdivided, complex riverside zone in which only particular points were accessible to the commonalty would exercise the minds and memories of the London courts in years to come, as thirteenth-, fourteenth- and fifteenth-century waterfront surveys reveal. But such legal niceties lay far in the future: in the tenth century, the Thames-side embankment was most probably a communal work, built and maintained as a necessary social obligation, as was the construction of defensive walls and bridges in many parts of England at that time.

Ships and ship-building in London, 900–1000

Archaeology can throw some light on the range of vessel types that would have plied London's river in tenth century: longships, cargo ships and dugouts. Three famous longships are known from Scandinavian burial sites at Ladby (Denmark), Oseberg and Gokstad (Norway). All were sleek double-ended clinker-built vessels propelled by oars set through oarports cut in the uppermost hull plank, but also with a mast supporting a single square sail. In general profile they would be broadly similar to the war fleet shown on the eleventh-century Bayeux Tapestry. The approximated dimensions of these longships were Oseberg (*c.*AD 820) 21.4m x 4.3m; Gokstad (*c.*AD 900) 23.4m x 5m and Ladby (*c.*AD 900) 20.6m x 2.9m (Delgado 1997)

As for the cargo ships, there is a find rather closer to home to illustrate this type, discovered in September 1970 on the Graveney Marshes, near Faversham in Kent (**colour plate 7**). Its study and prompt publication marked a milestone in British nautical archaeology (Fenwick 1978). This was an altogether smaller vessel, robustly-framed, being some 14m long but with a beam of *c.*3.9m. Like its Scandinavian contemporaries it was also clinker-built, but the iron fastenings that held the hull planking together had been driven through wooden pegs. There were other structural differences between this 'English' vessel and the alien longships: it had a straight (rather than a curved) stem and stern post, which provided a distinctive profile still evident in the bows of Thames passenger wherries 800 years later. The Graveney boat has been dated by radio carbon samples and dendrochronolgy to the tenth century, while the wooden platform upon which it was finally beached has been dated to *c.*AD 950. That it was a hard-working coaster rather than a royal war ship seems clear; indeed, its cargo capacity has been calculated at some 7 tons and residues of hop plants and unfinished millstones from the Rhine found on board (**18**). The latter suggest the vessel was capable of channel crossings as well as working the Thames and Medway.

For many of the families living and working along the Thames and its tributaries, the less complex dugout was still commonplace. The most recent find was made in Clapton on the River Lea in 1987 (**19**) and was a mid-tenth-century vessel some 3.75m long by 0.65m wide (Goodburn 1988). A replica made under the direction of Damian Goodburn took 45 person-days to complete and could carry up to 'four adults or the equivalent weight of pigs' carcasses', to use the boatwright's evocative phrase. At least two other dugout boats of tenth-century date are known from the Thames valley, one from Sewardstone and another from Molesey (Marsden 1996, 222).

As we have seen, documentary records imply that the town was growing as a port of real consequence in the tenth century and it is therefore reasonable to assume that it accommodated a thriving community of ship-builders. How this essential maritime industry was organised and where it was based at this

18 *This large assemblage of lava quernstones represents part of Saxon London's import trade with northern Germany. This group was recovered from the Thames Exchange excavations at Three Cranes Wharf.* TEX 88 Museum of London

19 *Full-sized replica of the tenth-century Clapton dugout. Such craft would have been common on the inland waterways*

time is not mentioned in any surviving written records, and thus the evidence for it must rely on archaeological discovery. For much of the medieval period, it is now known that the practises of vessel breaking, vessel repair and vessel building were closely interrelated. A vessel that had reached the end of its operative life would often be hauled up onto the foreshore and stripped of all reusable material, such as masts, sails and ropework, while iron fastenings would be recovered for recycling. Sound framing elements might well be reused in a new vessel, either directly or as templates for the new design. Consequently, the discovery of a significant concentration of vessel fragments on a waterfront site may well indicate a vessel breaking, repair or building site.

Such a concentration has indeed been found on tenth-century waterfront sites in London, all in the Queenhithe area, and has been studied by Damian Goodburn (1991) and by Hazel Kent, in an unpublished dissertation. The timber assemblage from the Thames Exchange and Vintry sites incorporates some fifty vessel fragments, including not only a variety of plank fragments, but also large and small frame elements, a 5m length of a broad, shallow keel, a moulded stem post and part of a side rudder. The iron fastenings found include a strip of unused roves (the washers used in clinker-building), clear and unambiguous evidence of shipbuilding and repair activity. A preliminary study of the timber fragments recovered from these neighbouring excavations suggests that a number of different vessels are represented, ranging in size from modest river craft to much larger sea-going vessels. Some had iron nails driven through wooden pegs, like the tenth-century Anglo-Saxon boat found at Graveney. Others had the hull planking secured only with iron nails and roves, considered by some to be a 'Scandinavian' style, sometimes using square-headed, sometimes round-headed nails. Others were secured solely with ash or poplar pegs, often seen as a 'Slavic' technique. Two sections of clinker planking from the Bull Wharf site had features of a non-local 'Frisian' style, utilising moss for the seam water-proofing held in place with roundwood battens and iron staples iron staples, and there was also an ash rubbing strake set proud of the uppermost hull plank, a feature best paralleled in the Netherlands rather than in English shipping. There was also a mast partner with a semi-circular cut to accommodate a mast up to 0.45m in diameter, a fragment that clearly represents a substantial sea-going vessel. By comparison, the ninth-century Gokstad ship had a mast with a diameter of 0.30m. All in all, study of this London assemblage was most informative, demonstrating a noticeable variety of vessel-building traditions represented on the tenth-century London foreshore, indicating the wide range of vessels that the beach market accommodated, and which the London shipwrights repaired or built.

Pottery in the Alfredian Port

The social, political and economic upheavals of the late ninth and early tenth centuries are mirrored not just by the dramatic relocation of the port, but also in a marked change in range and sources for the contemporary pottery supplies. When our period opens, London found itself on the frontier of the English kingdom. The most common ware found in Alfredian London is no longer East Anglian Ipswich ware, but that termed Late Saxon Shelley ware, thought to have been brought in from Oxfordshire or other production centres at some distance from London. This marks a pronounced change of outlook and direction for the port, away from the East Coast to a more land-bound hinterland, and so it was to remain until the Danelaw had been won back. Nevertheless, there is some evidence of wider contacts, shown by the occurrence of some Thetford ware from Norfolk, deep within the Danelaw. Continental imports include some Rhenish red-painted ware and Badorf ware, although the overall percentage of these ceramics suggests a substantially lower level of such contacts than in the eighth century (Blackmore 1999). Nevertheless, from these modest beginnings, traffic and trade could clearly grow. The relative lack of coin hoards from the tenth-century settlement suggests a period of relative peace in which mercantile interests could and should prosper. From AD 970, after arguably a rather slow start, the volume of imported pottery does show signs of increasing, at a time when the intensity of occupation in the intra-mural area was markedly increasing. But for London, life would never run too smoothly for too long. The English King

20 *A late Saxon boarded lane leading down to the water's edge, recorded at Three Cranes Wharf in the Vintry.* TEX 88 Museum of London

21 *Solid brushwood base of the Saxon waterfront embankment, seen here in cross-section, river to the right.* BIG 82 Museum of London

Ethelred (978-1016) had been threatened by a new wave of menacing Viking demands: in 991 'it was decided for the first time to pay tribute to the Danes because of the great terror they inspired along the sea coast'. The nightmare had returned and England could either play for time and buy the Vikings off, or battle it out. The following year – 992 – 'the strongest ships from every part of England were assembled at London with orders to catch the Danish fleet' (Garmonsway 1972, 126-7). Thus, for the City, the tenth century ends as it began, with London fighting for its survival. The outcome of this campaign is the focus of the next chapter in the port's eventful history.

5

NEW BRIDGE, NEW MASTERS

The eleventh century was a time of great political upheaval for the port and for the nation. England would fall first to the Danes, who ruled here from 1016-1042, and then to the Normans, following their invasion of 1066. These were warriors who used sea-power to their advantage. The die was cast in the closing years of the old century. In September, 994, for example, a fleet of 94 warships led by Anlaf king of the Norwegians and Swein king of the Danes attacked London (**22**). The *Anglo Saxon Chronicle* recalls that they were repelled by the citizens 'with the aid of God and his mother Mary'. While not disputing the importance of divine providence in such matters, it is clear that the Roman city wall also had a role to play in the security of the port. But recent archaeological research has thrown up another major contributor to London's defence, for it now seems that the first medieval timber bridge over the Thames dates from this period. Such a bridge at such a time would have been deliberately built to serve as a barrier to obstruct war fleets attempting to sail upriver. The structure would have been little more than a robust causeway suspended just above high-tide level, set over closely-spaced piles or caissons. The militia defending London would have manned the bridge, raining rocks, arrows and missiles down upon ships attempting to pass below, a manoeuvre only possible at the lowest tides. No longship could therefore sail through the new bridge with its mast up, since the bridge deck was too low, or with its oars extended since the piers were too close. Consequently such large vessels could only progress upstream when the tide was low and flowing in the appropriate direction. Anybody passing beneath the bridge under those conditions could not do so without the support of the citizen army.

There is ample documentary support for the effectiveness of a bridge built primarily as a defensive measure. In 1016, for example, the *Anglo Saxon Chronicle* records that the Danish war fleet came up to London from Greenwich, but the bridge successfully halted their progress. In order to press home their attack, the Danes were forced to dig 'a great channel on the south bank and dragged their ships to the west side of the bridge'. By this means the City was surrounded, although it held out valiantly until King Edmund's army was able to relive the siege. At Hibernia Wharf, just to the west of London Bridge, excavations in 1979-80 recorded part of a large 4m-wide channel

22 *Viking siege of Lundenburh: the riverbourne raiders are constrained by the bridge to the west and the Roman wall to the north.* Artist's reconstruction by Chris Unwin

running north-west to south-east, that seemed to be aligned on the natural inlet now modified as St Mary Overy Dock. Since it had silted up in the eleventh century, one interpretation is that it formed part of the Saxon defences of the bridgehead (Watson *et al.* 2001, 53-4). This may well be so, but if the southern abutment was indeed protected with a broadly continuous ditch, then that feature once deepened, could, ironically, have been utilised by Cnut's army as the channel through which their longships could have been dragged. An interesting find from this feature was part of an oar or paddle with an oval blade *c.*0.5m long that had been charred by fire (Marsden 1994, 159-160). Such a discovery could be said to support the military interpretation suggested here, with the ditch found in 1979 representing the western end of the siege works dug for Cnut during the battle for London.

Another example of a situation in which the defensive nature of the bridge is precisely described is found in the *Anglo-Saxon Chronicle's* entry for 1052. This is an account of a major disagreement (virtually a civil war) between Earl Harold and the then King, Edward the Confessor, who was in London at the time:

> Earl Godwine with his fleet sailed up the Thames against the tide. He reached Southwark . . . and there waited until the flood tide came up. During this time he had meetings with the citizens of London both in person and by deputy . . . and brought nearly all of

> them over to his side. So when everything was arranged . . . he weighed anchor immediately the tide came up and sailed up river along the southern bank, meeting no opposition at the bridge . . . .

In the event 'the wiser sorts on both side effected a peace between the King and the earl', but the importance of the bridge as a defensive barrier is clear from such contemporary descriptions (Garmonsway 1972, 180-1).

To return to the troubled events of the early eleventh century, in *c.*1000 Ethelred II reminded the nation of the importance of keeping fortresses and bridges in good repair (both obviously key elements in the national defence), and of the obligations connected to military service 'whenever the need arises' (Robertson 1925, 87). By 1008, the need had arisen: ships were being speedily built throughout England for its defence against imminent invasion; shipmen were to be provided to crew the vessels from every settlement: 'from Navestock and Neasden, 4; from Bromley, 1; from Tottenham, 1, from Clapham, 2; from Stepney and from Islington, 2; from Southminster 5, from Clacton, 2' (Robertson 1939, 145). Suitably manned, the new fleet mustered at London to await orders.

The Danish attack came the following year, moving into the mouth of the Thames and plundering the villages of Essex and Kent. They stormed London, but were driven back by the citizens 'with great strength', an event perhaps represented by the hoard of weapons dredged from the Thames on the line of the old bridge. The Danes therefore transferred their attention first to East Anglia and then to the Midlands, which they devastated. London's turn came again and again. On one occasion, only recorded in the thirteenth-century Olaf Sagas, an attack on the bridge itself is reported in which vertical piles or staves supporting the bridge decking were apparently pulled down once ropes had been attached to them by oarsmen who then rowed away (Watson *et al.* 2001, 80). In passing, it could be mentioned that such a method of attack might have been more effective on diagonal braces lapped onto the faces of the support piles rather than on the piles themselves. London then, battered and besieged, stood firm, but in the bitter end, it was all to no avail. The rest of the country was savaged, and London was ultimately forced to submit. King Cnut now had control of the last centre of resistance, a once prosperous port city with seemingly unbreachable defences. In 1018 it was decreed that England would have to pay £72,000 to the Danish army of occupation: London's share was a punitive £10,500 (Whitelock 1955, 286).

A bridge abutment on the southern shore

The construction of London Bridge was a defining moment for the town's defence but would also transform the fortunes of the port in peacetime, as later discussions will show. One of the major contributions that archaeological research has made to our understanding of London's development is in the study of this crucial feature. The recent detailed and perceptive report (Watson *et al.* 2001) has shown that the first medieval timber bridge over the London Thames dates to *c.*1000 rather than, for example, to the Alfredian restoration of *c.*900. The evidence presented for this in the published report is admittedly slight but consistent when studied alongside the phases of river erosion and the chronology of waterfront embankment building on both banks (**21**). The research is based primarily on the excavations at the south bank site of Fennings Wharf in 1983-4, where the spectacular remains of the masonry abutment of the late twelfth-century bridge were uncovered but not, alas, scheduled or preserved. This large site also recorded a long sequence of embankments and erosion horizons together with traces of at least four broadly successive rebuilds or repairs to an earlier timber bridge abutment. Of these, one represents a development before the Norman Conquest of 1066 and will be summarised here, together with the second one, dating to *c.*1070. The third and fourth will be considered later.

Only two disarticulated fragments of the first bridge survived on the south bank, since the long programme of rebuilding and repair had greatly disturbed the site of the abutment here. The first discovery was a squared oak beam some 5.3m long with evidence of joinery cut into it, found discarded in a sealed foreshore deposit. The second beam had been reused in a later phase of the abutment, but dendrochronological analysis demonstrated that both timbers had been cut from the same tree, and that that tree had been felled sometime after 987, but before 1032, i.e. around AD 1000. As to the form that bridge abutment would have taken, more evidence comes from consideration of its successor, represented by a squared beam at least 7m long, the baseplate forming the northern edge of a three-sided abutment, the southern side being formed of the earth and rubble ramp below the roadway. The baseplate had a long groove cut along its upper face, to take the feet of the stave or plank wall that would have retained the abutment infill. Two large square mortises at each end of the beam presumably accommodated piles driven through it to secure the plate to the foreshore. There were also two other rather slighter sockets set some 4.6m apart cut into the upper face, and these may well have held the upright posts that in turn supported the decking. If so, the width of that bridge would have been *c.*4.5m, around 15ft in old money. This is wide for a timber bridge of this date, calling to mind a later medieval description of the bridge in the eleventh century as 'so broad that two wagons could pass each other upon it' (Watson *et al.* 2001, 75).

Development on the northern shore: a piled bridge abutment?

The location of the new bridge also merits comment, since it lay well to the east of the initial harbour developments on the north bank. The position chosen reflects the narrowest crossing point of a wide tidal river since the largest Southwark island projected further northwards at that point, providing a firm and relatively high, dry ground for the abutment. Marshes and mudflats extended to east and west, areas that were regularly inundated with each high tide in the tenth to eleventh centuries. Thus it was the location of the gravel island on the southern shore that dictated where the northern bridgehead would be built, and consequently where London's next major waterfront development would be. Harbourworks were now constructed in the Billingsgate area for the first time, a direct response to the new bridge. This work has been published in detail elsewhere (Steedman *et al.* 1992) and will be summarised here.

Overlying the robbed out remains of the dismantled Roman quay, a rubble and clay embankment had been raised over the foreshore at Billingsgate, providing a dry surface above the level of the low tides, extending for some 20m east-west. It surface incorporated part of the broken-up remains of a clinker-built boat. To the west of this low embankment was a unique feature, a dense concentration of wooden piles projecting well above the surface of the foreshore (**23**) and interpreted in the published report as the base of a jetty (Steedman *et al.* 1992, 101-3). In each row there were five to seven piles set *c.*1m apart, and this dense grid of posts extended at least 13m southwards from the line of the Roman riverside wall. The pile feature seems to have had a relatively short operative life, since it was subsequently subsumed within a later eleventh-century heightening and eastward extension of the neighbouring embankment. The arrangement of the piles strongly suggests that they supported a series of east-west beams that could in turn have supported a decked superstructure.

This feature has been reconstructed by the excavators as a substantial jetty (Steedman *et al.* 1992, cover & figure 57), perhaps one that functioned as a ferry point when the timber bridge was undergoing repair or rebuilding (Watson *et al.* 2001, 74). The arguments against this interpretation are simply that such a jetty-like feature was not required before the bridge was built or indeed would not have been anymore practical as a landing place than the foreshore embankments that already existed. Another interpretation demands consideration, and that is that the piles represent not a jetty but the northern abutment of the bridge itself. There need not be any structural difference between a bridge and a jetty, bar the obvious one of length. As for width, the north bank feature was some 7.5m across, the same width as that proposed for the earliest version of the southern abutment. The 'northern abutment' could therefore have supported a decking some 4.5m wide with ease. Bearing this suggestion in mind, the published reconstruction of the 'jetty' can therefore be

23 *Possibly London's first timber bridge. Pile rows representing a Saxon bridge or jetty with the base of a later brushwood embankment piled around their bases, recorded near Billingsgate.* SM 75
Museum of London

seen as the unfinished northern end of London's first medieval timber bridge, a short-lived or perhaps even a failed attempt at providing a fixed link across the Thames. Indirect, indeed unwitting, support for this interpretation can be sought in an article published by Marjorie Honeybourne in 1969, long before the pile group was discovered. She argued from a study of documentary and topographical evidence (key elements of which have now been disputed) that the original timber bridge sprang from an abutment at the foot of what is now Pudding Lane, between the two waterfront churches of St Magnus and St Botolph's Billingsgate. The location she proposed was precisely where the excavators recorded the late tenth- or early eleventh-century pile-built feature (Hollaender & Kellaway 1969, 15-39, figure p.33).

Whether or not that suggestion is accepted, the archaeological evidence has clearly demonstrated that the harbour was dramatically transformed in the early eleventh century, with the construction of the new bridge and the consequent development of the associated embankments at Billingsgate. It is also possible to suggest that London's shipyards were relocated at the same time, since fragments of at least five vessels have been found broken up in eleventh-or twelfth-century contexts. The most substantial fragments came from the New Fresh Wharf excavations. The planks had been held together with wooden pegs rather than iron clench nails, and moss had been used to render the joints watertight.

Fragments of another pegged-plank boat were recovered from eleventh-century levels on the neighbouring Billingsgate site in 1983. Evidence of riveted plank boats came from the same site and from the opposite shore, where planking, part of the keel at least 2.5m long and a wide plank with an additional wale still attached were recorded reused in later features (Marsden 1994). All these vessels, although representing very different ship-building traditions, seem to have been built from timber felled in south-east England, and serve to demonstrate the variety of vessels in the eleventh-century harbour.

Ethelred II and the reform of the port

The previous chapter showed how in the tenth century, the primary settlement focus developed in the west of the town, around St Paul's. The streets that lead northwards from the Queenhithe waterfront were later known as Bread Street and Old Fish Street Hill, perhaps indicating the type of markets associated with the ancient *hithe* in that period. The evidence of the excavations considered in this chapter have shown that, with the building of the bridge, a new north-south axis was established on the eastern hill, and settlement rapidly expanded along this new Gracechurch Street-Bishopsgate alignment. London now lay at the lowest bridging point of the Thames, a new nodal centre for road traffic. It also found itself at the effective limit of navigation for sea-going traffic. Most ships coming up to London and arriving at the bridge would stop there, berthing on the beach above the high water mark. This seems to be the situation described in the broadly contemporary *Saga of Gunlaug Serpents'-Tongue* recording how 'Gunlaug and his companion sailed into the English Sea, and reached London's *bryggjur* (probably bridge, rather than wharves?) late in the autumn, and proceeded to draw their ship upon the shore' (Ashdown 1930, 191-2).

Such a geographical and economic conjunction therefore provided London with advantages no other settlement in the Thames valley could match. The construction of a timber bridge to obstruct Viking raiders had the consequence of stacking the cards heavily in London's favour: from the eleventh century onwards, in spite of wars and invasions, the port would have to prosper.

Our archaeological evidence, whether from the south or north bank, at present suggests that the first medieval bridge was built in c.AD 1000. This lies squarely in the long reign of Ethelred II (978-1016), the king who often bears the suffix 'the Unready'. If he was indeed the prime mover regarding the decision to build the bridge and if he provided the drive to complete it, then his bad press might require re-examination. There is an oft-quoted document that has a crucial bearing on our understanding of the early eleventh-century port: it is the IV Law code thought to have been issued during his reign but incorporating some slightly later additions (Robertson 1925). It provides the earliest unambiguous surviving documentary reference to the bridge at

London as well an informative list of the tolls to be charged at the newly-designated landing place at Billingsgate, next to the recently completed timber bridge. These regulations can be seen as part and parcel of a deliberately planned reorganisation of London's port, brought about by the construction of the bridge. They also provide a flavour of a beach market, an indication of the crimes and misdemeanours that must have beset the port previously as well as a picture of the diversity of craft on the Thames in AD 1000.

To take the last point first, it becomes immediately obvious that the craft in the harbour were not all of a uniform size. Small ships and small fishing boats paid ½d as toll, a larger ship with sails (presumably twice the capacity) and larger fishing boats paid 1d, while a merchantman that 'arrives and lies there' was charged 4d. Although this larger figure may imply those vessels were four times larger than the previous size class, it may just reflect the alien origins of such craft. The men of Rouen, for example, who brought wine or blubber fish, paid a duty of 6s for their large ships, or one-twentieth of the fish, if that was the main cargo. A ship with a cargo of planks, on the other hand, paid just one plank as toll.

The range of size-classes of craft implied by the range of tolls is supported by recent nautical archaeological research however, and this is summarised in figure **24**. Here tenth- and eleventh-century vessels are shown in profile, ranging from the small English dugout to a great longship, a Scandinavian warship (a rather less welcome presence on the Thames). The dugout, although probably the most common craft at a beach market, was presumably too small to attract the attention of the port reeve, and therefore does not merit a mention in the documentary record. The ½d, 1d and 4d tolls payable at the Billingsgate beach market probably refer to the middle range of vessels. The modest rowed coaster perhaps like the Skuldelev 6 wreck (Denmark) may be the ½d vessel-type. The more robustly-framed cargo vessel from Graveney (Kent), although only a metre or two longer, was considerably wider and has an estimated cargo capacity of some 6 tons, certainly twice that of the coaster: perhaps it represents 'the larger ship with sails' paying 1d. The fourth example is the *knarr* Skuldelev no. 1, a purpose-built relatively deep-draught vessel with an estimated cargo capacity of some 24 tons. This is, conveniently, four times that of the Graveney ship and therefore eligible for a 4d toll. The longships were built for speed, rather than cargo capacity, although such craft undoubtedly visited the port, perhaps transporting persons of rank, they did not 'arrive and lie there', as the regulations describe for the 4d ship, in order to sell off the contents directly from the hold. Since longships did not usually carry a cargo for sale, that type is also excluded from the port code.

It has been suggested that the issue of those harbour regulations relating so specifically to Billingsgate in the early eleventh century implies that a novel situation had arisen, requiring new legislation. Archaeology shows that the building of the bridge and the subsequent establishment of the new landing place did indeed provide the context for the reform of the port. The 'bridge

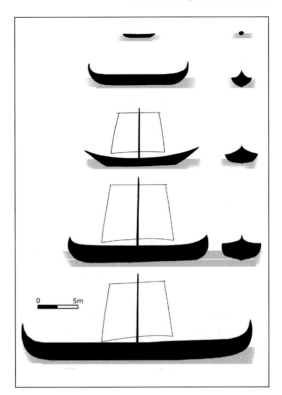

24 *Shipping in the eleventh-century port: diagram showing relative sizes of broadly contemporary craft that would have been seen on the late Saxon Thames, based on archaeological evidence from England and Denmark. J. Stripe, LARF*
From the top: *humble dugout (e.g. Clapton logboat); fishing boat (Skuldelev 6); coastal trader (Graveney); seagoing trader* knarr *(Skuldelev 1); longship (Skuldelev 2)*

effect' on London's trade is even detectable in the ceramic record. Around 1000, in spite of the political upheavals of the time, there is a marked increase in the volume of continental imported pottery found in London, with pottery from Normandy, the Paris Basin, Flanders and the Rhineland all recovered from eleventh-century waterfront sites (Blackmore 1999). That list of sources from which the pottery came is striking when compared with the wording of the harbour regulations, since they contain an account of restrictions on the alien merchants frequenting London's harbour. Men from Flanders, Ponthieu, Normandy and the Isle of France were obliged to display their wares and pay the appropriate toll, as were the men from Huy, Liège and Nivellas (**25**). By contrast, German merchants, subjects of the Holy Roman Emperor, enjoyed some of the same privileges as the English, and were allowed to buy wool and melted fat as well as up to three live pigs for the return journey. They were obliged to pay some tolls at Christmas and Easter, however, and that provides some indication of the cargoes being handled, as they were charged two lengths of grey cloth, one length of brown cloth, ten pounds of pepper, five pairs of gloves and two saddle kegs of vinegar.

The market was not just concerned with exotic cargoes from distant lands, as the list also records that hampers containing hens were charged one hen for toll, and hampers with eggs were charged five eggs toll, while the women who dealt in butter and cheese had to pay a penny during the fortnight before Christmas, and another penny the week before that festival. This seems a high charge, comparable with the larger fishing boats, and therefore implies that cheesemongers were engaged in a major London concern, the large-scale production and sale of dairy produce.

The fifth section of the code incorporates 15 clauses that seek to address the problems of coinage in the port. Study of these clauses provides a painfully clear picture of fraud and deception, from which it can be seen that the development of a cash economy (rather than the simple exchange of goods with a like value) was not easy. The basic problem was that the silver pennies in circulation were all too often defective in quality and weight, and consequently not worth their weight in silver as they should have been. There had been instances of counterfeit coins made from fraudulent dies, often using the name of a genuine moneyer. There had also been instances of genuine moneyers striking coins knowing them to be under weight or otherwise under value, often having been bribed by merchants. It was even clear that port reeves, the town officials responsible for the good order of the port, had been accessories to these frauds. If confidence in the coinage was failing, then traffic and trade would not prosper. This is the context that explains the presence of many coin balances recovered on waterfront sites. These attempts at precision balances were the traders' only chance of avoiding the worst of the counterfeit coinage. The measures prescribed to rectify the situation demonstrate how serious it was: moneyers shown to have produced defective coin were to have the offending hand chopped off to prevent them repeating the crime, while those that were caught working in the secrecy of the woods (rather than in the town) could lose their life.

The Code goes on to command that all the king's bishops, earls, ealdormen and all his reeves, 'both among the Danes and the English' to be on the watch for those who coin base money. This reference to a substantial Danish presence suggests that these sections of the Law Code were added during Cnut's reign, and implies a level of economic anarchy, at least during the initial years of the Danish occupation.

The coming of the Normans

England reverted back to Anglo-Saxon rule in 1042, with the accession of Edward (the Confessor) to the throne. He was the son of King Ethelred (the Unready), and great-great grand son of King Alfred; superficially therefore, his lineage was indisputably Saxon. However, his mother, Emma, was the daughter of the Duke of Normandy. Edward actually grew up in exile there, adopting much of the culture and language of that country. It was ruled by his uncle and then by his cousin Robert I (1027–35) who had a son called William, a blood relation who would also rule England. Thus Edward's reign introduced

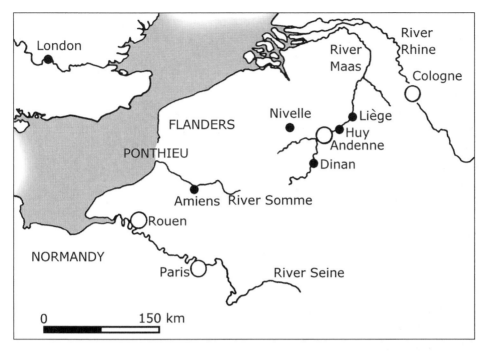

25 *London's Anglo-Norman cross-channel trading links, as represented by imported pottery found in the City. The open circles mark the main pottery production sites.* After Vince 1985, figure 11. By J. Stripe, LARF

London to the new king's Norman favourites, witnessed the development of an Anglo-Norman trading partnership and saw the town's first Romanesque building, Westminster Abbey consecrated on the banks of the Thames in 1065. While he was alive, Edward therefore promoted an ever closer relationship with Normandy, an entente that was not regarded cordially by many of his English subjects. He even promised the throne to his blood relation William, who was then Duke of Normandy. Following the death of Edward in December 1065, the Duke prepared and then launched a massive invasion to claim the crown, held all too briefly by Edward's brother-in-law, Harold Godwinson. The year was of course, 1066, the battle was at Hastings, the result, though close run, was a victory for the invader.

Having defeated the English army on the slopes of Senlac Hill on 14 October, William then marshalled his troops and set about subduing southern England, taking Romney, Dover, Canterbury and Winchester. His initial attack on London was driven back by the strength of the defenders on the bridge. There is also archaeological evidence for additional structures being constructed on the Thames waterfront, since a line of free-standing upright staves rising up to 2.5m above the contemporary foreshore was recorded, defending the embankment at Three Cranes in the Vintry. The dendrochronological study shows that the staves were cut from trees felled in the infamous winter of 1066/7. A similar-sized stave wall that had collapsed forwards was

63

also recorded on the Billingsgate waterfront (**26**). In this instance, the dendrochronologist was unable to be so precise since the outermost growth rings had been trimmed off the edges of the staves. Nevertheless it proved possible to suggest a date range of sometime between 1050 and 1070 for the felling of those timbers (Milne 1992, 26-7; 48-9).

Initially, London defences held firm. The Norman army withdrew, venting its wrath on Southwark and ravaging the countryside as far west as Wallingford where they finally crossed the Thames. The length of this major detour incidentally shows just how significant London Bridge was to north-south communications, since Wallingford lies a further 50 miles inland. The Conqueror's army then turned towards London, destroying all resistance, raping and pillaging at will. Now increasingly isolated, the capital knew what its fate would be if it resisted and lost. The documentary evidence is ambiguous, but there seems to have been some resistance followed by surrender on 'honourable' terms: London would be left in peace in exchange for acknowledging the brutal William as king. The discovery of part of a cemetery at the confluence of the Thames and the Fleet may date to precisely to this period: if so, that waterfront excavation would serve as a reminder of the Conqueror's terms. The bodies were crudely buried under piles of stones on the foreshore just outside the City wall: there were eleven bodies, but only three skulls and the group included men, women and at least four children (Mills 1996).

The new King then issued a charter in which he cordially greeted the Bishop of London and Gosfregth the port-reeve, the two leading officials, as well the townsfolk, described as 'both French and English', suggesting a significant Norman presence had already established itself there well before the Conquest. The charter went on to confirm the rights that London enjoyed 'in the time of King Edward', a phrase that referred to the previous year, but to a bygone age

26 *This tall oak stave wall has collapsed southwards into the river. Structures such as this may have been erected as part of the defence of the harbour during the troubled years of the eleventh century.* BIG 82 Museum of London

(Robertson 1925, 231). The upheavals of the second half of the eleventh century are even reflected in something as simple as the production and distribution of London's most common types of pottery, as the Late Saxon Shelley wares are replaced by products with different forms and fabrics from new kiln centres established to north and south of the Thames. There was no going back.

Mills and fisheries on the Thames

Although no returns for the City itself in the *Domesday Survey* of 1086, there are indirect references to the port in that great document. In the returns for Surrey (Morris 1975a), for example, London properties assessed with properties in Southwark list 111 holdings in the City, from which dues of between 2 and 40 pence were payable, reflecting a healthy property market. There is also a reference to the beach market on the southern shore, the rights to which were held by the Bishop of Bayeux in 1086. Previously, King Edward had held them, taking two parts of the income from the waterway 'where the ships moored'. Earl Godwin apparently took the third part, although the men of Southwark declared that before 1066 no one but the King took tolls on the shore or from the waterway (*in strande et in uico Aquae*).

Working upriver through the Thames-side Hundreds of Brixton, Kingston Elmbridge and Godley on the Surrey shore (Morris 1975a) as well as in Middlesex on the opposite bank (Morris 1975b), it is clear that the river and its tributaries continued to play a major economic role, since over 40 mills are mentioned. If the listed value is directly related to size and profitability, it seems that modest mills were operating at Thames Ditton (15d), Cobham (three worth 13s 4d); Kingston (five worth 20s); Stoke (one worth 6s and one worth 7s) and Battersea, where no fewer than seven mills were valued at £42 9s 8d, or the equivalent amount of grain. Larger mills were in operation at Staines (six worth 64s); Woking (11s 4d); Walton (two worth 12s 6d each); Stanwell (four worth 70s); Harmondsworth (three worth 60s) and Stepney (five worth £5 16s), with the largest concerns at Merton (two worth 60s), Mortlake (two worth 100s) and an additional one at Stepney (66s 8d).

Excavations on an eleventh-century waterfront site at Three Cranes Wharf recovered no fewer than 235 fragments of lava quernstone fragments (**18**). These had been fashioned from basalt lava, a non-native rock with a rough surface eminently suitable for the manufacture of hand querns as well as the larger millstones. All the London examples were broken before being discarded in the mud of the early eleventh-century foreshore, where they served as rubble for a phase of encroachment or as convenient stepping stones. Such stones were often transported as 'blanks' or rough-outs, then cut to shape once they were closer to their final destination. Study of the London assemblage showed that most stones, although broken, were unfinished. This leads to the suggestion that the stones might represent the detritus from a quern-stone finishing workshop in the immediate vicinity, the sort of specialist craft that a port like London would attract (Freshwater 1996).

The Domesday Book returns show how common mills were in the Thames valley, and it also demonstrates that fisheries were another major industry (Morris 1975a & b): Kingston had four, two worth 10s, a third described as excellent, and a fourth worth 125 eels, Byfleet had two worth at least 325 eels, Stanwell four (one worth 400 eels and three weirs worth 1,000 eels), Harmondsworth two (500 and 1,000 eels) and Petersham at least one worth 1,000 eels and 1,000 lampreys. There were other fisheries recorded at Walton and one at Mortlake (previously owned by Earl Harold), weirs at Staines and Shepperton, with fishing nets and dragnets worth 3s at Hampton. Freshwater fish was therefore a major commodity for the Thames-side communities, but there is also evidence for London's direct involvement in marine fishing, since there are also herring renders mentioned for Ditton and in the entry for Walkingstead, referring to duties payable on dwellings in London and Southwark. The recorded total for London is worth 2,500 herring, a figure to set beside those from coastal settlements such as Southwold's 2,000 (Suffolk), Brighton's 4,000 (Sussex) and the 60,000 from Dunwich (Suffolk).

Power over the port

London's new Norman masters stamped their authority on the port in no uncertain manner. As the great bulk of the White Tower rose at one end of the City waterfront, for which many bargeloads of Caen stone and other bulky building materials were shipped into London, another masonry tower was being constructed on an eyot in the mouth of the River Fleet, just north of its confluence with the Thames. This was the Fleet Prison, the foundations of which were recorded in 1988. It was a building some 12.5m by 10.5m across internally, with walls some 2m thick and turrets at each of the corners (McCann 1993). This was the architecture of power, grim masonry towers dominating a single-storey timber and thatch town, symbols of the uneasy relationship that now existed between London and its temporal lord.

To sum up, the new bridge gave eleventh-century London its unfair advantage, but there are factors other than the merely geographic that determine the fate of a port. A particularly pressing example in this period was the sudden imposition of an all powerful feudal monarchy, belligerent, antagonistic but wary of the 'vast and fickle populace'. The monarch needed a milch-cow, while London wished to be left as a law unto itself. The subsequent history of the Norman and Plantagenet port, in part at least the working through of these demands, shows that the one usually guaranteed the other.

6

PORT IN TRANSITION

The end of the waterfront wall

During the course of the twelfth century there were a series of significant changes in the topography of the harbour and equally significant changes in its mercantile infrastructure. These related developments, when considered together, mark a period of fundamental transition for London as the era of the 'beach market' gave way to the development of the merchant port. The archaeological evidence shows that as the old Roman riverside wall no longer dominated the waterfront, riverwards encroachment increased, masonry warehouses were introduced, larger cargo vessels were developed and the ceramic evidence suggests increased traffic and trade.

Since the 880s, London had relied on the repaired bulk of the great Roman riverside wall to protect its riverside flank. Such measures were essential to a town with a fortress mentality, to a town that had been besieged and occupied by riverborne invaders. But London was now part of the Anglo-Norman empire and its new masters had confidence in its future and saw the development of its harbour as a prime concern. The riverside wall was thus removed, partially undermined by the river, partially cleared by Londoners. A late twelfth-century commentator William Fitzstephen states that the 'most excellent river the fishful Thames, in which the tide ebbs and flows . . . has undermined the walls in that part.' (Wheatley 1956, 502). Whether or not the river was wholly to blame, it seems clear that London no longer felt the need to repair and maintain that defence.

The waterfront was now opened up for the first time since the early Roman period. The wall that for over 700 years had dominated the view of the City from the river and restricted the access of Londoners to the foreshore had gone (**27**). In its place an east-west street was (gradually) laid out in two sections, one either side of the mouth of the Walbrook. This provided a public thoroughfare (later called Upper and Lower Thames Street) that served variously as a routeway, fish market or rope walk. Excavations below Upper Thames Street in 1974 exposed a collapsed section of the Roman wall sealed by the first surfaces of the new Thames Street, which was dated to the twelfth century. On the neighbouring site at Baynard's Castle clear evidence was found for the gradual erosion of another rather longer stretch of the wall (Hill *et al.* 1980). Similar situations have been recorded on several other waterfront sites.

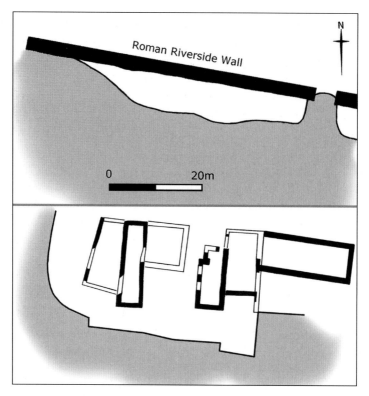

27 *Waterfront development and the Roman riverside wall: schematic plans of the Billingsgate sites showing, above, the eleventh-century timber and clay embankment providing dry ground at high tide to the south of the Roman wall (note the 'gate' in the wall and associated inlet); and, below, major encroachments and waterfront buildings in the late twelfth and thirteenth centuries, constructed after the removal of the wall: note earlier inlet now infilled. After Steedman et al. 1992. By J. Stripe LARF*

Twelfth-century harbourworks

With the removal of the riverside wall, partially by accident and partially by design, harbour activity was no longer confined to gaps and gates, but could now extend where it might. To the south, the process of encroachment began as the face of the embankments were advanced riverwards with the construction of timber revetments on the open foreshore. This process marked the 'privatisation' of the reclaimed land. Initially, some of these encroachments may have been made by individuals who owned or occupied the tenements immediately to the north of Thames Street, while other extensions may have been initiated by fishermen, merchants or others with a particular stake in waterfront development. What these new extended riverside properties had in common was that they were not designed to increase public access: that was now confined to the ends of the main streets that led directly onto the open foreshore. As the newly won private properties either side of the lanes pushed ever southwards, so the public lanes became ever more pronounced inlets (**6**).

The timber revetments built to retain the new generation of waterfront encroachments differed from the tenth- and eleventh-century structures either in style or in scale (**28**). The principal posts that supported those with a horizontal plank cladding were still set earth-fast into post pits cut into the foreshore, but the increased height of these structures (usually in excess of 2m) demanded additional support, often in the form of diagonally-set braces (**colour plate 9**). Even some of the stave-built revetments that were set in large grooved base-plates incorporated earth-fast posts at intervals to provide greater stability (Milne 1992, e.g. 53-67). A further example of late twelfth-century riverside development was examined on the east side of the River Fleet, close to the confluence with the Thames. Here, in 1160, the Knight Templars were granted land for the construction of a watermill. Excavations in 1988 recorded a substantial tract of reclaimed land, upon which the mill building would presumably have been set, together with part of a masonry lined tank and culverts, possibly representing part of the overflow system (McCann 1993).

London's timber bridge, damaged in a storm in 1097, was rebuilt only to be burnt in the Great Fire of *c*.1136, a ferocious conflagration that destroyed much of the timber-built port. Remains of the new bridge were recorded in 1984. The design adopted differed from the earlier version, incorporating a timber box-like caisson some 6m by 4m (**29** & **30**). This utilised substantial squared oak beams, laft-jointed at the corners, that had been cut from trees

28 *Excavating the substantial remains of a twelfth-century wharf in the Vintry.* TEX 88
Museum of London

felled some time after 1158. The resulting structure was not dissimilar to medieval waterfront structures recorded on several Norwegian sites, and was infilled with clay and chalk rubble (Watson *et al.* 2001, 76-7).

Cargo carrying, cargo storing

Another significant change was the introduction of masonry warehouses onto the waterfront, as will be described later. This event arguably marks the beginning of the end of the era of the beach market from a topographical perspective, marking a break with the period when ships had to serve as carrier, container and retail outlets. Working from the evidence of wreck sites found around the Baltic and North Sea, Ole Crumlin-Pedersen has suggested that the cargo capacity of ships increased significantly in this period, a development that is directly related to the introduction of waterfront warehouses. Before 1000 there is little archaeological evidence for vessels with a cargo capacity greater than 20 tons. By 1100, vessels such as that found in Hedeby harbour could carry 60 tons while the late twelfth- or early thirteenth-century ship found in Bergen, Norway has an estimated capacity of over 100 tons (Bill & Clausen 1999, 18). This new generation of what could be termed bulk-cargo carriers would have been used by wholesalers in conjunction with new warehouses rather than just operating from the vessels themselves, as would have been the case in the beach market era. Thus there is increased evidence for specialisation in cargo-carrying, cargo-handling, cargo-storage that, taken together, represents the dramatic rise of the middlemen, the specialist merchants. Thus a new, rich and influential class of commercial entrepreneur was inserted into the social order, widening that stratum of society that was not bound to the crown by feudal or military obligation.

Increased specialisation also begins to appear in, for example, pottery production, as many new kiln sites were established to meet the needs of an expanding population. The kilns closest to the capital tended to produce more tablewares, while those further out in the expanding hinterland in Hertfordshire or Middlesex, for example, concentrated on the less expensive cooking pots. This zoning might have also been reflected in London's effect on the wider agrarian regimes practised there, perhaps an increasing market-gardening zone closest to the town, with bulk products such as grain and fuel from the outer ring. On the twelfth-century London waterfront, the distribution of imported pottery also seems to mark the development of significant changes. There is a marked concentration of coarse wares and early glazed jugs from Normandy in the Vintry and also, pre-1200, in the Billingsgate area, together with material from Rouen and the Paris basin (Blackmore 1999).

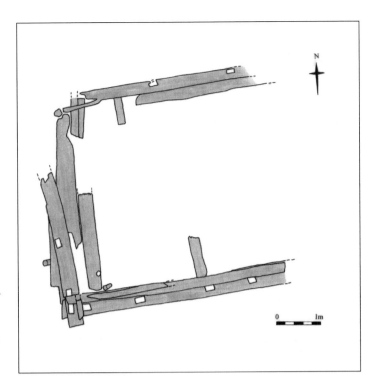

29 *Plan of the twelfth-century timber bridge abutment recorded at Fennings Wharf.* After Watson *et al.* 2001. K. Brandon LARF

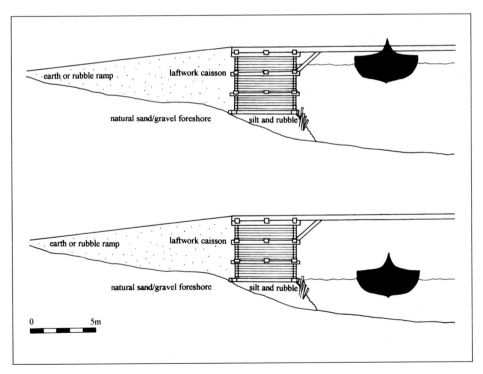

30 *A reconstruction of twelfth-century timber bridge abutment showing the river at high and low tide – ships could not pass through the bridge at high tide.* After Watson *et al.* 2001. K. Brandon LARF

Regulations and restrictions:
beach markets in the mid-twelfth century

A possible context for these related developments may be seen in the contemporary harbour regulations. London had grown used to the presence of alien merchants in the eleventh century. Although increasingly regular visitors, they were not always warmly welcomed, as is shown by the record of the additional payments and restrictions placed upon them. An early surviving set of such restrictions dates to a period after the 1130s, and concerns the men from Lotharinga, in Lower Germany (Bateson 1902). This document also encapsulates a moment of transition in London's economy, when the form and function of the beach market was showing signs of fatigue caused by conflicting pressures from different directions. On the one hand we learn how the powerful elements amongst the Londoners wished to maintain their tight control over the market in which their merchants were given the first choice of the merchandise brought in, with the merchants of Oxford second and those of Winchester third. This is a clear reflection of the extent of London's ancient hinterland. On the other hand, the restrictions heaped on the heads of the Germans reflect a changing situation in which the alien merchants were trying to stay in London for more than 40 days, rather than just sailing in and sailing out. The implication is obviously that German merchants were ignoring the waterfront market and taking their wares to a presumably more profitable location inland. The foreshore was no longer the primary focus of all trading activity.

The detailed twelfth-century document describes the procedures that these merchants were required to adopt and thus, by implication, draws attention to types of practice that were previously commonplace but not always acceptable to some of the more powerful factions in the city. There is as much to be read between the lines as upon them in these remarkable regulations.

Wine barrels had been arriving in the port that had clearly been open for some considerable time, to the detriment of the contents (and possibly the crew). The new regulations demanded that no tun could be breached until the ship was in the Thames and en route for London. The presence of the German traders had to be signified by flying a flag from the mast to identify them, and also by the crew singing *Kyrie eleison*, not only to give thanks for a safe voyage, but to prove their Christian credentials. Presumably pagan pirates would fail such a test. According to the 'old law' (a reference to Ethelred II's Law Code, see previous chapter) the merchants could travel as far as the Billingsgate beach market site at London Bridge, where the contents of first barrel opened would be sold retail at one penny per stoop. However, should the merchants wish to carry their cargo through the bridge to the markets at Queenhithe or Vintry, different terms applied. Having passed underneath the timber bridge, the ship had to moor in midstream before any produce could be sold for a period of a day and a half, measured as 'two ebb tides and a flood' (it will be remembered that it was only possible to pass through the bridge upstream on an ebb tide). This delay gave time for the authorities to be alerted and for the sheriff and King's chamberlain to board the vessel and have the opportunity to select the cream of the cargo, ostensibly for the King, should there be any cups of gold or silver, or precious stones, fine linen or similar commodities. It appears that the King was allowed a fortnight to decide whether or not to purchase the goods selected.

Nobody else was allowed on board the vessel during this period for trading purposes (unless they were buying their stoop of wine) on pain of a 40s fine. In this way the King, or at least his officials, maintained an initial monopoly on all such goods brought into the port. Once the King's interest had been so served, the residue of the cargo was opened up for the merchants of London to consider. Only after their needs had been satiated were the merchants of Oxford allowed to board the ship, and after them, those from Winchester, and after them, 'all merchants from within and without London'. This serves to suggest that a sense of order and a logical queuing system may have been lacking in the port prior to the passing of these regulations. Presumably a volatile mix of medieval merchants all boarding the boat at the same time was seen as unsafe as well as bad for business.

But the pecking order is itself of considerable significance, and serves to show how regulated the beach market had become, reflecting the all-pervading feudal order of Norman society rather than any economic rationale. The crown came first, followed by the London merchants, the mercantile equivalent of the baronial class. Indeed, a charter granted by Henry I in 1130 'let all the men of London and their property be quit and free from toll and from all other customs throughout all England and at the seaports' (Douglas & Greenway 1981). Such substantial privileges may not have counted for much during the succeeding civil war battled out between Stephen and Matilda (1136-1154), but the essence of the charter was confirmed in 1155 by Henry II. The London traders were determined to dominate their market, and were prepared to pay for royal patronage to achieve it.

To return the twelfth-century harbour regulations (Bateson 1902), if the port officials chose not to board the ship during those initial three tides, then the Lorrainer could sell and others could come and buy without forfeiture, although there would still be tax to pay. If the boat was classed as a *keel,* the largest of the traders, then two tuns would be taken for the King from below the mast (the main storage area) and one before the masthead. If the vessel was classed as a *hulk,* or other trader, then just two tuns were taken. For these, the King paid a reduced price depending on the quality of the wine. There were three classes identified: the best, the mean quality and the lowest. Needless to say, the King bought the higher quality at the lower prices. With the exception of the first barrel opened, a measure that served as a sampler as much as refreshment, the Lorrainers now had to sell the rest of the cargo wholesale, by the half or whole hoshead. The implication here is that on earlier visits to the London beach markets, the wine ships may have operated as temporary floating bars, a feature that would have annoyed taverns in the city.

The restrictive practices did not end there. To encourage the Lorrainers to remain on board their vessel during their stay in the port, and to sell all their cargo on the foreshore directly from the ship, it was decided that such traders would only have to pay the (relatively modest) tax on wine. This benefit was being actively promoted to clamp down on current practice which saw some of the Lorrainers leaving their ships with their goods, crossing Thames Street (the street on the landward side of the waterfront embankments that effectively defined the northern limit of the city's beach markets in the twelfth century), taking temporary lodgings elsewhere in the city and selling their cargo in the inland markets. Such a merchant now had to inform the port officials where he was staying and could not unpack his goods for sale for three days. The implication here is that the foreign merchants had been trying to avoid the arrangements whereby the King's officials were able to purchase the cream of the cargo directly from the ship as soon as it arrived in the harbour. But even if he had set up a temporary shop in the City, he could no longer sell cloth retail, only by the whole piece. Nor was he allowed to buy unwrapped wool, any previously opened wine barrels (i.e. only wholesale, by the tun), no unsalted (green) fleeces or hides, and no single lambskins taken out of its bundle. All such purchases had to be wholesale and neither could he buy more than three live pigs for his table, or fines were payable to the officials. The line that divides a fine from a tax or a tax from a back-hander was never clear in the later medieval port: these twelfth-century regulations set the tone for the complexity and petty corruption that would become part and parcel of the port's administrative machinery.

Some merchant Lorrainers were obviously trying to stay in the City longer than 40 days, another activity the new regulations were unhappy with, although some excuses for delayed departure were well-rehearsed and common enough to become enshrined in law: these were that debts owed or withheld should be resolved first, or that bad weather or 'some other evil' were allowable reasons for extended stays. It is perhaps not unsurprising to learn that some Lorrainers wished to pass straight through the City to trade outside its restrictive boundaries. Even these merchants were obliged to stay for one night within the city boundary first, and had to unpack all their goods, thereby displaying their wares to the intense scrutiny of the London officials.

There were fewer restrictions on the men ruled by the emperor of Germany (with the exception of those from Tiel, Bremen or Antwerp), who were allowed to engage in the retail market, selling pepper, wax and cummin by the quarter and cloth such as fustian by the yard or half yard. There were even fewer restrictions on the Danes who had clearly built up an influential power-base in London during their occupation in the mid-eleventh century. They retained the right of *Bosat*, that is, the right to set up stalls or houses and to stay for one year, rather than living and selling in boats. In addition, they enjoyed the same privilege advanced to London merchants, for they could trade in any English fair or market. The Norwegians also claimed *Bosat*, but were obliged to confine their trading activities to London.

Waterfront warehouses (31 & 32)

By the twelfth century then, selling directly from a boat was not the attraction it once was, although for a small-scale trader, market gardener or fisherman it was no doubt still acceptable. However, a professional merchant bringing in a large mixed cargo in a deep-draught ship, now seemed to prefer custom-built shops, stalls and warehouses for bulk storage and wholesale selling. Certainly an alien merchant allowed to live in London would need such facilities rather than accommodation in boats or tents. The restrictions placed on alien merchants by the Londoners, ostensibly to protect the City's own interests, ironically may have had the reverse effect. The alien merchants were thereby encouraged to band together for mutual support and benefit. The growth of these federations of foreign merchants began to alter the balance of the London

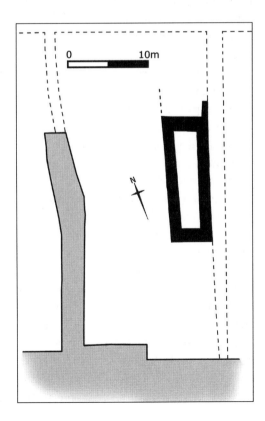

31 *Twelfth-century Wine Wharf at Three Cranes in the Vintry: foundations for an early waterfront warehouse alongside a lane leading down to the Thames.* J. Stripe, LARF

32 *Building on substantial foundations: the footings of this early twelfth-century waterfront warehouse comprised a beechwood raft with oak sill beams supporting masonry walls: the 0.5m scale rests on the rubble core.* TEX 88
Museum of London

market. None became more powerful than the merchant communities of the German Hansa, for they grew in strength and influence by developing monopolies of trade in many European ports. They were obliged to deal in bulk, using larger ships than the parochial English, who handled little of the country's export trade and fewer of its imports.

This significant development in economic practice, signalled by the introduction of masonry warehouses onto the waterfront, is represented by the substantial foundations of such twelfth-century buildings. On the Thames Exchange site, for example, although most of the stonework had been robbed and removed, the massive timber foundation preparation for the warehouses still survived. This comprised a spread of cleft beech planks supporting base plates cut from large oak slabs, a foundation designed to spread the load of the masonry walls over the newly reclaimed and rather unstable land (**31** & **32**). Dendrochronological analysis of samples from the beech logs suggested that they came from trees felled in 1136, just after a disastrous fire had swept through much of the timer-built town. Stone buildings provided more security against fire and theft and would obviously be an essential attribute for parties wishing to store valuable commodities for any period of time. Secular masonry buildings with stone-lined storage cellars have also been recorded both by antiquarians and by archaeologists on several London intramural sites of this date, at Corbet Court and Milk Street for example (Schofield 1995, 74). The introduction of masonry waterfront warehousing can first be seen at Queenhithe and Vintry above the bridge, and on both the west and east banks of the Walbrook confluence. Both those areas were particular merchant enclaves, one for the Anglo-French wine trade, the other the German merchant entrepôt.

It was therefore in these alien enclaves that bulk storage and bulk selling was introduced into the London commercial orbit in a way that was rare in the heyday of the beach market. These new warehouses represent a significant change in the infrastructure of the harbour, perhaps most graphically expressed on the site of the Hanseatic Steelyard (**33, 34 & 35**). Here a commodious aisled hall at least 18m long and 10m wide has been excavated, identified as the twelfth-century guildhall of the merchants of Cologne. The walls of the building survived up to 1m in height and had been set over alternating layers of rammed gravel and chalk. The internal floors were of chalk and mortar and the remains of an arcade was recorded on the eastern side if the hall, comprising square bases cut from imported French Caen stone, over which Greensand columns would have been set. It seems that the ground floor of the hall was used for storage while the upper floor would have provided the space for administrative and other functions. Part of the associated wharf frontage

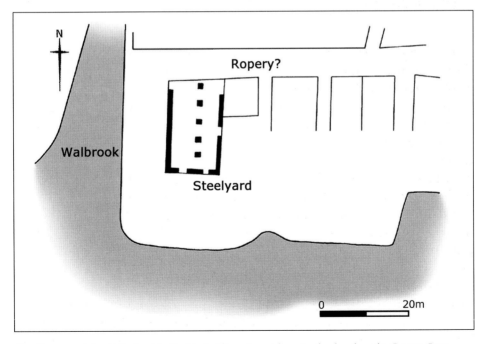

33 *German merchants Steelyard in the late twelfth century: schematic plan based on the Cannon Street Station excavations (UTA87). The aisled guildhall is set at the confluence of the Walbrook and Thames at Dowgate.* J. Stripe, LARF

34 *Recording the remains of the German merchants' twelfth-century entrepôt underneath Cannon Street Station.* UTA 87 Museum of London

35 *Part of the masonry footing of the arcade of the guildhall built for the merchants from Cologne in the late twelfth century.* UTA 87 Museum of London

may also have been recorded, constructed from a wall of upright timber staves erected to the south of an earlier sequence of clay and brushwood embankments (MoL 1990, 22-3).

London transformed

Our conclusion must be that the twelfth-century 'economy' was clearly running itself, without any help from pundits, chancellors or computer models. The London beach markets were not concerned with balance sheets but with bolstering a feudal social system based on extreme privilege, restrictive practices, protectionism, barter and back-handers. The charters granted by Henry I in 1130 and confirmed by Henry II in 1155 (Douglas & Greenaway 1981) showed that the London traders were determined to dominate their market, and were prepared to pay for royal patronage to achieve it. This was not an economy based on the principles of free enterprise, but it was on the move.

By the end of the twelfth century then, the topographical evidence, the archaeological evidence, the documentary evidence all seem to agree that London was now more than a beach market; it was an international port of consequence. By the end of the century, the City had also acquired a new identity to match its changing economic status: to mark its increasing self-confidence, it now had a mayor to govern it, a post held for over twenty years by Henry Fitz Ailwin (1189-1212). It also adopted its own saint to look after it, the martyred Archbishop Thomas who ennobled 'London by his birth and Canterbury by his death' at the hands of King's knights in December 1170. But there could be no more fitting symbol of the City's late twelfth-century transformation than the product of a 33-year building programme that began just six years later. This saw the old timber bridge replaced by one of the wonders of the age: a massive masonry bridge that lasted for over 600 years. The timber bridges had proved their worth as defensive measures, but had been susceptible to fire and flood and structural failure. London undertook some serious long-term planning and was now building in confidence for the future.

A contemporary if biased description of the late twelfth-century port was penned by one William Fitz Stephen just before work on the new bridge began. It provides a fitting finale to our study of the Anglo-Norman harbour:

> Amongst the noblest and celebrated cities of the world, London, the capital of the kingdom of England, is one of the most renowned, possessing above all others abundant wealth, extensive commerce, great grandeur and magnificence . . . . The artisans of the several crafts, the vendors of the various commodities, and the labourers of every kind, have each their separate station, which they take up every morning. There is also in London, on the bank of the river,

amongst the wineshops which are kept in ships and cellars, a public eating house: there every day, according to the season, may be found viands of all kinds, fish large and small, coarser meat for the poor, more delicate for the rich . . . . To this city, from every nation under heaven, merchants bring their commodities by sea (Wheatley 1956, 501).

7

TO GOD AND THE BRIDGE

London's new masonry bridge was not just an impressive architectural achievement and a symbol of the prosperity of the expanding port, but also spoke of its piety. The chief architect was one Peter, the chaplain of Colechurch, and a prime feature of the structure was the great chapel built over its largest pier. The chapel was dedicated to St Thomas Beckett, to whom London was devoted: the saint also appeared on the Common Seal of the City. In its first century, Londoners such as Alexander and Matilda Palmer who wishing to bequeath property for the upkeep of the great bridge declared that the gift was 'to God, the Blessed Thomas the Martyr, London Bridge and the brothers and sisters there serving God'. Others put it more succinctly as 'to God and the Bridge' (Masters 1972).

There were other masonry bridges in England at this time: the *Grand Pont* at Oxford dates to 1091-2, the bridges over the River Lea at Stratford and over the Wear at Durham were built a generation later, and that work began on the masonry foundations of Kingston Bridge in *c.*1170 (**colour plate 10**). Consequently, it cannot be said that London Bridge was the first stone bridge built in England, but it was the most famous (**36**). The documentary evidence states that work began on this great project in 1176. However, the dendrochronological study of samples from piles associated with the southern abutment excavated in 1983-4 shows that work did not begin on the Southwark shore until 1189-90. It therefore follows that work commenced on the City shore and worked slowly southwards. Once the techniques of piling and constructing the foundations for the pier bases had been perfected, then a simultaneous programme of work could start in the south and work northwards. Suggestions as to how this remarkable engineering feat was achieved have been discussed elsewhere (e.g. Nash 1981; Watson *et al.* 2001, 85-9).

Given that the northern abutment of the stone bridge (unlike the southern end) may have been established on a new site to the west of the original timber structure, it is possible that the timber bridge remained in use for a further decade or so after work began on its masonry replacement, especially if it were set at an oblique angle to it. Retaining the old bridge for as long as possible would have benefited road traffic and the new pier construction work. Only when the line of the new bridge reached that of the old would the timber-

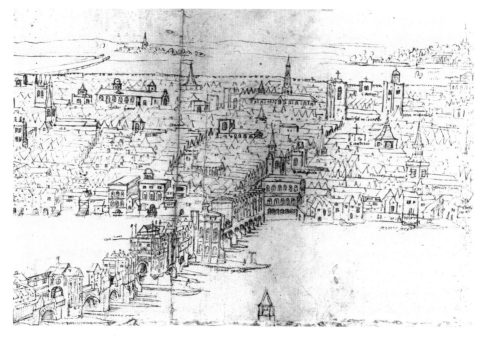

36 *London Bridge in the mid-sixteenth century: the largest pier was the one supporting the chapel. A section from Antonis Van der Wyngaerde's panorama of London.* The Ashmolean Museum, Oxford

work be removed, after which work on the southern abutment could begin. The dendrochronological study of foundation timbers recovered in 1983-4 could suggest that this point was not reached until 1189. The southern abutment itself measured some 19m from east to west at its maximum width, projected 11m northwards and would originally have stood 4.5m above the foundation level. The ashlar facing was set over oak sill beams and comprised a mixture of materials including Kentish ragstone, Wealden 'marble' and Purbeck stone, while the core infill comprised chalk rubble (Watson *et al.* 2001, 90-1).

By 1209, London had a new masonry bridge linking the City to the southern shore (**37**). Study of the surviving sixteenth- to nineteenth-century plans and drawings implies that it was *c.*270m long, comprising some 20 arches supported by 19 rather irregularly-set piers set on large oval artificial islands, termed cutwaters. There is an obvious anomaly with that plan however, since the largest pier, the one that accommodated the chapel, does not appear to be set in the centre of the span. There seems to be general agreement (e.g. Home 1931; Watson *et al.* 2001) that the chapel was on the ninth pier from the north or the eleventh from the south. This pronounced lack of symmetry could therefore reflect the practical consequences of building over an uneven bed of an aggressively tidal river. An alternative view is that the chapel was initially more centrally set, and that the abutment on the City shore was set further to the north than is shown on the earliest accurately surveyed maps of London, such as the *Ogilby & Morgan* survey of 1676. This suggestion is supported by archaeological excavation in the Billingsgate area that recorded the alignment of the waterfront in the late twelfth to early thirteenth century. If the northern abutment was built in line with that (i.e. below the southern edge of the church tower of St Magnus the Martyr), then there would be sufficient space to the south of it for an additional pier. Presumably the abutment and pier were enveloped by waterfront encroachment by the fourteenth and fifteenth centuries, a common fate for medieval bridges as at Kingston and Exeter, for example. The basal levels of the very first bridge pier to be constructed in the

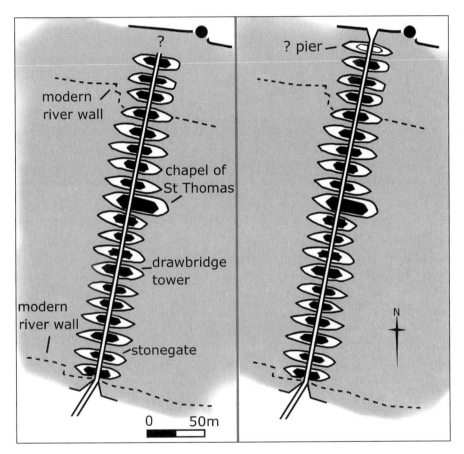

37 *London's new stone bridge. The diagram on the left shows an outline of the bridge based on the excavation of the south abutment and an eighteenth-century survey, suggesting a span supported on 19 piers (after Watson et al. 2001). Dashed line marks the alignment of the modern waterfront; solid line marks alignment of the twelfth-century waterfront, based on archaeological evidence; black dot marks position of the earlier piled timber feature excavated near Billingsgate, perhaps an eleventh-century bridge abutment on the north bank (see **23**). Note the north end of the stone bridge recorded on post-medieval maps does not extend as far as the twelfth-century riverbank: the diagram on the right rectifies that anomaly by adding a hitherto unsuspected twelfth-century pier. J. Stripe, LARF*

late twelfth century might therefore still survive beneath the modern buildings, a potential discovery of some significance for future waterfront archaeologists. If this revised plan of medieval London Bridge is accepted (it is no more than a suggestion), then the bridge would have been rather longer at 300m, and the chapel would lie, arguably where it belongs, right in the centre. The pragmatism of the medieval engineers might have been responsible for irregularities in the pier positions, but perhaps the location of the chapel was determined by pious purpose and accurate surveying.

Building history

Work on the bridge did not stop once it was completed in 1209. There was a major fire in 1212 that destroyed the houses that were being built upon it; following a severe winter in 1279-80 that saw the Thames frozen over, five arches collapsed. To help pay for the urgently needed rebuilding, tolls were charged from 1281 at a farthing per foot passenger, a penny per horseman and a ½d per pack of goods. Further embellishments in the fourteenth century included the rebuilding of the chapel of St Thomas from 1384-96 and a new drawbridge in 1388. Since 1405, there had been further work on the Drawbridge Gate, and the drawbridge itself was renewed by 1426 (Masters 1972).

   Meanwhile, emergency repairs were being undertaken on the span beyond the Chapel. For a while, all iron-shod wheeled traffic was banned from the bridge, but in January 1437 disaster struck: two arches at the southern end actually collapsed. By the end of March, a timber structure had restored the crucial link, and this 'temporary' bridge continued in use until 1466. The excavations at the Fennings Wharf site showed that the southern abutment had been substantially rebuilt in the fifteenth century, a major development presumably associated with this phase (38). A large number of elm piles were driven into the foreshore just to the east of the twelfth-century abutment and, over a foundation of oak sill beams, a new ashlar wall was raised, in which the masonry blocks were held together with iron clamps. The northern face of the abutment was thereby increased in width by $c.5$m.

   The Bridge, like much of the Thames waterfront, was also subject to a programme of continuous routine maintenance. The Bridgehouse Account Rolls record the work of the 'tidemen', the team responsible for the upkeep of the starlings, dangerous work only practical at low tide involving the use of piling rams mounted on sheer-legs to drive home the wooden piles that protected the piers. Then there was the delivery of the huge quantities of stone required by the gangs labouring on the continuing maintenance and repair of the superstructure (Spencer 1996, 213). The most common cargo listed was ragstone from Kent, and a modest fleet of stone barges made the regular

38 *The stone bridge at London was considerably larger than that at Kingston, as this view of the foundations of its south abutment shows. The piles are being sampled for dendrochronological analysis on the Fennings Wharf site.* FW 84 Museum of London

journeys to Hoo, Gillingham or other Medway ports to collect the stone. Often two vessels would travel together, apparently effecting the round trip in six to seven days if required, as in 1388, but usually taking rather longer. Large quantities of chalk were also required and each year a separate consignment of northern stone (from Yorkshire) arrived, usually in July or September. Rather less regular were cargoes of Beer or Portland stone from Dorest, Quarr from the Isle of Wight, or Caen from Normandy. Timber was brought in from eleven sites in Surrey, eight in Kent, six in Middlesex, three in Buckinghamshire and one in Berkshire. Thus the Bridgehouse records show the extent of the hinterland that the expanding city relied on for the supply of its building materials.

Navigating the bridge

The closely set starlings that protected the piers were a navigational hazard, since they impeded the flow of the river creating a weir-like effect at some states of the tide. It was thus dangerous for small vessels to attempt the 'shooting of the bridge'. In 1429, for example, *The Chronicle of London* recalls that a barge carrying the Duke of Norfolk and his substantial retinue set off from the river stair at St Mary's (now Southwark Cathedral), but collided with one of the starlings on London Bridge and overturned. Several were drowned, but the

Duke himself and two or three others scrambled onto the piles surrounding the starling, and were hauled to safety on ropes let down from the bridge.

Larger vessels needing to pass beyond the bridge would need to wait until the drawbridge was raised; information on this complex manoeuvre is contained in the detailed monthly accounts complied by the Bridge House Estates. The account roll for 1381-2 records the collection of 1d per vessel moving to and from Queenhithe, Vintry and Westminster, for example (Harding & Wright 1990). The grand total for that year is c.2,220 pence, which gives a clear indication of the volume of traffic on that part of the late medieval river, as well as how lucrative toll collection could be. That figure presumably represents two journeys per vessel, since what goes up must come down. But is it likely that the drawbridge was actually raised over 2,000 times per year? This seems impractical, given that vessels could only attempt the passage through the bridge when the tide was flowing at an appropriate speed in the appropriate direction. Perhaps what happened was that vessels wishing to move upstream would anchor in a line waiting for the tide to turn. Once the pennies had been collected, presumably by the Bridge House boatman, the drawbridge would be raised to allow all the vessels through in convoy. Such a manoeuvre may well have taken an hour or more to make best use of the tide.

Ships passing through the bridge, coming into or leaving a port need to signal their movements. Before the now familiar sirens were invented, medieval seamen made do with rather more modest but equally effective instrumentation, the long signalling trumpet. A remarkable late fourteenth-century example was recovered from the Billingsgate excavations in 1983, made up from a copper zinc alloy in four sections. A hole had been bored in the rim of the bell, suggesting that a pennant or flag had been hung from it (**39**).

Once all the ships had passed through the bridge in convoy, the drawbridge would be lowered to allow road traffic to cross again. The procedure would be repeated some four hours later to facilitate the passage of vessels back down stream. Thus the bridge would be closed to road traffic for at least an hour or more twice a day. The stalled road users could therefore watch the delicate progress of the ships between the cutwaters, or retire to the many riverside inns conveniently positioned at either end of the bridge (and on its span) until the land link was restored.

The monthly average of vessel movements through the bridge in 1381-2 was 184, or some seven ships each working day. Those figures do not take account of considerable fluctuations, however, with over 200 per month in October and November (230, 262), in March and April (257, 286), and in June and July (253, 210). The busiest week was in mid-June, when vessel were passing through at a rate of 25 per day, while the quietest months were, not unsurprisingly, January and February, with just 81 and 102 ships respectively. For five weeks in the year, the bridge was not opened at all, either because there was no traffic, as at Christmas, or because of bad weather.

Politics and pageantry

As the principal entry point for a proud city, the bridge also had a significant ceremonial role to play, as in 1357 when the Black Prince crossed the Thames in triumph with the captured French King, or in 1415 when Henry V was welcomed home after Agincourt. Thus London Bridge symbolically linked the port to external events that shaped and reshaped the country's future. In 1421, for example, the City put on a great pageant to commemorate the triumphal arrival of Henry V and his French queen Katherine. Preparations for this great occasion required the labours of a carver, a plasterer, five joiners, 13 carpenters, up to 16 wood stainers and four cloth painters, not to mention the assorted costumed 'virgins' needed for the parade (Watson *et al.* 2001, 122). But the bridge was also used for another form of political display, that of the heads of traitors and enemies, a practice that seems to have begun in the 1280s after the beheading of Llewellyn ap Gruffydd and then his brother David. These trophies served to repay the port for its contribution of 6,000 marks for Edward I's war in Wales. Other such souvenirs displayed in the harbour included the head of the Scottish warrior William Wallace in 1305.

There were also a series of events on London Bridge that had a more direct effect on the course of English history. In 1263 for example, a period in which many Londoners felt increasing antagonism for the poor administration of

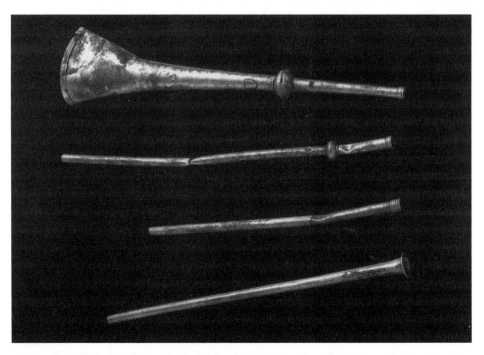

39 *Sounding the alarm: a ship's trumpet, found in four sections, on the Billingsgate waterfront.* Museum of London

Henry III, Queen Eleanor was pelted with stones and insults as her barge tried to pass below the bridge. This incident on the Thames inflamed an already volatile situation that then boiled over into civil war: the London militia marched out to the Battle of Lewes in 1264 to support Simon de Montfort's cause against the crown. The defence of the Bridge in later uprisings also proved to be a turning point. During Jack Cade's rebellion in 1450, there was a furious battle between the Londoners and the rebel army in Southwark. This resulted in a great loss of life and the destruction of the drawbridge and much else, but the rebellion was put down. There was a rather too familiar replay of events in 1471, during the assault by rebels led by Thomas Fauconberg, supporting the Lancastrian cause. The Stone Gate on the Southwark shore was attacked on Sunday 12 May, and again the following Tuesday, when 14 houses between the gate and the Drawbridge were destroyed. On both occasions the rebels were repulsed. The Bridgewarden's accounts for the heroic defence of the Bridge reveal costs of 38s for gunpowder, 76s for 51 sheaves of arrows; 44s for canvas soaked in vinegar to protect the drawbridge from 'wildfire' and 2s 7d for 62 loads of water used to dowse the flames. Other costs included payments of 44s to the two Aldermen who directed the defence, 6s 8d for writing a letter to Edward IV concerning the incident and its outcome, and 4s to send it by horse to the king, who was then at Coventry (Masters 1972, no. 20). The medieval port of London was not just an engine of the economy; it was a force to be reckoned with.

8

MERCHANT PORT

From Magna Carta to the Great Custom

The great flowering of art and architecture for which the thirteenth century is renowned was based on a robust cash economy in which the King, the church, the barons, the merchants, townsfolk and peasants all engaged. London established itself as a major driver of the economic momentum: one eighth of the total national revenue in 1203 was collected there. The influence of the port was therefore widely felt. The London merchants, for example, allied with the baronial class to confront King John, and ensured that their interests were well represented in the Magna Carta signed so reluctantly at Runnymede on Thames in 1215. They demanded that: 'London shall have all its ancient liberties and free customs as well as by land as by water' (*clause 10*); that 'henceforth all fish weirs shall be cleared completely from the Thames & the Medway and throughout all England, except along the seacoast' (*clause 33*); that 'there be one measure for wine throughout our kingdom, and one measure for ale, and one measure for corn, namely the London Quarter' (*clause 35*) and also that 'all merchants . . . shall be able to go out of and come into London safely and securely, and stay and travel throughout England, as well as by land as by water, for buying and selling by the ancient rights and customs, free from all evil tolls, except in time of war . . .' (*clause 41*).

King John's reign saw the loss of Normandy in 1204, ending in civil war and an invasion by the French from 1215-17. London's relationship with Henry III (1216-1272) varied from cordial to uneasy to outright opposition: indeed there was a strong London faction that rode out in support of Simon de Montfort during the civil war of 1258-65: the Provisions of Oxford include the complaint concerning 'the City of London and all other cities of the King that have gone to shame and destruction through tallages and other oppressions'. Edward I (1272-1307) was slow to forgive the City for the wrong it did him and his father, but needed London's money to support his wars against Wales, France and Scotland. For these, new taxes had to be raised, such as the taxes on the export of wool, fleeces and hides, as stipulated in the Great Custom of 1275; the port had a key role to play in bankrolling the Plantagenet cause.

The material wealth of London and the disposable income of its inhabitants increased markedly in the thirteenth century, in spite of a series of political setbacks. This statement is supported in dramatic fashion by the archaeological evidence, for this shows a clear contrast between the relative poverty of the finds assemblages of twelfth-century date (Vince 1991) when compared to the range, quality and exuberance of the material from the succeeding century, be it pottery, metalwork, dress accessories or even shoes (e.g. Egan & Pritchard 1991; Egan 1998; Grew & de Neergaard 1988). Even the ponderous Norman architecture is succeeded by the more inventive 'Early English' styles, and multi-storey timber-framed buildings make their appearance on the London streets. This was a town transformed: this was a consumer culture.

London's economic impact on the surrounding counties continued to grow in tandem with its population. Its firewood was drawn principally from Middlesex and Surrey, with Kingston and Ham developing as important distribution centres for this bulky commodity. The hinterland that supplied grain to the capital was noticeably more extensive, routinely extending as far west as Oxfordshire, as far north as Hertfordshire and Bedfordshire and east into Essex. Again, river transport was an important consideration. As for livestock, the drove roads that led to London reached even further into the English countryside (Galloway 1999). London was thus sustained by these rich hinterlands and they in turn prospered on the profits of the port.

The port expands

The economic pattern that had begun to evolve in the previous period developed rapidly in the new century. Expansion was the watchword, and encroachment moved forward at a startling pace on the waterfront, not just in the core area already described but extending eastwards beyond Billingsgate and westwards beyond Queenhithe. The most common type of structure used to effect this great advance was now a full-height timber-framed revetment, often braced from the landward as well as the riverward side (**40**). This was a time when London's house builders were experimenting with multi-storied framed buildings: the complex range of contemporary riverfront revetment design mirrors this period of architectural innovation. These waterfront structures were then clad with horizontally-set planks, often pegged to the upright posts. Tipped in behind the planking to make up the ground level were cartloads of midden material taken from the City's rubbish dumps and stable sweepings. This was hardly appropriate landfill material, but it was clearly available in quantity and presumably at no charge. And it was this unsavoury medium that significantly increased the size of the port. The rate of encroachment was sufficient to concern the City fathers in 1244, who saw the increase as a potential hazard for navigation (Chew & Weinbaum 1970, no. 343), although the archaeological evidence shows that Thames-ward encroachment continued unabated for the next century or so. Indeed, the rubbish-packed

40 *The thirteenth-century timber-faced wharf recorded at Billingsgate, viewed from the river.* BIG 82
Museum of London

reclamation zone soon extended so far south as to comprise two separate sets of properties, a northern one accessed from Thames Street and a southern one facing the Thames, accessed by a new private lane laid out alongside it.

As for the commonalty, they still needed to draw water, take their livestock to the river, make use of the public latrines. Such activities were now centred not on the common embankments but just at the end of the lanes that were regarded as common (as opposed to the privately-owned one). There were, in consequence, complaints when these lanes leading down to the Thames were obstructed, hindering access to the river (e.g. Weinbaum 1976, no. 443). The riverward end of some of these lanes remained as inlets, that is with ramps or slipways leading down to the Thames. These were used by Londoners to water their horses for example. Some of the others were infilled and extended south-wards in tandem with the neighbouring properties; these now had a river stair or jetty extending from their foot. It was relatively easy to draw water or hire a ferry from those points. Alongside the common stairs and landing places, the majority of the waterfront properties were now served by their own private river stair (**colour plates 11** & **12**) The largest private watergate on the Thames served the Tower of London, and was built next to the Wakefield Tower (**51**), a reminder the river traffic was as important to the Crown as to the daily life of medieval London.

Thus, apart from the common lanes and common quays, the waterfront was now in private hands and built up with multi-storey commercial, residential and industrial buildings, such as the vast dyehouse recorded on the Swan Lane site close to London Bridge (**41**) This building, with its series ranks of hearths, exemplifies the scale of urban industry in this period, for this was not a shed in the backyard but a full-blown factory (Egan 1991). The textile industry was big business and labour intensive, and London had a controlling interest in it.

The City's new waterfront façade was much enhanced by the new masonry bridge. However, the bulk of the piers constricted the flow of water through the bridge, making navigation rather hazardous. This served to enhance the twin focus of the port, with the western harbour still at Queenhithe and Vintry but with the major port facilities to the east at Billingsgate. Here, as elsewhere in the City, substantial buildings with storage undercrofts were now the norm.

The western half of the waterfront was dominated by the enlarged profile of St Paul's minster church. To the tower was being added a massive spire that could be seen by mariners approaching the City for some miles distant. This symbolised both the piety and the prosperity of the port, as did the presence of a string of smaller parish churches along the waterfront, not to mention the remarkable chapel dedicated to St Thomas, actually built on the bridge, and accessible directly from the river.

The wards were responsible for the security arrangements and the maintenance of good order in the harbour. East of the Bridge it was the men of Billingsgate and Dowgate, west of the bridge, men from Vintry, Queenhithe and Castle Baynard, while the bridge itself was policed by men from Candlewickstreet and Bridge wards. Crossing the Thames by night was forbidden, and the sergeants at Queenhithe and Billingsgate ensured that all the boats there remained moored throughout the night. By 1278, prostitution had been banned from the port, or at least from the intra-mural settlement, but flourished in the stews of Bankside on the Southwark shore.

Merchant port

By the thirteenth century, the development of the merchant port was all but complete: bureaucracy and middlemen had become commonplace. London's new merchant class accumulated large fortunes and exercised considerable influence. This is shown by the following examples of merchants who all served as Aldermen and Mayors but also enjoyed strong court connections. John de Gisors (mayor 1246; 1258-59) was a major wine importer and included the crown amongst his clients. He was appointed Royal Butler from 1236-56 and was strongly opposed to Simon de Montfort, unlike many in London. He held a great messuage on the Thames in the Vintry and his family later owned Gerard's Hall in Basing Lane, the undercroft of which was recorded in 1852 (Schofield 1994, 158). Gregory de Rokesle (mayor 1274-81; 1284-85) was a goldsmith who also shipped wool in quantity, but became known as one of England's leading wine importers. He served as the Royal taker of wines in Southampton and was appointed Royal Butler in 1275. When he died he left a chantry at All Hallows Haywharf, in Dowgate (Williams 1970, 323-336). The shadow cast by the wine trade on the archaeological record is indirectly represented by the evidence of pottery: during the early thirteenth-century, northern French pottery is the most common imported ceramic (**42**) and even the local 'London-type' wares potters were producing jugs in the French style. However, from the 1250s onwards, Saintogne pottery from south-west France (**43**) marks a pronounced change in the focus of the port's overseas traffic (Vince 1985).

Wine was thus a major element for the import trade, but wool and cloth were also big business. Adam de Basing (mayor 1251-2) was a prominent Draper whose family fortunes were founded in the twelfth century. He dealt extensively in wool, but primarily supplied the court with high quality materials such as cloth of gold, chasubles, mitres, copes, vestments and banners. Another family whose name survives in the City street map was in Andrew Buckerel of Bucklersbury (mayor 1231-37). He exported hides, but also dealt in wool and French wine, and made sufficient profit to pay for the expenses of Henry III coronation, as Royal Chamberlain.

These summary biographies point to a crucial aspect of London's buoyant economy, the servicing of the English aristocracy. It was not just the crown that demanded a lavish lifestyle but so too did the rest of the court, the barons and

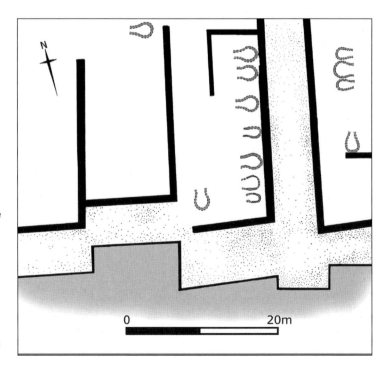

41 *Waterfront industries: a thirteenth-century dyehouse complex recorded on the Swan Lane site, where evidence of some 50 key-hole-shaped hearths were found, presumably for heating dyeing vats.* After Schofield 1995, figure 250. By J. Stripe LARF

0   20m

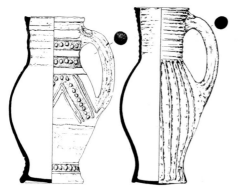

42 (Above) *Rouen jugs found in London represent traffic with northern France.* Vince 1985, figure 16, Museum of London

43 (Right) *Saintogne jugs found in London represent the Bordeaux trade.* Vince 1985, figure 22, Museum of London

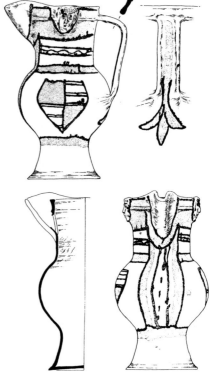

the bishops. London was a magnet for the medieval élite, many of which had an established residence there. These opulent town-houses became 'centres of conspicuous consumption' and ensured that a substantial proportion of the wealth recouped from rural estates was spent in London (Barron 1995). As an example, the Bishop of Winchester's waterfront palace can be cited, part of the Great Hall of which still survives in Southwark. It was built in the early thirteenth century and at almost 9m wide and over 40m long, was one of the largest in the land. Seventeen other bishops, both archbishops, at least twenty-two abbots and six priors all had a major residence in or close to the medieval capital, not to mention an unknown number of secular lords, knights and other prominent personages (Schofield 1995, 34-5). Several of these mansions graced the waterfront, notably in the western half of the City, and along the Strand to

Westminster. Examples for which there is some archaeological evidence would include Bigod House at Broken Wharf, owned by the Earls of Norfolk, the Bishop of Baths Inn (Arundel House), the Archbishop of York's house at York Place, and of course, the Palace of Westminster itself. The port's merchant community provided the imported wine in the required quantity, its craftsmen and women obliged with clothing, tableware, jewellery and furniture of the appropriate quality, and there was always work for the best architects, masons and carpenters. Consequently London's economy fared better than any other town in the kingdom.

The pronounced development of the merchant port manifested itself not just in the acquisition of personal fortunes, but in the very topography and fabric of the waterfront, both in its extensions and in its sub-divisions; in the rise in the number of warehouses and counting houses; in the increasing size and frequency of ships, in the range and quantities of cargoes passing through the port, in increased hustle and bustle. This is also the period for which there is increased documentary evidence both for regulations and for violations of the rules of the port: we are introduced to *forestallers*, those who buy up produce just before it reaches the official market, *engrossers*, those who purchase in bulk solely to sell it on at a higher price, and the *regraters* who bought produce in one market just to sell (at a profit) in another (Archer *et al.* 1988, 5).

The revitalised merchant port is also evident in the artefact record, as thirteenth-century waterfront sites produce significantly more lost coins than in earlier periods. For example, Alan Vince has catalogued just 11 twelfth-century waterfront coins compared with 47 thirteenth-century specimens (Vince 1985, 80). The coinage was dramatically reformed in 1279, when the London mint produced new silver pennies as well as new round halfpennies and farthings (fourthings). Previously, such small change had been produced simply by cutting pennies in halves or quarters as required, a system widely open to abuse from those who chose to clip the cut edges of the silver coinage. Further evidence of economic expansion is provided by the presence of lead tokens and copper jettons, which make their first appearance in the London markets in the thirteenth century. So too do such items as steelyard weights, of which three are illustrated in the London Museum catalogue in 1940 (plate 38). They are globular in shape, made of bronze with a lead core, and are embellished with heraldic devices to announce their authenticity. The arms are those of Richard, Earl of Cornwall (the younger brother of Henry III) or his son Edmund, and clearly demonstrate official interest in such matters. Indeed, it was the same Richard from whom the City had been obliged to purchase Queenhithe harbour in 1240, and the same man who controlled the London mint from 1244. The earliest examples of the steelyard weights have shields with double-headed eagles on them, and date to the period after 1257, when Richard had been elected 'King of the Romans'. He had been a strong advocate for the German merchants working in London, and had persuaded his brother (Henry III) to grant them their first charter in 1260. Henry had previously given permission for Merchants of Koln to attend fairs and markets throughout the kingdom and also to establish their Gild Hall in London. The German merchant enclave was known as *The Steelyard*, and this name seems to have been transferred to the official weighing machinery in the vicinity. Richard died in 1272, and his son Edmund seems to have taken over his role, since a third of surviving steelyard weight bears not only the arms of the Earl of Cornwall but also those of his wife, Margaret de Clare. Another example from the British Museum has the arms of Edward I's beloved wife Queen Eleanor (d.1290), again demonstrating a very real royal interest in the regulation of the port.

Fragments of tally sticks have been recovered from several London sites, some dating back to the thirteenth century (Egan 1998, 276). They comprised strips of alder or hazel wood, in which a series of notches had been cut to record a particular transaction, either a sum of money or a series of quantities. For example, a v-shaped notch the thickness of a little finger could represent £20, a smaller notch the thickness of a grain of barley, £1, while pence would be marked by cuts without notches. The stick would then be cut obliquely. The larger section, including the uncut base, was known as the *stock*, and would be retained by the party that was owed payment. The smaller part, the *foil*, was held by the other party until such time as the debt could be settled, the two halves matched and then cancelled. The largest fragment found on the London waterfront was 390mm long and recorded a complicated transaction represented by notches arranged thus: 10 small, 11 medium and 1 large, followed by 10 medium, 1 large, then 10 medium, 1 large, then 7 medium. It is uncertain precisely what was being bought or sold, but clearly it was a considerable sum (Egan 1998, no. 914).

A number of personal seal matrices have been found in London (**colour plate 13**), on which the names of men (and occasionally women) are recorded in reverse. These would be impressed into bees wax applied to documents or goods to authenticate them. These seals appear in London from the thirteenth century onwards, and became a standard part of a merchant's accoutrements as the merchant port developed. Some of the earliest examples belonged to *Willi Fabri*, William Smith of Southwark, a *John of London*, *Walter of Reigate* and also *Matilda Islebel*. The later examples include bronze seals lost by foreign merchants as well as Londoners, and record the names of *Albert Beien*; *Arnold of Wulven*; *Beatricis*, daughter of Hugh; *Johan Demeken*; *John Tuwetfelde*; *Pautonerius of Podio*; *W Lawrence*. The loss of a seal matrix was a serious business if it fell into the wrong hands so a new design would have to be made as soon as possible. Unless they had clearly been cancelled, the lost London seals in the museum collection therefore represent a series of major domestic crises for the individuals concerned, like losing all your credit cards today.

1 *Obsolete warehouses, last vestiges of the great Victorian port of London, under demolition in 1972.*
Museum of London

2 *Tower cranes dominate the skyline as the mile-long London waterfront is redeveloped over a 30-year period: new buildings rise on the Trig Lane/Sunlight Wharf site in 1987*

3 *A unique archaeological opportunity: the waterfront redevelopment programme opened up massive riverside sites for the first and last time. The scale of the challenge is shown on this view of the Baynard's Castle site in 1972, where the excavation programme was restricted to just one month.* Rescue

4 *Remarkable preservation: the waterlogged conditions on the London waterfront sites preserved the timber wharves and foundations of the medieval riverside tenements, as shown here on the Trig Lane site in 1974. The view looks north-west towards the land, over the remains of a sequence of fourteenth- (foreground) and thirteenth-century (background) waterfront revetments.* TL 74 Museum of London

5 *The broad brushwood base of the Saxon waterfront embankment recorded near Queenhithe.* BUF 90 MoLAS

6 *Finds from Lundenwic: a group of large loom weights, representing London's burgeoning textile industry, dated by association with mid-Saxon pottery found on the Savoy site in 1924.* Museum of London 17-18. Copyright Museum of London

7 *Half-scale replica of the tenth-century Graveney boat on the Thames. Such craft could ply their trade around the coast and inshore waters*

8 *The Thames Archaeological Survey team recording the mid-Saxon fish trap discovered on the open foreshore at Chelsea.* Museum of London

9 *The face of the late twelfth-century waterfront at low tide: the excavator stands on the foreshore to the south of a front-braced timber-planked revetment facing a wine wharf at Three Cranes Wharf in the Vintry.* TEX 88 Museum of London

10 *Kingston Bridge was originally built, like the great stone bridge in London, in the late twelfth century. The excavations here show the landward abutment and two piers as rebuilt in the fourteenth century, before they were all subsumed by later waterfront encroachment.* HOR 86 Museum of London

11 *On the foreshore to the south (left) of the front-braced wharf in the Vintry, the footings of an early thirteenth-century jetty can be seen.* TEX 88 Museum of London

12 *The structure in the foreground is part of a scissor-braced trestle that supported an early thirteenth-century waterfront jetty projecting out into the Thames from wine wharf in the Vintry (see P11a).* TEX 88 Museum of London

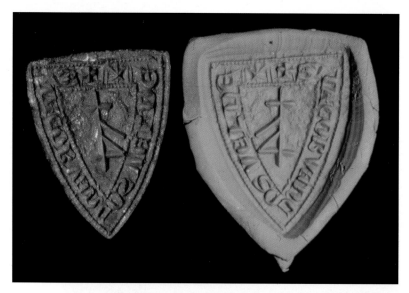

13 *The seal of a Dutch merchant Jacob van Cosveloe, together with an impression taken from it.* Museum of London

14 *Fourteenth-century seal matrix for the Westminster Staple with a positive impression taken from it.* Museum of London

15 *This fourteenth-century seal matrix for the Port of London would have been used by customs officers such as Geoffrey Chaucer.* Museum of London

Port practice

The *Liber Albus* (Riley 1861) has much to say on the everyday procedures in the revitalised late-thirteenth to early-fourteenth-century port: aspects of the traffic in grain, salt and wine will be reviewed here. The grain trade dealt in wheat and rye imported for bread, barley for brewing and oats for animal fodder. London's grain hinterland in this period stretched out some 20 miles for road traffic, but as far as 60 miles from the centre for waterborne transport with major intermediate markets at Henley, replacing Wallingford upriver, the Kentish ports of Maidstone and Faversham downstream, with coastal ports of Rye (Sussex) Sandwich, New Romney (Kent) to the south and as far north-east as Great Yarmouth (Norfolk) (Campbell 1993). By 1280 there were four recognised grain markets in London, two of which were inland at Cheapside (St Michael-le-Quern) and Gracechurch Street (All Hallows). The other two were in the harbour at Billingsgate and at Queenhithe, held on the common land between Thames Street and the River, the site of the ancient embankments in the days of the beach market.

These waterfront markets took place on Mondays, Wednesdays and Fridays, and opened as the church bells chimed half-prime (Archer *et al.* 1988, 9). The standard practice at Queenhithe is recorded in the *Liber Albus* thus: the bakers and brewers provided the 24 staff needed to measure and then distribute the grain. The two activities were inter-linked, since the charges levied both for tax purposes and for porterage were directly related to the precise quantities involved. Measurement therefore had to be both public and reliable. This involved the provision of eight chief master-meters, armed with the requisite tools of the trade, a set of measures incorporating a quarter, a bushel and a half-bushel, and a strike (the tool used to level off the heaped grain), together with his horse, the preferred beast of burden. Each Master had three assistants constantly on stand-by, each with a horse and at least five sacks to shift the grain from the ship to the meter. The meters and their assistants were not supposed to interfere in the negotiations between the buyers and sellers, but clearly did from time to time. For the unwary, they also sometimes charged higher rates for their services than they should: these rates were set at three-farthings (¾d) per quarter for carriage from Queenhithe north to Cheapside and east to the Walbrook, 1d in the outer zone from Cripplegate to Billingsgate, and 1¼d to the suburbs from Temple Bar to Smithfield.

The trade in salt was also significant, but required a smaller eight-man team. This comprised four meters each armed with a bushel measure, a strike and a spud, and each supported by a single assistant with a ready supply of 'good and sufficient sack', i.e. not ones that were split and leaking. The approved practice here was that salt should be brought from the ship to the meter's bushel-measure in two sack-loads, with the third load heaped on top and then smoothed flat with the strike. The sharp practice, by contrast, was to use more than two loads of half-full sacks, in which the actual volume of salt poured into the bushel was bulked up with increased air trapped by the smaller loads. They also occasionally interfered with the deals being set up between buyers and sellers, and had been known to charge 'beyond one farthing more' for their services especially in regard to carrying the salt to the zones already described for the corn trade.

The authorised salt meters of Queenhithe enjoyed a monopoly that extended from London to Yanlet Creek, the eastern limit of the port at the confluence of the Medway. For this privilege, they had to pay a fee to the Bailiff of Queenhithe of five shillings, while each of the assistants paid up to two shillings. Even the casual labourers had to pay 'an amercement of two pence at the least or three or four pence at most'. If any of these 'poor labourers' were convicted of any wrongdoing, they could be dismissed forthwith. Once the salt had been measured, the Bailiff then charged the merchant 2d for every five quarters of salt (one ciphe), followed by a further 2d tax per ciphe for the King, unless the merchant was a freeman of the City. Only after the salt had been off-loaded, all of the cargo carefully measured and all dues duly exacted, could it be carried to Salt Wharf to be sold.

The movement of large wine barrels was also a labour-intensive exercise. It was decreed that a team of at least 12 men would always be on standby, ready to lift a tun from the vessel onto the quay. For this activity there would be a charge of no more than 2d, which included transport to one of the cellars on the adjoining quayside. Beyond that however, the charges naturally increased: to a property on one of the other lanes between Thames Street and the river, it was 2½d; to a cellar north of Thames Street in the parish of St Martin Vintry, 3d, to other cellars in lanes running northwards from Thames Street, 4d, to cellars of the Ropery (i.e. east of the Walbrook), 6d; elsewhere within the City, 10d. These prices are very much higher than those charged for the porterage of grain, and reflect the specialist nature of the work as well as the bulk and profitability of this particular import. If the merchant provided his own cart, he would benefit from a substantial reduction, and then would be charged just 4d for the carriage of one tun or of two pipes, barrels which were half the size of the standard tun.

Transportation was by no means the only additional cost now faced by merchants: there was also a range of tolls and taxes.

Pesage: (Riley 1861, 199) This was levied on all bulk items brought to London by merchant-strangers, and sold in gross by the half or whole hundredweight. Such material was usually weighed on the King's beam, the buyer paying the sheriff a halfpenny for every hundredweight weighed. The *Liber Albus* records that those purchasing consignments of ten hundredweight paid one penny, for eleven hundredweight 1½d, while for twenty hundredweight, 2d was payable 'and so on'. Clearly large cargoes were commonplace and by implication, large cargo ships. If the buyer was unable to take his bulky cargo to the King's beam, then he could 'at his own cost cause the King's beam and weight to be brought to the house where the vendor is staying'.

Scavage: (Riley 1861,196) This toll was paid to certain officials 'on behalf of his lordship the King' for the 'shewing' or inspection of imported goods prior to their sale in London. This was charged per 'kark', a quantity which varied from three to four hundredweight depending on the commodity. The *Liber Albus* lists the impressive range of imports, representing the very wide extent of London's trading contacts: pepper, sugar, cummin, almonds, brazil (a red dye), quick silver, ginger, cetewale (a medicinal herb), liquorice, spices, vermillion, glass, figs, raisins, shumac, sulphur, ivory, cinnamon, incense, pyoine, anise, dates, chesnuts, orpiment, olive oil, gingerbread, rice, turpentine, cotton and whalebone were all charged at 12d per 'kark'. By the early fourteenth century alum was 16d and grain was half a mark per kark. The list continues with a catalogue of fine goods including sundry small wares, Spanish wool and squirrel pelts, wadmal, canvas, cloths and caps, marten skins, rabbit skins, fur trimmings, woolfels, linen, fustian, felt, lymere (saddlers cloth), parmentery (tailor's cloth) pile, kersey, hapertas, material from Limoges and from Reyns, skins and silk. All the latter were charged at 12d per load. Comparison with a less detailed list of mid-thirteenth-century charges shows that this particular levy doubled in 50 years: on alum, it rose 8d to 16d, on pepper and fine wares from 6d to12d and so forth.

Tronage: The King's tron was normally used for weighing wool. Quite apart for the royal customs duty due on wool, a sack of wool of three to four weys which was being exported from London by a foreign merchant, was also liable for tronage charged at 11d by the Sheriff. However, if the merchant was exporting more than one such sack, he need only pay 10d for the others. For the smaller two-wey sacks, the levy was 6d for the first and 5d for the others. Wool that was to be sold in the City itself was not liable for tronage by the sheriff.

Thus is can be seen that there were tips, tolls, taxes dues and customs payable at every turn in the thirteenth-century town, whether it was from the foreign merchants paying 50 marks per annum to simply land and store woad in the City to the charge of 3½d on every Jew buried in London. This last regulation concerned a very particular minority group: being non-Christian, the contemporary laws of usury did not apply to them. They were therefore 'able' to lend money and charge interest on the loan, an essential banking service for the medieval port. The focus of the community was not actually in the harbour, but is recalled in the 'Jewry' place name near Guildhall and in the archaeological discovery of features such as the remains of two ritual baths (*mikveh*) found nearby (Blair *et al.* 2001). Their religion and their profession did not win them many friends however, and when they lost the protection of the crown the whole community of 16,500 Jews was forcibly expelled in 1290.

Life and death in a thirteenth-century harbour

The accounts of court sessions held in 1244 (Chew & Weinbaum 1970) and 1276 (Weinbaum 1976) reviewed cases of murder, suicide and death by misadventure spanning the previous 20 years. The summaries of each case incorporated in these surviving rolls, together with those from the medieval coroners court (Sharpe 1913), provide a telling insight into the daily life and labours on London's waterfront, highlighting as these post-mortems do, the most common activities on the quayside and the importance of the Thames to the town.

Many Londoners would need to draw water from the tidal Thames, which would be fresh and suitable for drinking when the tide was out, i.e. the freshwater was flowing downstream. However, only three Londoners are recorded as having fallen into the river and drowned while drawing water: the unfortunate William Aubyn, Isabel Scrul and Henry Green in 1236, 1269 and 1276 respectively. Given how common such an activity was, this is a thankfully small number. Watering horses was rather more dangerous, with five deaths recorded between 1230 and 1264: the groom Adam of Norfolk, Guy of Elmdon, Nicholas Bat, Richard of Stepney and John of Newport. Judging by the names it is possible that some of these men were not Londoners but had just ridden in, and may not have been used to the strength of the river's current. Four more drowned between 1258 and 1278 while bathing in the river, a task that could have been undertaken at any state of the tide: Warin, Simon Godgrom, a woman called Edith, who only wanted to wash her hands, and poor Katherine de Brackele, aged nine.

In 1253 Robert de Haselyngfeud was simply walking on the banks of the Thames when he slipped and drowned, as did William, aged 14, in 1237. Three more fatalities are recorded for Londoners who fell from the jetties or river stairs, perhaps a consequence of poor maintenance of these much-used facilities: Ralph Baggand (1231), Badde (1240) and Muriel, wife of William of Staines (1267). Ten bodies were found in or by the river over a 50-year period (1231-78) representing others who may simply have fallen in the Thames from the river stairs or unprotected quayside, even from London Bridge itself, in the case of Gilbert Cloke. There was an unidentified girl, three women and four men. The most tragic discovery of all was the body of a male infant who had been tied by the foot to Nicholas Bat's quay, allegedly by one William Croll in 1255.

However, the greatest number of waterfront deaths in the period from 1226 to 1277 was caused by falling out of passenger boats. The figure of 19 fatalities in half a century no doubt masks a much larger number of near misses and unrecorded heroics, but shows how common water transport was to Londoners in this period. In 1261, John, a servant of Roger de Essewelle, and five others were together in a boat on the Thames. John and another man sitting in the stern of the boat were drunk, fell into the water and drowned. Little of the circumstances of the other accidents are recorded, other than the unfortunate Henry, Geoffrey, Edmund, John, Ralph, William, Martin and a boy called Bartholomew who all fell from the small undecked boats that were an essential feature of the medieval river. In 1263 two boatmen including John Poytevin were ferrying passengers to a ship moored at Westminster when John fell into the water and drowned. Hugh de Rotherherde was drowned after his boat was swamped in September 1276, and in May the following year, Robert Fauk de Leusham met a similar fate.

These craft are referred to in the records by the general term of *batella*, but they varied in the values quoted from 2 to 10 shillings. Consequently, it is possible to argue that they may well have represented a range of different sizes and types of vessel, rather than just standard-sized rowing boats for carrying passengers. Indeed, the records of some of other recorded drownings also mention cargoes being carried as well as passengers. For example in 1231, Henry of Tutbury and Alan the Fuller fell from a boat carrying chalk; in 1251 Robert Russel fell from a boat over-loaded with wood and two other passengers, while even more tragically in 1269 Walter le Estrays, William le Batiler of Greenwich and Maud le Estreys all drowned having been on a boat with two others and another over-large cargo of firewood. Another working vessel, this time a fishing boat was involved in an accident in 1240. The boat (valued at 10s) and net were recovered, but neither of the crew members was found.

Moving onto the larger class of vessel, *navis*, also a common sight in the port, another eight deaths are recorded. We read that in 1232 a man from Stanmore fell from ship near Dowgate and drowned; in 1272 Roger de Chevendre of Sheperton was sailing in a ship when he drowned, as did one Robert son of Roger, in the following year. A more explicit industrial accident is recorded in 1236, when Robert le Portour fell into Thames while carrying coal from a ship. The stresses and strains of moving heavy cargoes also contributed to other deaths: in 1257 Oliver of Winchelsea, Richard Franklin and others were together on a ship on the Thames near the Tower; the ship was carrying at least eight tuns and one pipe of wine. A quarrel broke out amongst the crew, during which Oliver hit Richard with a staff and threw him into the water. A similar sequence of events is recorded in 1273 when John Coubley and others were onboard a ship moored at Laurence Hardel's wharf in the Vintry, loading it with wine, when a quarrel broke out among them:

Stephen le Esert came up to strike John, who fell into the water while trying to avoid the blow and was drowned. Another ship moored at the Vintry was laden with millstones belonging to John Gisors. Simon Stanhard was helping to unload the millstones and had pulled one up to the upper part of the ship when the rope broke and the stone fell, crushing Simon to death. The final fatality, in 1262, was that of William Spiring who, presumably along with others, was trying to drag a ship lying on the foreshore into the deeper channel of the Thames when the rope broke and he fell into the water. Taken together, these accidents provide a telling glimpse of the hardness of life in the harbour: it is not known how many near misses or broken limbs the loading and off-loading of London's riverborne wealth demanded.

Ships, boats and barges

Thus our list of thirteenth-century vessel-related deaths from the port of medieval London, 19 from the ubiquitous passenger boats, eight from more stable working boats and eight from the larger sea-going ships, provide a glimpse of the range, variety and proportion of craft in the contemporary Thames. In addition to providing a summary of each case and an evaluation of the verdict, the sessions also recorded the *deodand*, a legal valuation of the item associated with the death, be it a boat, ship, horse or whatever. These figures provide interesting comparative values for such modes of transport. The values quoted for the boats and ships vary from 2 shillings to 40 shillings, providing an indication of the size range, with the largest ships being perhaps some 20 times larger than the smallest *batella*. Interestingly, the values quoted for the general *batella* class varies considerably, from 2 to 10s, which suggests that the term *batella* or boat does not refer to a particular craft, but covers vessels of a wide range of sizes and types.

Further confirmation of such variety is implied by the late thirteenth-century customs of Queenhithe and those of Bridge and Billingsgate (Riley 1861). These documents provide an overview of the general size-classes of vessels in the port, listed generically by the mooring charges levied on them. There are eight types mentioned. Beginning below the bridge, the first two are presumably seagoing ships (*Great Vessels* and *Vessels with Bulwarks* were both charged 2d), the third a *coaster with bails*, perhaps to support a removable awning was charged 1d. The fourth class of vessel was navigated with oars projecting from *oarports*, holes cut into the uppermost strake of the hull. This, a substantial boat operated with several pairs of oars, was charged 1d and was clearly differentiated from the more modest 'boat' which was the fifth type. Three more are referred to above the Bridge. The sixth type is a vessel navigated with *tholes*, a reference to thole pins or rowlocks set on top of the uppermost hull strake. Such vessels had a shallower draft than those with *oarports*, and represent upriver craft not usually found below the bridge. It was charged 1/2d and thus was presumably smaller than the seventh type, a scout or *shout* (1d) which again seems only to appear above the bridge, and therefore is likely to be another though more substantial upriver inland craft. The eighth vessel type was a *waterman's boat*, the ubiquitous ferry, obviously smaller than any of the other generic types mentioned in these contemporary lists.

Moving down the nautical social scale, the archaeological evidence has produced a ninth class of vessel seen on the Thames. A dugout boat from Kew, once thought to be of prehistoric date and displayed in the London Museum as such, has now been dated to the mid-thirteenth-century (Marsden 1996, 222). This form of vessel was the most common craft on the Thames for millennia, although by the late medieval period, it was largely superseded by the plank-built boats used by most riverside families.

The tidal Thames

That the Thames was tidal in this period is clear from the archaeological evidence, through study of the foreshore deposits and the identification of micro-organisms such as *diatoma* that have a particular preference for saline or brackish water, as well as the study of the waterfront structures, the piles and baseplates of which could only have been set at low tide. There is also documentary evidence that the thirteenth-century Londoners were keenly aware of the river's tidal nature and were able to calculate the rhythm of the tidal cycle. The state of the tidal flow, which determined the salinity or freshness of the water, was obviously an important consideration for Londoners or livestock wishing to drink it. It was also a most important factor with regard to the movement of large vessels, for they would need to be brought up to the port with the tide, while the start of their return journey would not be practical until the tide had turned. A document compiled by John de Wallingford, a monk working at St Alban's Abbey from 1231 to 1258, includes a table that provides a means of calculating the time of the *fflod tide at London brigge*, based on the phases of the moon (*quantum luna lucet in nocte*) operating on a 29-day cycle, a lunar month. The document records that the time of high tide changes each day by *c.*48 minutes (Dyson 1996).

Today, it is possible to purchase a set of tide-tables in which the times of high tide at London Bridge are presented with equal mathematical confidence: these calculations, like those in the thirteenth century, are a guide rather than a precision instrument, as heavy rain, drought and storms can and do alter the time at which the tide turns, as well as the height or depth it reaches. Today, high tide at London Bridge turns between 1 and 2pm after the new and full moon, and between 6 and 7am after the first and third quarter. The ancient table seems to show that the tide turned one to two hours later, suggesting that the tidal head has moved significantly since the thirteenth century. This, it must be admitted, is speculation: what is of real interest here is that the compilation of the ancient tide table shows that thirteenth-century Londoners were sufficiently engaged with the Thames to appreciate the regularity of its lunar-assisted cycle. No doubt their less literate Saxon forebears were equally attuned to the vagaries of the river upon which they depended for so much.

9

FISH ON FRIDAYS

Fish formed a crucial part of the medieval Londoners diet, since Christians were not supposed to eat meat on Fridays or other fast days, including Lent (**44**). The fishing industry was consequently a major concern (Salzman 1923; Steans & Foreman 1991), while its regional nature and considerable diversity is shown by a thirteenth-century poem which praises 'the Eels of Cambridge; Herring of Yarmouth; Plaice of Winchelsea; Merling of Rye; Dace of Kingston; Loches of Weybridge; Barbels of St Ives; Salmon of Berwick; Cod of Grimsby; Mullet of Dengie' (Kowaleski 2000). The fish brought to the London markets was therefore caught in a variety of locations, offshore, inshore and from the Thames itself. The most common marine species eaten in London was unquestionably herring (either fresh or salted), probably comprising between 50 and 60 per cent of the total fish consumed here. It was caught from September to November in shoals by drift nets (sometimes known as 'flews' or 'norwards') up to 60m long and up to 10m deep. The nets were cast from boats with crews of eight to 12 fishermen, or from larger vessels with up to 26 oars (Dulley 1969). This was a volume industry as by the late fourteenth century it has been estimated that there may have been up to 40,000 fishing boats catching herring in the North Sea, supported by some 500 ships loaded with casks of fish distributing the catch across northern Europe (Unger 1980, 167). The principal centre of the English herring industry was indisputably Great Yarmouth (Norfolk: see figure **1**). Here fleets from the Thames and the Cinque Ports were repaired, and it was where merchants and mariners bargained and battled. The Fish Fair lasted for some seven weeks from late September to mid-November, attracting at least 500 vessels from all over England and elsewhere in Europe (Kowaleski 2000).

The second most common fish sold in London was plaice and other flat fish, often caught in complex trammel nets, cunningly designed to ensnare bottom-feeders, or in the large fixed traps called kidells that caught the fish as the tide turned. The season lasted from April into August, which overlapped with the mackerel fisheries, running from April to June. Mackerel was the third most common fish on offer and, like herring, was caught in shoals in drift nets. Other species such as cod (melwel) were caught with long lines by 'hookmen' working from 12-man boats, often operating with four 100m-long lines simultaneously. This work lasted from November to Easter, after which their attention turned to conger for the summer months. These seasonal supplies of fresh fish from offshore and inshore sources were regularly supplemented by harvesting the 'fishful Thames', which produced large quantities of eels and salmon, for example some of the evidence for this part of the fishing industry as recorded in the returns for Middlesex and Surrey in the *Domesday Survey* has already been described in chapter 5. There was in addition, a thriving market in London for preserved fish such as herring, smoked and salted. This staple was known as stockfish, and was common enough to lend its name to the section of Thames Street that was the focus of the market, *Stockfishmongers Row*, near London Bridge. As for shellfish such as oysters, whelks and mussels, these were still being sold directly from the boats that brought them in, as in the days of the beach market, until the fifteenth century by which time they could be sold by street hawkers (Archer *et al.* 1988, 9).

The *Liber Albus* (Riley 1861) lists the scale of fees charged for the different kinds of fish brought by non-Londoners into the port, which gives an indication of the varying availability and preferences for the various species. Herring was expected in vast quantities: for each boatload, whether fresh or salted, a charge of 100 herrings was payable. Vessels with mackerel, merling or haddock paid 26 fish and those bringing cod (melwels) or rays paid just one fish. Boats that brought in five panniers of whelks were not only charged one pannier but 1/2d as well. If any foreigner, including men from the Cinque ports, brought 100 or more salmon to Queenhithe, he had to give two salmon: 'one of the very best and one of the middling quality'. Boats with under 100 salmon were charged pro rata, although those with a haul of fewer than 25 only paid strandage. Craft carrying the produce of the inshore and river fisheries such as

44 *Fishing with nets from an open boat at sea.* J. Stripe, LARF

sea bass, conger, dory, surmullet, turbot, shad or eels were also only charged for mooring. Dealers bringing fish into London by pack horse paid one fish per pannier plus ½d for the horse, but if a cart brought salmon in belonging to a foreigner, the bailiff would take the second best salmon plus 2d for the cart. Pack horses from Rye could carry fish in baskets called dossers: wrapped in seaweed or canvas fresh fish could be transported overland to London from the Sussex coast in four hours (Kowaleski 2000, 31).

The evidence for the fishing industry in London also includes the study of bones recovered from excavations, and represents a range of fish species. These include all those mentioned specifically in the customs accounts for Queenhithe and Billingsgate just discussed, and one or two others. The archaeological list includes: herring, whiting mackerel, rays, roker, smelt, roach, conger eel, cod, gadoid, red sea bream and black sea bream, ling, gurnard, ballan wrasse, halibut, brill, plaice, flounder, salmon and eel (Locker 1992). Shellfish such as whelks or mussels are also common, while discarded oyster shells were so common that they were gathered up and used in the building trade as a levelling agent in masonry wall construction or as makeup deposits below yard surfaces.

The larger sea creatures, such as the whale, porpoise and sturgeon, were crown property whenever caught or discovered stranded at low tide in the estuary. Henry I did, however, grant the Bishop of London the right to porpoises taken on his lands. In 1245, Henry III ordered 100 slices of best whale, 25 pieces of sturgeon and two porpoises from the Sheriff of London, and in 1254 a whale stranded in Milton (Kent) was sent to Westminster for the royal larder. The king was also prepared to sell those parts not required for royal consumption, since at the end of the thirteenth century it is recorded that whale meat 'of this year's salting' was being sold in the London market at 2d per pound or 16s the hundredweight. Meat of last year's salting was half price and porpoise sold at half a mark a hundredweight (Salzman 1923, 265-6). All this suggests that the strandings or deliberate capture of these sea mammals was not that uncommon: consequently whale meat was an accepted part of the diet for some medieval Londoners. The archaeological evidence supports this assumption. In addition to the whale bones recovered from mid-Saxon settlement sites in Lundenwic, City waterfront excavations ranging in date from the eleventh to fourteenth centuries have provided fragments of pilot whales, the rostrum of a rorqual, the rib of a sperm whale and vertebrae from a porpoise or dolphin.

It is no surprise to report that the fishmongers were a prosperous and highly influential company, providing the medieval City with a major staple and several mayors. They also retained a keen interest in other mercantile pursuits, using their knowledge of ships, coastal and cross-channel traffic to good effect, echoing the importance of fishermen in the early development of overseas trade. This is shown in the records designating the trade of those engaged in London's wool and wine trade. In 1313, for example, although the woolmongers and the drapers are listed (as might be expected) as the leading players in the export of wool from London, the fishmongers held third place. As for the import of wine between 1318 and 1323, the fishmongers held second place behind the Vintners (Williams 1970, 150-153). Arguably the fishing community had always been prepared to diversify as circumstances dictated.

The location of the original fish market lay north of Fish Wharf, where Friday Street joins Old Fish Street. By the twelfth century, following the building of the bridge, a new fish market was established in Bridge Street (New Fish Street, or Fish Street Hill). A third site, the covered market at le Stocks near St Mary Woolnoth, had been built by 1283 to serve the expanding population, as Vanessa Harding has shown (Archer *et al.* 1988, 4). Something of the workings of the market that the Fishmongers Company closely regulated can be pieced together from the tolls and taxes charged and from other incidental fragments of legislation and litigation. In 1320, for example, the *Liber Custumarum* records that the fishmongers had been bringing fish in their own ships to London to sell both wholesale and retail from their own tenements on Fish Wharf 'from time wherof memory does not run'. Many came to the market, 'foreigners as well as denziens'. The poor folk of the city were allowed to buy fish here, before carrying it out of the City to sell it on to those unable to buy wholesale; the good folks, the officers of the King and others who lived in the City came to buy their store of salt fish and fresh fish there since you could buy ten herrings for one penny, whereas elsewhere in the City one penny would only pay for six or seven at most. The fishmonger's demand in 1320 to operate an exclusively wholesale market at their wharf, i.e. to sell fish only by the basketful, was thus hotly contested by the Londoners (Riley 1860, 605-7).

A fishmonger's wharf (45, 46 & 47)

The fisherman's quarter was originally focused in the western end of the harbour, around Fish Wharf, Old Fish Street and Friday Street, the latter lane leading to the original fish market. Although Trig Lane, the medieval water-front alley, initially known as Fishing Wharf Lane, has been obliterated by modern redevelopment, the set of wooden stairs that marked its riverward end survive in the shadow of the Millennium Bridge, still providing public access down onto to the foreshore. No less than four major archaeological projects have been conducted around these stairs during the rebuilding of the water-front from 1970 to 1999. In 1974-5, work was concentrated on the property immediately west of Trig Lane itself and the foundations of a 5.2m-wide four-teenth-century building were recorded. It had obviously suffered fire damage, since an internal chalk floor that showed clear signs of scorching was sealed by a thick layer of burnt material including spread of burnt oyster shell. This

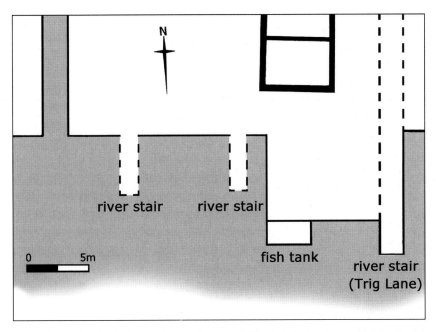

45 *Fishmonger's wharf: plan of a fourteenth-century fishmonger's house, quayside and foreshore fishtank (see 46) recorded to the west of Trig Lane.* J. Stripe, LARF

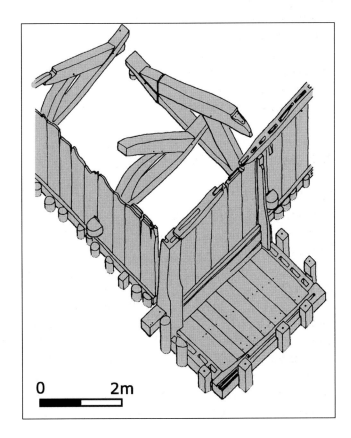

46 *Fishmonger's wharf: south-west corner of a fourteenth-century timber wharf (see 45) with the base of a fish tank extending out over the foreshore.* J. Stripe, LARF

47 *The timber face of the fourteenth-century fishmongers' wharf, viewed from the river, looking north-east. The foundations of the contemporary waterfront building can be seen below the chestnut paling fence.* Photograph by D.F. Harrison

suggests that oysters were being stored or processed in the vicinity (Milne & Milne 1981).

The associated timber-faced wharf frontage was initially less than 4m to the south, and there was direct access to the foreshore for this and the neighbouring properties via individual sets of private river stairs or jetties. Mooring posts set into the foreshore at this point shows that river transport was important to the occupier of the building. By the late fourteenth century, part of the waterfront was advanced by some 6m southwards, with the construction of an elaborate vertically-timbered back-braced revetment, behind which over 70 cubic metres of midden material was dumped as infill. This new wharf facing survived to a height of *c*.1.7m in the excavation, but would have originally stood some 3m proud of the foreshore, since there is evidence that an additional 'second storey' of vertical planks had been set into a base plate over the top of the surviving timberwork. An additional structural feature of particular interest was set at the south-west corner of the new projection, the base plates of a timber platform 3.4m wide, constructed as an integral part of the original design. Study of the grooves and mortises cut into the edges of the platform showed that it had support vertical timbering, forming a water-tight tank (Milne & Milne 1982, 29-36). This has been interpreted as the remains of a large fish tank, designed to retain water at low tide, and thus keep a catch fresh. All the evidence therefore suggests that here was a building, wharf and associated fish-tank, cleverly designed and built with high-quality materials, for a prosperous fishmonger. The complex almost certainly represents one of those tenements from which the Londoners could once purchase fresh fish directly from the monger. By way of a postscript, it is worth noting that the fish-monger's building recorded on this site had been replaced by a dye house a century later, demonstrating how the expanding textile industry displaced many of the former waterfront activities.

Hook, line and sinker (48 & 49)

Over 50 medieval fish hooks have been recovered from London waterfront excavations, half of them from sites in the Queenhithe/Vintry area (near Old Fish Street Hill) and half from the Billingsgate area (near New Fish Street Hill). According to a late fifteenth-century treatise on fishing, hooks could be made from reworked needles. Apparently shoemakers' needles robust enough to penetrate leather hides were 'the beste for grete fysshe' (Steane & Foreman 1991, 146). The London fish hooks varied in length from 32mm to 75mm, all were barbed and all were made of iron, rather than the copper alloy sometimes used for Roman fish hooks. Such a size range in this medieval assemblage confirms that a range of small, medium and large fish was being caught. This variety is also evident in the different types of net and line sinkers recovered from the upper, middle and lower reaches of the Thames as well as from the

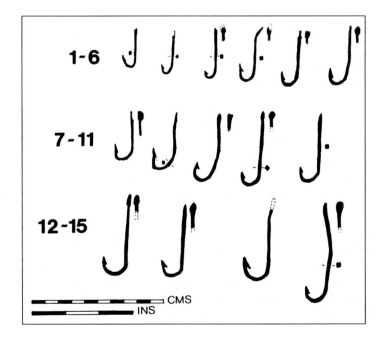

48 *Fish hooks from London: the range of sizes reflects the range of fish caught.*
After Steane 1991, figure 12.3

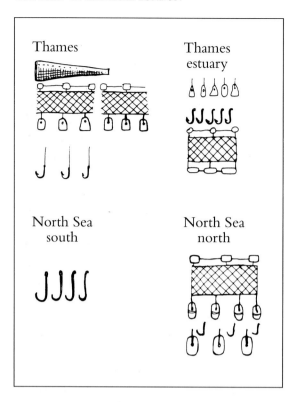

49 *Medieval fishing tackle representing inland, estuarine and marine traditions. After Steane 1991, figure 12.10*
a) Thames: fixed engines on weirs; net weights: stone for Upper Thames; brick for Lower Thames hooks: angling
b) Thames Estuary: lead sinkers; hooks for angling and for long line fishing; cylindrical lead weights
c) North Sea (south): big hooks for large fish; no evidence for net weights
d) North Sea (north); grooved net and line sinkers; hooks corroded by sea water

estuary and North Sea. Research by J. Steane (1991) suggests that weights made from stone (often limestone) are common on the upper Thames region above Pangbourne, below which weights shaped from ceramic material including old peg tiles becomes the standard type.

Lead is used for sinkers and for the cylindrical weights along the foot of fishing nets used in the estuary or out at sea. A group of over 1,000 such cylindrical weights were recovered from the Blackfriars III wreck in 1970. All were weighed and measured, and the lengths group into three size classes; there were 223 less than 1in long (14-23mm), 733 less than 1½in (i.e. between 24-33mm) and 152 less than 2in long (34-45mm). It is therefore possible that nets with three different mesh sizes are represented. It is known, for example, that peternets had a mesh 2in (51mm) wide 'and not more narrow', while the treineke nets had smaller mesh of 1½in (c.38mm). An alternative explanation is that a single net incorporating a wide range of different-sized weights is represented. If the latter is accepted, an interpretation preferred by the excavator Peter Marsden, that a net of at least 56m in length is suggested.

The heads of two fifteenth-century eel spears (glaives), have been recorded by Steane and Foreman from the Thames, one with five flat blunt tines, the other with seven. Both had serrated edges on just one side of the tines, to wedge rather than damage the captured eels (Steane & Foreman 1991, fig. 1).

Fighting the fishermen

The most lucrative and effective fisheries in the Thames itself incorporated a variety of installations to trap the fish. Unfortunately these substantial structures proved to be a navigation hazard, as was explicitly stated in *c*.1403, for example: 'the common passage of boats is impeded and many people perish' (Riley 1861, 440). The medieval legislation designed to regulate these structures refers to them by names including the term 'kiddels'. Clearly there was a major conflict of interests between the Thames fishermen and the townsfolk: the latter declared that 'the greatest detriment and disadvantage did accrue unto the aforesaid city of London, and unto the whole realm of England, by reason of such kidells' and persuaded Richard I to 'enact that all kiddels that were in the Thames should be removed, wheresoever in the Thames they might be: and in future no kidells should be placed anywhere in Thames' (Riley 1861, 428). That unequivocal position was maintained by King John (a clause to that effect appears in the Magna Carta of 1215) who added a £10 fine, presumably because the earlier legislation, however impressive in its sweep, had no teeth (Riley 1861, 428-9). But in spite of the fines, the fishing and the friction continued. There were still so many kidles in the Thames and Medway in *c*.1237 that London sent a sheriff and armed men to destroy them, and to arrest those who used them. On Saturday 6 January no fewer than 30 kidells were found beyond Yanlet Creek, running into the Medway, and some 28 master mariners from Rochester, Strood and elsewhere were arrested, tried, fined and all their valuable nets were burnt. In 1253 the sheriffs of London once again destroyed all the kidells between London and the Sea. This was one of the years that the Thames flooded, rising 'to a greater height than it had ever done'.

The periodic purges of the fish traps in the Thames continued in the four-teenth century. In 1327 for example, the citizens were exhorted to remove all kiddels in the waters of the Thames and Medway. In spite of these demands, the kiddels were replaced. In 1332, John Godard of Hamme was arrested by the wardens of the fishmongers for fishing with a kidell, as were John Wygen & John de Stokflete.

The legislation of 1352 demanded that such engines that were an impedi-ment to shipping should not just be removed, but be 'wholly abated and not reinstated'. The fines were increased to 100 marks for each offence, a penalty that was also to be applied to those who heightened or extended their engines. Given that the offenders were being caught and fined, it seems that they saw such sums as a price worth paying: presumably the cost of the catch was appre-ciably greater than the fines levied. Certainly there is a change in tone in the next phase of legislation from 1390 onwards, as this is now regulatory rather than prohibitive. Fisherman or garthman were now being told not to set traps in the Thames that would catch immature fish, such as the fry or brood of the salmon. Indeed, there was to be no taking of any salmon from 8 September until 11 November. In September of 1338, for example, three nets taken from the river of the east side of London Bridge were destroyed in Cheapside as the mesh was deemed to be too small. To make the policing of these regulations more effective, the sub-conservators were now allowed to keep half of the fines they collected, a shrewd policy that should have provided the necessary incentives to ensure its wide implementation.

Although by 1394 further calls to remove all Thames kidells were being made between Staines and the Medway, the fishermen were fighting back. Four years later, as a result of a series of major disputes, a compromise was being thrashed out. A survey was to be taken of all 'the gorces, mills, stanks, stakes, kidells' which had been made 'in ancient times' (i.e. before the reign of King Edward I, 1272-1307): those that were too high or too narrow would have to be amended accordingly, rather than being destroyed. Although no new traps were to be sanctioned, it is clear that an unknown number had survived and been maintained for over a century, in spite of all the prohibitions. Events in the early fifteenth century show why the City was unable to have its own way; the answer lay in the sheer weight of numbers of the fishing community, and that they were prepared to fight as fiercely for their independence as any Londoner.

It was in 1406 that Alexander Boner, the sub-conservator appointed to oversee the Thames fisheries, came across 16 nets which he had removed and was about to take to London to check if the mesh size was legal. The account of what happened next, although no doubt embellished, is unambiguous. Nets were valuable items, and the local fishermen did not take kindly to such interference. They mustered at speed, summoned by the ringing of the bells in the riverside churches, from Erith, from Barking, from Woolwich, and from elsewhere in Essex and Kent, 'to the number of 2,000 persons . . . arrayed to make war with bows, arrows swords, bucklers, clubs and doors and windows in place of shields'. They fired 'a great number of arrows at him on the said water of Thames' and chased him to Barking in divers boats filled with men in arms. Alexander landed and gave the nets to the constable, 'but the mob did take the nets'. A number of individuals was subsequently arrested and brought to trial on 21 February. They apologised, but clearly presented a strong case, as they were promptly pardoned and given licence to use the 16 nets until the following Easter. In an attempt to save face, the mayor declared that in future, all new nets would have to be approved by him. The credence the fishing community gave to that order can be readily imagined.

10

PESTILENCE AND WAR

London and the Hundred Years War

Ominous events overshadowed life in the port in the fourteenth century: a sharp famine in 1317, the renewal of hostilities with France in 1337, and the terrible outbreak of the pestilence in 1348. Neither the outcome of the war or the visitation of the plague could be predicted; external forces rather than economic planning were once again shaping London's history.

There was little in Edward II's reign (1307-1327) that London would wish to remember. The major famine in 1317 hit England and its principal port hard. The *London Chronicle* records that there was such a great dearth of corn and other foodstuffs 'the poor people eat for hunger cats, horses and hounds'. To complete the misery, the weakened population were subsequently ravaged by an outbreak of pestilence (but not on the scale of what was to follow 30 years hence). The Scots then invaded Northumberland and a detachment of London troops were despatched to York to repel the invasion. It was hoped that the new king, Edward III (1327-77) might herald a better future. Certainly the new regime proved able to defeat the Scots by 1333. However, since his mother was a daughter of King Phillip IV, Edward considered that he had a legitimate claim to designate himself King of France, a title he assumed in 1337. This act launched the gruelling episodic campaign now known as the Hundred Years War, a war that had profound effects upon the history and economy of northern Europe. In 1337 the import of cloth and the export of wool were prohibited: these draconian measures brought the core trade of Ypres, Bruges and Ghent to a standstill. But Edward III then invited the unemployed Flemish weavers to settle in England to ply their craft here, a move that significantly expanded English cloth production.

French ships had attacked the English in the Thames estuary, had sacked Portsmouth in March, raided Guernsey and had also captured five 'great ships' of the English that had been moored off the Scheldt estuary. But on Sunday 4 October 1338 some 50 French and Genoese ships attacked Southampton, a major port on the south coast, burning, killing, raping and stealing. The shock waves were felt across the nation, especially in its port communities. English seamen mounted a revenge attack on Le Treport and burned 30 ships in Boulogne harbour, but the Kent coast was attacked in return.

As for London, it set about preparing its defence in earnest. We know with hindsight that the French did not attack London, but way back in 1338, the Londoners did not know that: the defence measures were for real (Sharpe 1913). It was decided that a better watch on the Thames was needed. With this in mind, Simon Turgys was assigned, with a retinue of six men by day and twelve by night, to guard the postern by the Tower. From the Lion Tower to the Stonewharf by Woolwharf, Stonewharf to the Bridge, and Ebbgate to Castle Baynard, as well as London Bridge itself, were assigned to the aldermen and men of the wards along the river. Henry Darcy, Sir John de Pulteneye, Richard de la Pole and Reginald de Conduit were picked to oversee the watches. At the same time, it was also decided that piles should be put in the river to prevent more than one ship from passing at a time. Richard de Hakeneye and Richard de Rothyng (both aldermen) and Alan Gille and Henry de Preston (both commoners) were chosen to supervise the work. In addition to these security measures, everyone with a quay along the Thames was ordered to build a wooden brattice (temporary wooden palisade or battlement) for defence. William de Brikelesowrth asked whose duty it was to fortify the quays, as he had Baudries Wharf leased to Petronilla Turk, and she would not pay for the building of a brattice. It was decided that it was de Brikelesworth's responsibility as owner, and he paid £10 6s 8d to John de Totenhman to build the brattice on his quay. Meanwhile, the Tower's river frontage was also strengthened from 1336-42. The entire length of inner curtain from the Bell to the Salt Tower was heightened and crenellated as was the southern wall from the Byward to St Thomas Tower.

In November 1338, men from each ward were appointed to collect money from the religious houses and 'others holding property in the City' for London's defence (Sharpe 1913). A year later, in November 1339, men from each ward were chosen to assess the men of their wards and levy money from them. The amounts collected from the waterfront wards were: Tower Ward – £25 16s; Bridge – £24; Billingsgate – £21; Queenhithe – £12; Vintry – £23 14s; Castle Baynard – £7. If these sums can be taken as indicative of disposable income (rather than a measure of selective tax evasion or inefficient collection) then it suggests that the greatest wealth on the waterfront was concentrated below the Bridge in the Pool of London (**50**) and at Vintry. The extreme western end of the waterfront seems to be valued at half or a third of that of those wards in the heart of the harbour.

In the event, the very real threat posed by the marauding enemy fleet was spectacularly dispensed with following the famous, if bloody, naval victory recorded at the Battle of Sluys in 1340. Here, in the estuary of the River Scheldt, the great armada gathered together by Philippe VI to invade England, was effectively destroyed by Edward's hastily contrived force. His fleet included the London ships *La Jonette*, the *Cogge of All Hallows*, the *St Mary Cog* owned by William Hansard, the fishmongers' warden. Buoyed up by this success, the

50 *The Plantagenet Port.* Artist's reconstruction by Chris Unwin

City provided a further 26 ships and further money for the war the following year. London ships were soon in action again, ferrying the troops led by Walter de Manny to Brittany. In 1346, the English archers, including a contingent from London,

> . . . won another historic victory at Crecy. This led to the siege of Calais, supported by London's levies, ships and 3,000 marks: the town fell in 1347. Edward III was triumphant, returning to England with more than enough booty to pay off his war loans (Home 1927, 131-2).

The national rejoicing was short-lived. *The London Chronicle* records that 'in the year of our Lord 1348 was the great pestilence at London, which endured from the feast of Michlemas unto the month of August'. The Black Death was the most unwelcome of imports, working its way from Constantinople across the well-worn trade networks of Europe, arriving in Dorset in August, and then brought into London's harbour by infected sailors. The death toll in the port was such that the parish churchyards could not cope. New cemeteries had to be opened up, including the one just outside the Tower, which was investigated in 1986. This archaeological excavation at the Old Royal Mint site revealed a sobering site (Grainger & Hawkins 1988). Large trenches had been dug to accommodate the obscene numbers of victims: over 800 were recorded here. In spite of the horror of the situation it seems that a remarkable sense of good order and reverence prevailed in 1349. Bodies were not tipped into hastily-dug hollows, but each individual was laid out east-west with as much dignity as the situation could afford. The calm regularity of this mass cemetery showed that London did not break down into anarchy.

The long-term effects of the Black Death on society and on the economic trajectory of Europe were considerable. In the short-term, however, it seems that London absorbed the trauma as best it could and tried to get back to business. The all important wool trade from England was reorganised, for instance, and was focused on ten wool staples, the ports that monopolised the export of this major commodity. Naturally the Thames had a major role to play, and in 1353-5 a new facility was set up at Westminster to accommodate the lucrative traffic, within the shadow of the King's palace on Thorney Island, next to Edward III's bell tower. A programme costing some £800 was required to build this new facility, incorporating a hall and chambers for the mayor and constable of the staple (**colour plate 15**), together with the wharf and its weigh-house, landing stage and watergate (Colvin 1963, 552).

Although the French had been defeated, temporarily at least, the seas were still not safe as the Spanish had been attacking the Bordeaux wine fleet. Edward led out an English fleet that, once again, had London ships within it, large vessels with fighting crews of 70 to 100 men. The navies met up in the Channel off Winchelsea and Romney, and the English sank or captured 24 enemy vessels. As for the French army, that too was destroyed six years later by the English at Poitiers. London and London Bridge provided a spectacular pageant to celebrate the event in May 1357, as the Black Prince brought his captive, the King of France, to Southwark, and thence over the Thames in triumph. The contrast between war ravaged France and the highly prosperous port was not lost on the French monarch (Home 1927, 122-3).

The truce following the Treaty of Bretigny in 1360 brought this phase of the long and savage war to a close. The next phase was to be less successful for the ageing Edward and for London. With the resumption of hostilities in 1369, convoys were organised to ensure the safe passage of the wine fleet to and from Bordeaux. This involved the provision of 15 ships and 5 barges 'furnished for war', of which 14 vessels were English, the others from Bayonne. The escorts were under the command of Admirals Philip de Courteney and William de Nevil, and would accompany English merchants 'as often as they wish to make the voyage out or home'. The cost of this service was not cheap, since the fleet levied a charge of 2 shillings for every tun of wine that arrived safely.

The general level of insecurity felt was marked by the renewal of the warning beacon system in the Thames estuary in 1377. A fleet of French, Spanish and Scottish ships had begun harrying shipping off the east coast. Edward III had died, the new King, Richard II was an 11-year-old boy. The ruling Royal Council was slow to respond but a London merchant, John Philpot, sprang into action, armed a fleet of ships from the Thames with 1,000 men, and sailed out to attack the raiders. His fleet surprised the pirates, and he was able to capture no less than 50 richly-laden Spanish ships. The following year, London elected him mayor as he was the kind of merchant the Plantagenet port needed (Home 1927, 139). The insecurities and suspicions remained, however. A Genoese merchant was murdered in London in 1379. He was attempting to establish a major storage base for oriental merchandise in Southampton, an act thought not to be in the best interests of English merchants. The following year was far worse because a combined French and Spanish fleet raided Gravesend and Tilbury, far too close for London's comfort. By way of a rather belated response, Cooling Castle in Kent was rebuilt with key-hole gun ports to accommodate hand guns (a novel feature for a castle) while the rest of the defences in the estuary were reviewed.

The instabilities that war engenders could obviously have a negative effect on a town that depended on traffic and trade. A protectionist measure termed a 'Navigation Act' was passed in 1382, for example, stating that all merchandise being exported from England may only be carried on 'ships of the king's allegiance'. Any alien who tried to transport English goods would now forfeit them to the king (Douglas 1969).

Tower Wharf (51)

The fourteenth century left its mark on the London waterfront, as archaeologists have discovered during their rescue excavations, but some of the changes are still visible for all to see. These relate to the Tower of London, its new river wall, watergate and wharf.

Towards the end of the thirteenth century, Edward I decided that the Tower needed to be dramatically enlarged and set in train an energetic expansion programme. The visible increase in the size and bulk of the King's fortress in the City presumably related to the lesson that the Londoners were required to learn concerning their support for Simon de Montfort's cause in the destructive civil war. One of the topographical consequences was dramatic change to the waterfront on the Tower's southern side, change that became even more marked during the course of the fourteenth century. This development included the construction of Tower Wharf itself, a direct consequence of the Hundred Years War making its impact on the London waterfront.

The process began with the decision to infill the original moat, building a new outer curtain wall, and cutting a substantially wider moat to the east, north and west of the enlarged precinct. The latter project on its own cost at least £4150, but some of that expense was off-set by the sale of the excavated clay (the King's Earth) to London tilers.

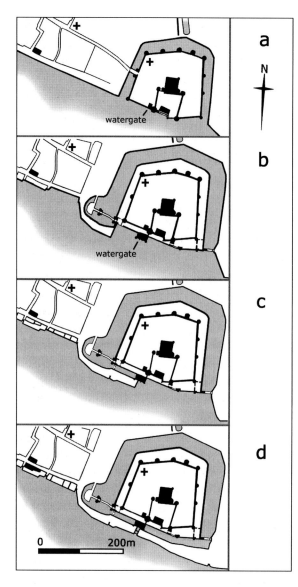

51 *Waterfront development at the Tower of London. After Tatton-Brown 1975, figure 2.*
J. Stripe, LARF
a) late thirteenth century: the Thames laps the southern curtain wall and the principal watergate next to the Wakefield Tower.
b) early fourteenth century: land has been reclaimed from the river and a new curtain wall built over it, as well as an enlarged Watergate (St Thomas Tower) projecting out into river. First stage in construction of Tower Wharf has also been completed to the south of the new landward entrance.
c) mid-fourteenth century: wharf refaced in stone and extended as far as the Watergate.
d) late fourteenth century: wharf extended across south face of the Tower, partially obscuring the Watergate.

Expansion space on the southern side, overlooking the Thames, was achieved in the manner perfected by the King's neighbours over the preceding centuries: encroachment into the river itself. Initially then, the Thames had lapped up against the foot of the Bell, Lanthorn and Salt Towers, with the main watergate for the complex being then the 'Bloody' Tower, set immediately east of the large Wakefield Tower. The fourteenth-century river wall was set some 15m to the south, and comprised the elaborate outworks for the new landward entrance to the west (the Lion, Middle and Byward Towers) as well as a new watergate. This was the St Thomas' Tower (now known as Traitors Gate), projecting right to the edge of the contemporary deepwater channel, and thus providing complete protection for the royal landing place at all states of the tide. The whole length of the southern wall was rebuilt 'broader and higher' between 1324-5. At either end of this wall, where the moat would disgorge into the Thames, tidal mills had been constructed, operated by the sluices within the revetments designed to retain the water within the moat at low tide. The mill at the eastern end, however, closest to St Katherine's hospital, was replaced by a stone dam or sluice in 1354-5 (Colvin 1963, 716-25).

As for Tower wharf itself, the earliest surviving reference to it is in 1335 when a request for extensive repairs over a length of 28 perches is made. This refers to the section repaired in 1336 at a cost of 41s by John the Clerk, running from Petty Wales (to the west of the Tower moat on the City side) to the Byward Tower. The wharf at this stage does not seem to be stone-faced, and thus would have been revetted in timber, as was the contemporary wharf to the south of Wool Quay. With the official 'declaration of war' in 1337, matters moved on. An enlarged quay was now urgently required for shipping the King's munitions to France, and thus in 1338-9 the modest wharf previously described was extended eastwards as far as the watergate at St Thomas Tower. Again, the work seems to have been an earthen and timber quay, and was to remain so for a further 25 years. When the time came to repair it between 1365-70, it seems that the decision was made to reface the whole length in ashlar stonework from Petty Wales to the watergate. Payments of up to £24 were made to the mason Maurice Young for 16 perches of new walling 'next to the Thames River' for example (Colvin 1963, 726-7).

The building of the final section, the length from the watergate eastwards to link up with the land 'towards St Katherine's', began in June 1389. This was during the period when the Clerk of Kings Works was none other than Geoffrey Chaucer, and the architect was Henry Yevele. Both men are better known for their Canterbury connections, the one for his *Tales* and the other for his work on the cathedral. Unlike the City wharves that were a direct extension of the land into the Thames and therefore required just one river wall, Tower Wharf comprised two walls, one facing north, the other south. The building contract for this project survives (Salzman 1952, 469-70) and provides details of the process. The walls were set in foundations approximately 1m deep but the ground here sometimes had to be 'firmed' by driving piles into it to ensure the walling did not subsequently subside. The walls themselves were 8ft (2.5m) thick at their base, diminishing to 5ft (1.5m) at the top, some 16ft 6in (5m) above the footings. These walls therefore had a pronounced batter on their outer face, a feature also recorded on contemporary masonry river walls excavated on City waterfront sites. Every ten feet, long 'end stones' were inserted, a reference to the compartmentalised method of building such wharf structures, in an attempt to keep some of the working areas as dry as possible. The infill material also had to be added incrementally 'as the work proceeds' and not all in one go. The material chosen is described as 'earth and rubble', presumably a rather more solid mixture than the much cheaper rich organic midden waste, so prone to compaction, beloved by the citizenry in their waterfront encroachment programme to the west. This long extension to Tower Wharf was to be complete in two years ('unless', as the contract comments, 'payment is interrupted', perhaps an all too familiar feature of the Kings Works). For each perch of 16ft 6in, payment of £9 13s 4d would be paid. However, the foreshore was not level then, anymore than it is level now, and thus it was agreed that, if the walls are more or less than 16ft 6in in height, 'then payment shall be proportional' (Salzman 1952, 469).

The contract is therefore quite clear about the height of the wharf: it was designed to rise some 5m above its foundation level. This figure merits comment, since broadly contemporary structures recorded by the archaeological team on the Trig Lane site, for example, stood no higher than c.3.40m, while other documented examples of fourteenth- and fifteenth-century wharf structures, such as those at Broken Wharf in 1347 (Salzman 1952, 434) or Billingsgate in 1404 (Chew & Kellaway 1973, no. 645), were only c.3.65m tall. It has also been suggested that the tidal range of the Thames at that period could have been as little as 3.50m (Milne & Milne 1982, fig. 43). Taken together, the evidence therefore seems to suggest that Tower Wharf, at least in its late fourteenth-century form, was designed virtually as a deep-water quay. It was set so far south into the tidal stream that vessels may not have been grounded at low tide, since little foreshore would have been exposed here as the tide ebbed. However, such a suggestion requires further study.

The general outline of Tower Wharf today is thus broadly that completed by Geoffrey Chaucer and his team, although considerably heightened. As such it represents a major medieval waterfront structure, a remarkable survival, built to serve the King's needs in his wars with France. For those able to visit the foreshore to the south of the wharf, it is possible to see sections of medieval walling at the base of the present river wall, although much of the upper work has been substantially refaced in later periods.

Custom House (52 & colour plate 14)

Another major consequence of the wars, whether with France, Wales or Scotland, was the need to pay for the King's army, and this led to increased control, increased taxes and the reorganisation of their collection. The Crown appointed men to collect the monies due on such items as wool, wine and cloth. In most provincial ports two officials were usually able to cope, but in London at the end of the fourteenth century there were no fewer than 42 officials appointed, such was the level of trade passing through the port. Even though England's wool trade was in decline, London's share of that commodity had increased to outstrip all other rivals, while the expanding cloth trade

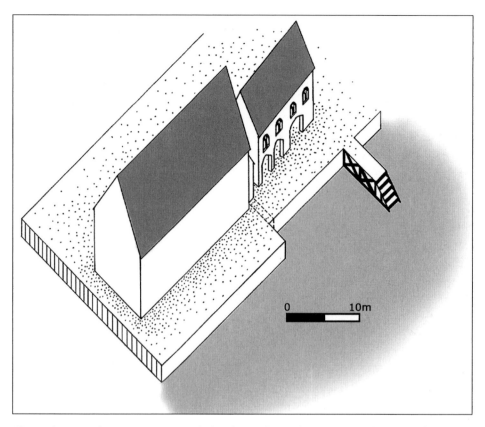

52 *Wool Quay and its Custom House in the late fourteenth century: a reconstruction based on the excavations in 1973, looking north-east.* After Tatton-Brown 1974. J. Stripe, LARF

benefited the port at all levels. The collectors of the custom were not career civil servants, but substantial businessmen with a vested interest in ensuring that the tax was recouped efficiently. In 1377 for example, the crown borrowed £10,000 from a consortium of London merchants, including John Philpot (the buccaneering mayor) and Nicholas Brembre. These same two gentlemen were then appointed to collect the returns due on wool. They were, in effect, using the London customs tax to repay the debt the King owed them. Since the wool tax would normally produce a return of some £18,000 per annum in this period, the Londoners felt – quite correctly in this instance – that their loan would thus be repaid promptly and in full. The King, for his part, would rest assured that the customs collection would be rigorous, he would be relieved of his debts, and would also make additional profit on the proceedings (Hollaender & Kellaway 1969, 177-194).

The reorganisation of the port also left its mark on the London waterfront, in the form of the new Custom House, which was constructed in the fourteenth century. In 1303, Edward I developed a new custom, increasing the duty paid by alien merchants who shipped out some 65 per cent of the English wool exports. The customs administration in London had probably been based at Wool Quay since 1275, but the documentary evidence only becomes clear on this point from 1318, as Tony Dyson has shown (Tatton Brown 1974; 1975). A building known as the Woolhouse, a hall with chambers, a house and a garden, is actually mentioned in Adam Blakene's will in 1295, and was situated on the northern side of Petty Wales (now Thames Street), directly opposite Wool Quay. By 1344, the Woolhouse was owned by the Turk family who also owned the quay to the south, and may have been responsible for the initial waterfront encroachments here.

By 1382, John Churchman had a Custom House erected on the riverside site, 'newly built for the quiet of the merchants . . . to serve for the tronage of wools in the Port of London'. The following year he added a chamber for a latrine, with a solar over the counting house, containing two more rooms and garret, 'as a further easement for the customers, controllers and clerks'. Archaeological excavations in 1973 exposed substantial fragments of chalk and ragstone foundations incorporated wooden piles up to 1.5m long, defining a building 24m east-west by 10m wide, with an extension 17m long by 9m wide. The excavator was tempted to associate those remains with the hall of 1382 where the tron was kept, and the extension of the following year (Tatton-Brown 1974, 139-141). Between the two sets of foundations, the archaeologists found a well-built timber-framed and planked drain c.0.5m across: the silt filling contained an unusual find, a small medieval buckler c.0.3m across, which would have been used for fencing rather than for battle (Tatton Brown 1974, 201-4). To the south were the remains of timber riverfront revetments and a braced jetty, although some of these features represented late thirteenth- or early fourteenth-century activity, before the Custom House itself was built. The discovery of the late medieval Custom House is of no little interest, if for no other reason than the plan of a building has been recovered in which one Geoffrey Chaucer, poet and civil servant, served. He was the Controller of Customs from 1374 to 1386, the man who ostensibly watched over the work of the often rather more powerful collectors. Indeed, it is not impossible that the timber drain may have been utilised by him.

Life and death on London's river

Something of the social context of more mundane aspects of life in this tumultuous century is recorded in such documents as the findings of the city's courts. Following the outbreak of the war with France, attitudes to aliens in London became more intolerant as a number of incidents show. In December 1337, for example, sailors from a convoy of foreign galleys which had just arrived in the port were attacked in Tower Ward. Again, in the following month, in the house

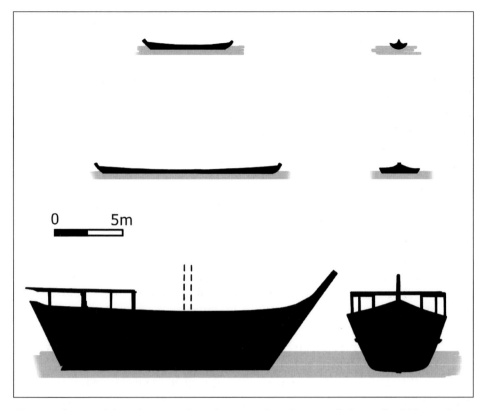

53 *Boats, barges and ships: diagram to show relative size of vessel types on the late medieval Thames (from the top): passenger wherry, river barge; cog or seagoing merchantman.* J. Stripe, LARF

in the Vintry, Laurence Dardge of Bayonne was searched in connection with the theft of 29 bales of cloth stolen from the Spanish vessel *La Naude*. In 1381, however, during the riots which followed the 'Peasants' Revolt', *The London Chronicle* records a terrible slaughter of 'Flemings and other aliens as they comen to honde' by a mob rampaging through the Vintry on Sunday 15 June.

The coroners courts (e.g. Sharpe 1913) also provide insights into life and death on London's river. On 14 September 1367, John Farnham boarded a vessel at Botoloph's Wharf, intending to travel to Essex. The tide was against them and as they waited patiently for it to turn, several of the passengers fell asleep. Suddenly a storm blew up swamping the crowded boat. John's body was washed up at Limehouse just over a week later. There was a similar fatal incident in 1322, after a couple had boarded William Stedman's boat and were being taken upriver to Kingston when a storm blew up near Putney, casting the husband into the water. A more avoidable fatality is recorded in November 1336 at St Lawrence Wharf near St Dunstan's. Elias Ide, seaman, climbed the mast of his ship, the *St Mary Cog* of London while the tide was out and he was drunk – he fell to his death. The body of another seaman, this time from

Holland, was discovered on 4 September 1373. Although it was found well to the east of the City near Wapping, it still came to the notice of the London coroners as it was found just 32ft within the liberty of the City.

Even for the non-seafaring Londoners, the Thames could be dangerous. On a hot June day in 1322, Robert le Layre went to Fish Wharf and down Trig Stairs to bathe in the river. He was found floating near Queenhithe the next day by a boatman. On 31 May, William Wombe waded into the river near Hay Wharf to wash himself, a not unreasonable or presumably uncommon activity given his occupation as a latrine cleaner. Unfortunately he lost his footing, and was washed up dead near the Fleet Bridge.

Just fetching water could still prove to be fatal. In 1324, Young Elena Gubbe took two earthenware pitchers down to the Laundry Bridge in St Martin's Vintry to collect some water on 18 October, but fell in and drowned. Her father eventually found her body on 1 November. And poor Mary, the 9-year-old daughter of Agnes de Billingsgate, also drowned while collecting water in an earthenware jug when the Thames was in full flood in 1340. It seems that there was no parapet or other form of protection on the quayside. On December 21 1300, for example, Lawrence the poulterer chased Johanna de Cherringe to Billingsgate, where she fell into the Thames – the corpse was found on Christmas Day. At high tide, the river might often top the quayside. In 1338, Richard Wrotham, the son of a cornmonger, was walking on the wharf at Billingsgate, 'the Thames being full and flooding the said wharf', but the boy lost his footing and drowned. Even for more experienced hands, the unprotected quayside could be hazardous. Henry le King, a shipman, fell from a plank projecting from Wool Wharf over the Thames in full flood in 1340. Then there was the case of Thomas Ballard, a shipman from Cliffe (Kent). He stood upon a manure heap piled on Billingsgate Wharf, as he tried to unfasten the boat moored there. However, the dung heap collapsed throwing him into the Thames.

Even the presence of Edward II himself contributed to at least one death on the ill-lit London waterfront. In 1321, for example, Elias de Beverley was making his way towards the Tower to meet his master, the King's Sergeant at Arms. He did not realise that the drawbridge was raised, as the King was lodged in the Tower that night, and fell into the water. Another nocturnal adventure is recalled in 1338, when John le Brewer stole money from two Florentine merchants. The thief fled to St Paul's Wharf and waded into the river, the tide being low. His intention was to make his way westwards under the cover of the wharves to Fleet Bridge, but the tide moved faster than he did. When his body was eventually recovered, he was found to have 160 stolen florins as well as the seal of one of the merchants, John Bescardi. The Thames was thus an unforgiving neighbour, as our last fourteenth-century example shows. Richard, the 8-year-old son of John le Mason, was crossing London Bridge after dinner on his way to school. By way of a game, he swung on a beam projecting out over the river, but his hands gave way. He was washed up at Queeenhithe four days later (Sharpe 1913).

On a more uplifting note, it is worth recording that the Thames also played a role in the literary life of the nation, for it was the congenial meeting of Richard II, travelling in his royal barge, with the poet John Gower in his ferry, that led directly to the penning of *Confessio Amantis*. This poem was written not in French or in Latin, as *Speculum Meditantis* or *Vox Clamantis* had been, but in English.

A riverside survey (54)

At a council meeting in 1343, that is, after the Battle of Sluys had lifted the immediate fear of a French invasion, but before the pestilence had ripped through the City's population, more mundane matters were on the agenda. Certain aldermen and several commoners expressed grave concern over the 50 common (as opposed to private) lanes that led from Thames Street to the river. They should have provided ready access for all who needed to reach the river for transport, for washing clothes, for watering livestock, to make use of the public latrines or to draw water for their masters. The mayor and alderman asked the sheriffs to consult 'discrete and wise persons from each ward' to collect information as to which lanes had traditionally extended to the Thames, but were subsequently blocked or obstructed. That survey, published in Latin in the *Liber Custumarum* (Riley 1860, 444–53), and now (thankfully) translated by Tony Dyson, throws considerable light on the daily comings and goings in the early fourteenth-century harbour. Of the 13 lanes that had *not* been obstructed, all lay to the west of the bridge in Dowgate, Vintry and Queenhithe wards. By contrast in the heart of the harbour in Tower, Billingsgate and Bridge wards, there was much to report. The City's most easterly watergate, the inlet just outside the Tower, lay in the area where numerous cargoes were transhipped from horse and cart to barges. Consequently pedestrian access to the river was gravely impeded by piles of dung and by the shipping moored there. The situation was made worse by the ruinous state of Walter le Meleward's quay, forming one rather unstable side of the inlet. St Botolph's wharf in Billingsgate, one of the largest landing places on the river, used to be open 24 hours a day but, to the great inconvenience of the city, had been closed at night by the keepers of the quay, John Sparlyng and Richard de Eure. The situation was made worse by the fact that almost all the neighbouring lanes were obstructed by the erection of fences or narrowed by building encroachment.

Beyond the bridge, the inlet at Ebbgate (in Bridge ward) now had privies from the properties of John de Pulteneye and Thomas atte Wyche overhanging it so that the waste from them 'fell upon the heads of people passing along'.

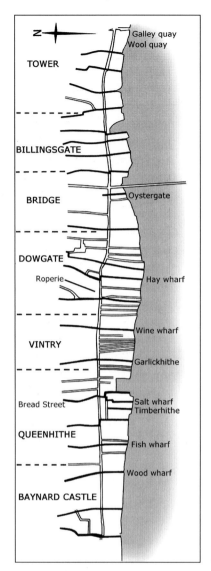

54 *Waterfront wards and wharves: schematic plan of London's medieval harbour showing place names associated with particular commodities. NB: north to left.*
J. Stripe, LARF

Armenterslane in Dowgate ward had been blocked by a cookhouse built over the jetty at its southern end. The nearby Granthameslane, once used by anybody handling large quantities of firewood and so forth, had been quite deliberately blocked by the stones and iron bars thrown across the lane so that horses and carts could no longer get down to the water. Three Cranes Lane had been narrowed by building works while the jetty at its foot, an important ferry terminal, was badly damaged, even though it was agreed that the commonalty were responsible for its repair 'by ancient precedent'. By contrast, the lane and jetty at Hay Wharf, just to the east was 'without impediment'. On Salt Wharf, however, the lane that approached it had been so narrowed that the carts that had formerly brought dust and dirt down to the river could no longer pass there. As for one of the most westerly watergates in the city, in Baynard Castle ward, one side of the narrow inlet had been refaced in stone to the detriment of many vessels that cluttered up the moorings there.

To this litany of physical impediments must be added that other characteristic of the medieval harbour – the hassling for legal and illegal dues. A right of access to the river did not necessarily mean that it was free. It is clear that charges were regularly levied, both on those using the lanes and wharves from the landward side as well those landing there from the river. If the land was deemed to be common, then the right to collect such monies was usually consequent upon paying a set fee to the city, that sum in theory going towards the cost of the upkeep of the wharf, rebuilding of the river stair or paving of the lane. For example, the fee for collecting such a custom at Salt Wharf was worth 3 marks *per annum* and at the rather busier Queenhithe with its public latrine, 6 marks. In both instances the 1343 survey found that fee was being illegally retained by the collectors. This was also the case with the annual fee of 13s 4d at Oystergate, where the reed sellers congregated (and were no doubt charged for the privilege), but there was further deceit on the neighbouring Stephenes Lane. Here the line of a common lane that once had a river stair at its foot had been deliberately diverted to pass onto the neighbouring private quay, whereupon one Adam delighted in charging 'a large fee from men wishing to approach the Thames'. A similar trick was uncovered at St Botolph's Wharf, where a diversion forced all who were making for the Thames with their goods onto the neighbouring private quay, where once again 'a large custom' was requested. Because the payment of tolls and customs were such an everyday demand in medieval London, it was difficult to know how many of the dues were officially sanctioned or not; much depended on the demeanour of the collector. At the Laundresbrigge, for example, the very persuasive Ralph de Berners took a custom from all men and women washing clothes and drawing water there, although nobody knew why he was allowed to charge them. The council promised to call him to account.

London weighting (55)

As has already been noted, London has long been a centre for the regulation of weights and measures, as might be expected of a major international port. A wide range of weights have been recovered from archaeological sites in the City, some stamped or decorated, some made from copper alloy, others from lead, some circular, or square, some 'hide-shaped', shield-shaped or even conical. The precise standard or system represented by those varied weights is hard to deduce, even though it is known that *avoirdupois* weights were being officially stamped at Guildhall from at least 1357, while *Troy* weights were under the careful control of the Goldsmiths from the 1370s. Depending where

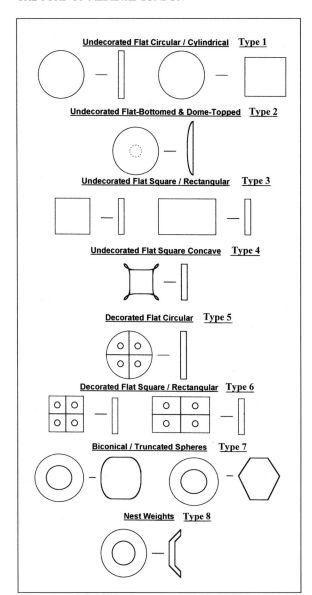

55 *London weighting: eight different types of weight recovered from sites in London, representing the complexities of the systems in use in the medieval port.* Source: Drinkall & Stevenson 1996

you were and what you were weighing, a pound might comprise 14, 15 or 16 ounces, while the pre-1327 Assize of Weights and Measures discusses a London Pound of only 12 ounces. In late medieval Bruges it was just 439g for a 14-ounce pound, the Florentine *grosso* was *c.*453gms, an Antwerp pound was *c.*471g, while the Paris pound seems to have weighed in at *c.*490g. The 'pound of pence' used for weighing spices, confections or medicinal items comprised 240 pennies, that is, to the value of 20 shillings. To firm up on this particular measure before 1350, long before the introduction of electronic accuracy, a common, readily-available standard was introduced *in lieu* of acceptable pennyweights. It was decreed that the weight of a full sterling penny would be the 32 grains of wheat (dry in the midst of the ear) or 22½ grains of barley. By 1351, this weight of the penny had been devalued to 18 grains of barley, and by 1412, just 12 grains. The implication seems to be that those who wished to balance their accounts in this way would have to carry the appropriate measure of dry grain (Egan 1998, 300-322).

A number of coin balances (or parts of such instruments) have been found in London, usually made from copper alloy. They could comprise a single arm, or could be folded to fit in a carrying case. The scale pans suspended from these balances were circular or triangular, and some had been stamped as confirmation of their accuracy. A third type of balance incorporated a weighted arm with a tray for the intended coin (*trebuchet*). A fragmentary London example seems to have been tampered with on the underside of the counter-balancing arm, so that the balance would only be in equilibrium with short-weight coins. The fact that this particular instrument had been broken up and discarded strongly suggests that the deceit had been exposed, the perpetrator punished and the offending balance destroyed (Egan 1998, 328-9).

Piracy in the fourteenth century

The fourteenth century had more than its fair share of wars, pestilence and other troubles, and the port of London suffered directly and indirectly in all of them, as this chapter has shown. Its trading activities were also adversely effected by piracy (e.g. Brett-James 1944), which had grown worse during the thirteenth century. Sea journeys were always risky, but shipping had to contend not only with bad weather, but Englishmen could be attacked by French or Flemings, by Norwegians, or even other Englishmen; the Cinque Ports often battled with the men of Yarmouth or Lowestoft. The Calendar of Close Rolls lists over 100 attacks on merchants in the early years of the fourteenth century, which impacted unfavourably on trade. For example, in 1309 it is recorded that Flemings stole 91 casks of wine belonging to English merchants. Among the English ships captured by the men of Flanders was *Le Bon An*, carrying wine from Bordeaux, and *Swallew*, carrying wine and wool: both were attacked off Margate with significant loss of life. The standard reaction was one of direct reprisal, as in 1304 when a Yarmouth merchant lost a cargo worth £260 to Zeelanders. Subsequently, Zeeland ships, goods and property up to that value were seized in a number of ports, including London, to provide compensation for the victim.

Sometimes it was the English who were the pirates; Chaucer's Shipman was clearly not the only Englishman who strayed outside the law. In 1315 for example, the *Santa Maria* of Fontarabia bound for Gascony was wrecked off Dungeness. Its rich cargo worth some £2,000 was stolen by Cinque Ports shipmen. This was the same year that William Bidyk, along with other London merchants, had chartered a ship to take wool worth £600 to Antwerp. He hired the ship *La Petite Bayard* from John le Prair, loaded the cargo and sailed down the Thames in late summer without mishap. But then they grounded off Margate at low tide and were attacked by 22 armed men led by the Admiral of Calais. Those of the English crew who were not killed or injured, tried to make their escape to the town, after disabling the vessel by taking the sail and rudder with them. The French caught up with them and seized the tackle as well as the ship. This was valued at £40, and its cargo was worth 2,000 marks.

On 2 November, Edward II sent a written complaint to the King of France demanding compensation. Since no reply was received over the next three years, Edward threatened that goods to the value of £2,000 would be seized from French merchants in London. He also sent similar instructions to the ports of Southampton, Ipswich and Great Yarmouth, which had all suffered comparable losses. Although negotiations continued, they were ineffective, and the order was put into operation on 28 August 1320, some five years after the initial attack. Chaucer's merchant had 'hoped that the sea would be kept free of pirates from Middleburg to Orwell' and his contemporaries in London no doubt shared similar sentiments.

Merchants and merchandise

The archaeological evidence supports the documentary evidence for London's widening trade network in this period, war or no war. The discovery of a fourteenth-century seal of *Jacob van Cosvelde* on the foreshore illustrates the Flemish presence in the port (**colour plate 13**). But from 1350 onwards, the proportion of imported pottery recovered from excavations markedly increases and although there is an emphasis on ceramics from the Low Countries and the Rhineland, wider horizons are also represented. This is shown by some Italian Maiolica and material from the Iberian peninsular, such as the Valencian luster-wares and Andalucian *alberelli*. (Vince 1985; Blackmore 1999). Even more dramatic evidence is found in the British Museum, which displays a bronze jug adorned with arms of King of England, a badge of Richard II and a Lombardic inscription. It was almost certainly made in a London bell-foundry in the late fourteenth-century, but ended up in sub-Saharan West Africa. It was discovered amongst the treasure of King Prempeh, following the sacking of Kumassi. It presumably ended its long journey to Africa, not directly from a London merchant, but through the hands of the more adventurous Portugese traders. Nevertheless, the world was growing.

So how did London's trade fare in this sad century? This chapter concludes with an insight into the affairs of London's fourteenth-century merchant class, and the demands the crown and military expeditions made upon it. The source

56 *Late medieval harbourworks: the rear (north) face of a fourteenth-century stave-built riverfront revetment exposed on the Trig Lane excavations, looking south-east towards the river. Note the large triangular back-braces that would have supported the (missing) upper level of the 3m-tall structure. See also* **67***.* TL 74 Museum of London

is provided by the chance survival of the ledgers of one Gilbert Maghfeld. He took out a lease in 1372 on a substantial property in Fresh Wharf, in the parish of St Botolph's, Billingsgate, extending from Thames Street to the river. By 1386, he had increased his holdings in the area to include six shops on the neighbouring Billingsgate quay. The foundations of several of those buildings were recorded by the Museum of London some 600 years later, just after a major study of his accounts was published in 1971 (James 1971). Gilbert Maghfeld was a successful ironmonger, principally concerned with the importation of iron from Bayonne and Bilbao, in exchange for grain and cloth. However, about a quarter of his imported cargoes were made up with other valuable items, including wine, beaver pelts, saffron, licorice, woad, wax, linen, copper, millstones, green ginger and even some Spanish asses.

His staff included Thomas Croft, another London merchant, John Barleborough his agent in Flanders, and Stephen Angevin, his agent in Bayonne. Half of the iron he imported was sold to wholesalers in London, a third to other merchants from East Anglia to Hampshire, but only one-sixth directly to blacksmiths. His Lombardy woad was sold to dyers and drapers from

Suffolk and Wiltshire, and his wine directly to customers such as St Giles Holborn, St Mary Graces, Waltham Abbey, the Sheriff of Middlesex, or the Mayor of London. He also shipped out linen for drapers and millstones for manorial lords, imported herring and stockfish from Boston, sold lead to plumbers, wainscot boards to carpenters and silk to silkworkers. He thus had direct dealings with merchants in London, in southern and eastern England and overseas, as well as with wholesalers, craftsmen and consumers.

Much of his business was conducted using credit which would be settled periodically, often in kind rather than in cash. In fact, less than a quarter of cloth trade used hard cash. Linen exported to Bordeaux was simply exchanged for two pipes of wine, his own goods for expensive furs, for example. Such bartered transactions seem to recall distant memories of the beach market.

Gilbert's success as a merchant, however, brought obligations and ultimately bankruptcy. In June 1394, Richard II began preparations for an expedition to Ireland. England's most prosperous port had to support the crown's endeavours, to the tune of 10,000 marks. In addition to contributing £50 directly to that levy, he was also required to help fit out three ships, *George of the Tower*, and two others both called *The Trinity*, at a total cost of £360 9s 10¼d. He died in May 1397, owing £500 on his London customs returns. The crown therefore seized £80-worth of goods from his widow and £500-worth from his servant Thomas Craft to make up the arrears. Clearly the king depended heavily upon the proceeds of the port.

11

HARBOUR CONSTRUCTION

Harbour advances

As was shown in chapter 2, London's riverside harbour was dramatically extended riverwards throughout the medieval period (see **7** & **57**). The motivation for the significant increase in the size of the City's waterfront has been studied, and reasons proposed included the need to win land, or to maintain a sound frontage. Superficially, the most obvious reason would seem to be to win new land and in 1345 we learn that Gilbert de la Brewere built a quay into the Thames specifically 'to enlarge and improve his property' (Chew & Kellaway 1973, 392). Many of the larger advances recorded would obviously fall into this category, and this could therefore include much of the thirteenth- and early fourteenth-century work.

However, several instances have been noted where the quayside has been advanced by only 2m or so, no more than was required to insert the new braces in front of the older, often dilapidated structure. In such cases it seems that the work was more concerned with repairing the frontage, rather than winning new land. Again, there is documentary evidence to support this suggestion, in particular the court proceedings summarised in the *London Eyre of 1244*. These specifically state that the waterfront extensions were permissible, 'since land and tenements could be protected against the sea ebbing and flowing night and day' (Chew & Weinbaum 1970, 343). This introduces the problem of who was responsible for their maintenance, the City, the property owners or their waterfront tenants? The answer here lies in the sheer variety of the structures recorded, as well as in the lack of uniformity in the alignment of much of the waterfront itself. All that clearly precludes the role of a uniform civic authority designing, or physically undertaking, the work. This is in marked contrast to the evidence from the Roman port of London, where a far less indented and noticeably more uniform embankment construction programme was effected. It also seems to differ from the major phase of brushwood and clay embankment construction, dated to the later tenth and eleventh centuries, which again seems to represent a more uniform endeavour. In the later medieval period, however, it seems that the responsibility for the maintenance of the wharves and flood defences rested with the owners or occupiers of each individual waterfront property. This was a period in which even the upkeep of the City

57 *Medieval engineering: note the system of braces and wedges used in this timber-faced wharf erected in the late twelfth century.* TEX 88 Museum of London

wall was no longer the direct responsibility of the City itself, but fell to a number of different Guilds, each responsible for a particular section.

A further question that needs consideration is whether the remarkable range of medieval timber revetments recorded over the last 30 years was built by shipwrights or housewrights, or whether some other specialist group of craftsmen was used. The earliest documentary record of a named waterfront worker in London is that of Ailnoth the engineer, who was contracted to repair not just the wharf but also the wall and King's landing stair at Westminster in 1188 (Harvey 1954, 130). A similar range of tasks was allotted to a City carpenter, one Richard Cotterel, who built the wharf, jetty, fence and sheds at Broken Wharf in 1347, and to three carpenters who worked in Southwark in 1389, constructing two watermills and a millhouse in addition to the timber-faced wharf (Salzman 1952, 467-9). Even Hugh Herland, one of the most famous carpenters of the late fourteenth century, 'the disposer of the King's works touching the art and mistery of carpentry' and the man responsible for the magnificent hammer beam roof in the Palace at Westminster, worked on the waterfront when he assisted with the harbour works at Great Yarmouth (Harvey 1954, 130). Returning to London in the fifteenth century, the contract to build a timber wharf at Vauxhall in 1476 makes use of two carpenters who had previously worked on the roof at Westminster Abbey (Woodward-Smith & Schofield 1977).

Thus the handful of surviving written records that relate to waterfront carpentry all suggest that London's riverfront installations were designed and built by the same persons responsible for building elsewhere in the City. This proposition is supported by the direct evidence, a detailed study of the structures themselves. Since over one hundred examples of these riverfront structures have now been observed or recorded, it seems reasonable to assume that a broadly representative sample of the wide range of designs and techniques has now been established. The sheer variety of structures, the discrepancy in their quality and the manner in which broad changes in revetment design mirror similar changes in house construction, all show that waterfront structures were not the product of a special woodworkers guild, such as shipwrights or coopers, but were seen as part of the house builders craft. As a consequence, the remarkable sequences of riverfront revetments recorded in London can be studied both as examples of harbour engineering as well as of contemporary house building practice (Milne 1992).

Three distinct types of timber-built river front revetment have been identified in London from the Saxon period to the sixteenth century: the earthfast, stave-built and framed structures, while masonry revetments have also been recorded from the late thirteenth- to sixteenth-century contexts. The earliest medieval waterfront structures, like most contemporary Saxon houses, incorporated earth-fast posts (**58**). These were unsquared posts with just the bark stripped off set in post holes, or alternatively, wooden piles driven into the foreshore. They retained wattlework or a cladding of cleft (not sawn) planks. The tradition of erecting pile-retained revetments continues to this day especially in areas where the river is non-tidal, but the practice of building earth-fast revetments was generally superseded in London by timbers set into a baseplate, a technique first utilised in stave-built structures in the late tenth or eleventh century (**59**), and fully-framed structures by the thirteenth century.

With the need for taller riverfront revetments came more elaborate structures (**60** & **61**). From the twelfth century, the principal timber posts were no longer used in the round, but were squared up, which allowed complex joints to be cut in. This was an important development, since the taller revetments needed to be braced, sometimes from both the riverward and landward side using a combination of diagonal braces (**62** & **63**), or sometimes just from the landward side using horizontal anchor-beams (**64** & **65**). As with contemporary house construction, the increasingly elaborate waterfront framework needed to be prefabricated, a point supported by the recording of examples of assembly marks incised on the revetment timbers (**66**). The plank cladding could be retained by setting it horizontally into grooves or rebates cut into the squared posts, or pegged into place in the twelfth century. It was not until the thirteenth and fourteenth centuries that the cladding was fixed with iron nails, by which time sawn boards were being used.

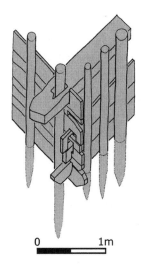

58 *Tenth-century riverfront revetment with planking retained by piles driven into the foreshore.* TEX 88 J. Stripe, LARF

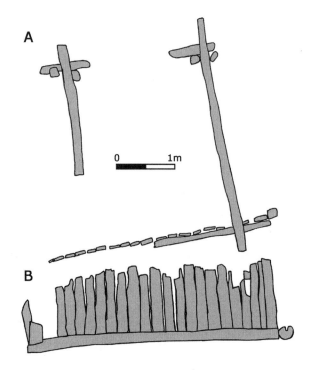

59 *Eleventh-century stave-built revetment: a) plan view of backbraces; b) front elevation viewed from the river.* BIG 82

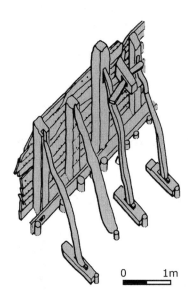

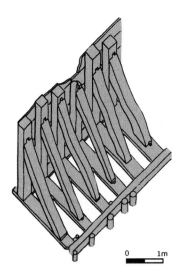

60 *Thirteenth-century riverfront revetment with plank cladding retained by front-braced posts set into post pits dug into the foreshore.* CUS 73 J. Stripe, LARF

61 *Fourteenth-century riverfront revetment with plank cladding retained by front-braced posts set into a baseplate.* CUS 73 J. Stripe, LARF

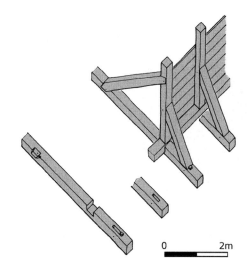

62 *Thirteenth-century riverfront revetment with plank cladding retained by front-braced and back-braced posts set into a baseplate.* THE 79 J. Stripe, LARF

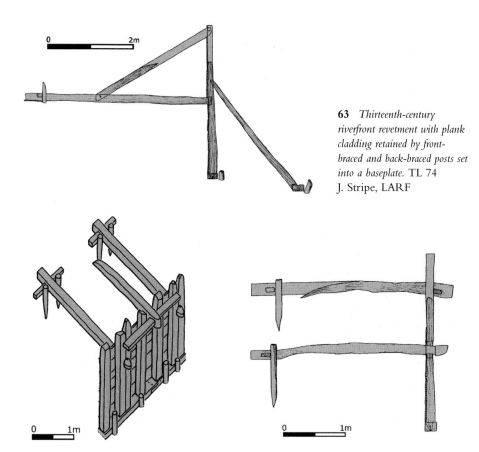

63 *Thirteenth-century riverfront revetment with plank cladding retained by front-braced and back-braced posts set into a baseplate.* TL 74 J. Stripe, LARF

64 *Fourteenth-century riverfront revetment with plank cladding retained by back-braced posts set into a baseplate (see also* **65***).* TL 74 J. Stripe, LARF

65 *Side elevation of the fourteenth-century riverfront revetment with plank cladding retained back-braced posts set into a baseplate (see also* **64***).* TL 74 J. Stripe, LARF

The most complex timber harbour works date to the period after the Black Death, a time when good quality timber was relatively cheaper than it had been previously. By the late thirteenth century, for example, the demands of an expanding population were all but outstripping the ability of the native woodlands to provide a sustainable supply of high quality building timber. The late fourteenth-century fishmonger's wharf at Trig Lane was a fully pre-fabricated structure incorporating a wall of sawn vertically-set staves retained from the landward side by large widely-spaced triangular braces. The upper level was designed to be replaced when it decayed without disturbing the lower structure, and it also incorporated a complex fish tank as an integral part of the design (see **46** & **67**). This inventive, elaborate but eminently practical fishmonger's wharf is surely as worthy of our technical admiration in its own terms as the contemporary glories of the magnificent hammer-beam roof at Westminster Hall.

Masonry river walls (69 & 70)

The construction of a masonry river wall required a significantly larger financial outlay than a timber structure. A timber revetment erected on the Thames at Vauxhall in the fifteenth century cost approximately £1 10s per perch (Woodward-Smith 1977, 283-4) for example, whereas the late fourteenth-century ragstone wall built at Tower Wharf cost £9 13s 4d per perch (Salzman 1952, 469). However, the masonry walls proved an excellent long-term investment, requiring far less maintenance and repair than the timber structures. Consequently, the amount of land won from the river after masonry walling was introduced was significantly less than in the days when timber revetments were being regularly built and replaced. Before the Black Death, only a few riparian owners had the resources to face the harbour in masonry, but from the late fourteenth century onwards, stone walls became increasingly common.

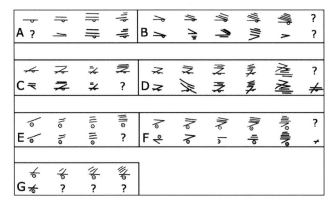

66 *Sequence of assembly marks incised on the fourteenth-century riverfront revetment timbers. The marks were traced over a 16m-length, demonstrating that the structure was prefabricated and constructed from west to east. The lower motifs were actually recorded; the upper line of motifs suggests what the complete figure may have been.* TL 74 J. Stripe, LARF

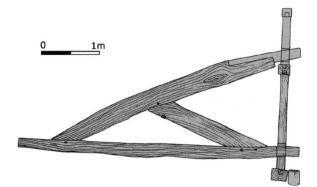

0 _____ 1m

67 *Side elevation of a fourteenth-to fifteenth-century riverfront revetment showing its construction in two distinct levels. See also* **56**. TL 74 J. Stripe, LARF

The earliest archaeological example of medieval masonry river walls in London was recorded at the confluence of the Thames and the Fleet. This was the area into which the Blackfriars expanded their precinct in the late thirteenth century, an event that involved the rebuilding of the town's defensive wall. The base of the new north–south section of that wall was washed by the waters of the River Fleet, and thus has all the characteristics of a harbour wall at that level. Construction began between 1279 and 1286, producing a wall some 2m wide just above foundation level. The lower courses were of well-cut ragstone ashlar, forming a battered face. Above the waterline the facing was of ragstone interspersed with flint nodules, while the reverse (landward) face comprised chalk blocks, a facing that was subsequently sealed by dumping to make up the level of the reclaimed land to the east (McCann 1993, 73). The more southerly section of this wall, which was completed in the early fourteenth century and included a tower, was observed in New Bridge Street in 1984. This also incorporate a battered, well-cut ashlar base as well as dressed ragstone rubble with flintwork in its western (riverward) face, backed by vertically-set chalk-blocks for its eastern (internal) face. Some 80m to the south of that site an east–west wall was recorded in 1985 in Queen Victoria Street, constructed directly over what had been Thames foreshore deposits. The foundation was of poured mortar and ragstone rubble, the riverwards face was battered, the core comprised chalk rubble, and the landward face was vertically-set rough rubble walling that was subsequently sealed by the associated reclamation deposits. The mid-fourteenth-century masonry wall recorded on the Whitefriars site in 2001 and the contemporary wall recorded just west of Boss Alley (Milne & Milne 1982) also had battered river faces. The latter wall was partially founded on a pile-retained timber base-plate, as was the fourteenth-century wall excavated on the Arundel House site, to the west of the City (Proctor 2000).

A noticeable change is recorded in the late fourteenth-century river wall at Tower Wharf, for this had a vertical face (Salzman 1952, 469) as did the fifteenth-century waterfront walling at Trig Lane (Milne & Milne 1982) and at the East Watergate, near Baynard's Castle (**69** & **70**), where timber rubbing posts had been set against the riverward face (Milne& Hobley 1981, 14-5). The masonry was supported on substantial timber base-plates at Trig Lane and Baynard's Castle, as was the case for the vertically-faced waterfront walls at Whitehall Palace, dated from 1512 to 1546 (Thurley 1999, 164-8).

Watergates and river stairs (68)

Getting onto the foreshore or into the river itself was an important consideration for many medieval Londoners, and the form of the riverside access points also changed over time. The earliest 'watergates' recorded by the archaeologists were no more than gaps between sections of riverside embankments; as later encroachment extended those embankments riverwards, so the gaps became, by default, increasingly pronounced inlets. Some of the larger of these waterfront indentations were retained, as at Billingsgate or Queenhithe. However, many of the lesser examples became increasingly constricted by repairs and encroachment along their edges. Such inlets were then infilled, at least in part, and a lane would be laid out at wharf level following the line of the ancient inlet, but now with the river stair or jetty constructed at the foot. By the thirteenth century, there were thus two general forms of waterfront access: ramped inlets that could be used by Londoners, their livestock or wheeled vehicles, and river stairs that could, obviously, only be used by people. One indirect effect of the pattern and chronology of waterfront encroachment was to restrict the watering of horses, for example, increasingly to the extreme eastern and western edges of the City waterfront, where the reclamation zone was narrowest and where inlets (imaginatively named 'watergates') were established in the thirteenth and fourteenth centuries.

Archaeologists have recorded evidence of many river stairs on the Thames-side sites. Some of these represent the 'common' stair at the foot of a 'common' lane, usually one that had its distant origin in a deliberately designed gap between sections of tenth- or eleventh-century embankments. The majority, however, were 'private' stairs, facilitating access onto the foreshore from a discrete waterfront property. The remains might comprise a timber platform on the foreshore from which a diagonally-set stair would have ascended directly onto the wharf. A more elaborate version incorporated a short jetty projecting horizontally over the foreshore at wharf level, the decking being supported by diagonally-braced trestles. The actual stair itself would then descend from the foot of the jetty. These structures were constructed as truncated versions of the common types of timber bridge known to have been used to span castle moats, for example (Rigold 1975); surviving documentation from London sometimes uses the same term, *pontes*,

68 *Posts and baseplates from a sequence of waterfront jetties marking a much-used private river stair. This example descended onto the sloping foreshore to the south of a fourteenth-century fishmongers' wharf near Trig Lane. View from the river looking north-west.* TL 74 Museum of London

69 *Masonry river wall built in the fourteenth century, on the western side of Boss Alley.* TL 74 Museum of London

70 *Masonry river wall, with timber rubbing posts, recorded on the East Watergate site at Baynard's Castle.* BC 72 Rescue

to describe them. These jetty stairs could be associated with mooring posts, since it was possible to board a boat moored there at any state of the tide. Indeed, it is worth stressing that a substantial proportion of late medieval London's imports and exports passed over the quayside utilising shallow-draft river craft moving between the projecting jetties and the large sea-going ships moored in mid-stream. Thus the plethora of waterfront jetties, public and private, formed a crucial element in both the form and function of London's harbour (**71**).

Revetments and the river (72)

As we have seen, each late medieval timber-built riverfront revetment comprised a braced framework designed to withstand the ebb and flow of the tidal Thames, together with the plank or stave cladding to retain the earthen dumps thrown up behind it. Such structures were therefore subject to pressure from both the landward and the riverward sides, and the size, spacing and position of the braces reflect that. However, the structures also have a direct relationship to the level of the contemporary Thames, and thus their study can tell us about ancient river levels. The Thames was tidal in this period, and thus the lower part of the revetments was immersed twice daily, while the uppermost part remained dry. The timber in the zone between the high and lower water mark was therefore subjected to regular swelling and shrinkage while the higher timbers were not. The physical breakdown of the fibre of the wood in all vertical timbers that extend from beneath the low water mark to above high water level is an inevitable consequence. The decay zone is readily identified as much in modern waterfront timberwork as in medieval revetments, and is coincident with the level of the mean high water mark. In a determined effort to overcome this pronounced problem of structural failure, the later medieval structures were actually built in two levels, with the upper one set at the mean high water mark. When these structures began to decay, only the upper level had to be replaced, rather than the whole structure. Thus, those particular structures have the actual level of medieval high water designed into them for latter-day archaeologists to discover.

An even more obvious point to note is that the earliest structures, such as the late ninth- or early tenth-century revetments from the Vintry/Queenhithe sites, are not as tall as later structures, and also that the contemporary ground surface that they protected lay at a lower level. This suggests that the river level changed during the medieval period, an assumption supported by the identification of river-laid flood deposits sealing occupation features on several waterfront sites. Indeed, study of the Roman quays in London has shown that the mean high water may have reached +1.5m OD in the first and second century, substantially lower than present-day values. However, there is also

71 *Accessing the river: this seventeenth-century panorama of the London waterfront shows a range of sizes and types of river stairs and jetties – the medieval waterfront had twice the number of projecting stairs.* Guildhall Library

evidence of a fall in river levels in the late Roman period, and the tidal head may have lain east of the City by the late fourth century. Such a situation would not have benefited the late Roman port. When the tidal head began moving westwards again is as yet unclear, but it is assumed that seventh-century Lundenwic would have been established on or below the contemporary tidal head, so that vessels arriving and leaving the port could take advantage of the ebb and flow. The lowest waterfront surface yet recorded in Lundenwic lay at about +1.2 or 1.3m OD, whereas the tenth-century waterfront surfaces in later Saxon London were at +1.5 to +1.7m, and an early eleventh-century external quayside surface in the Vintry lay at +1.7m OD.

These approximate figures could lend support to the suggestion of a modest but discernible rise in river level from AD 600 to 1000. If subsequent research verifies that, then it follows that the tidal head (and consequently the limit of navigation for seagoing vessels) can be assumed to have moved westwards in that period. By the mid-eleventh-century, significantly, there is consistent evidence that the riverside surfaces protected by waterfront embankments were laid at a higher level than those in the tenth century, even when they were set to the south of earlier structures or on sites with no previous major waterfront development. On the Billingsgate site, for example, external surfaces were established at +1.9m OD, while the internal surface of a late twelfth-century waterfront building was at just above +2m OD. Although other interpretations

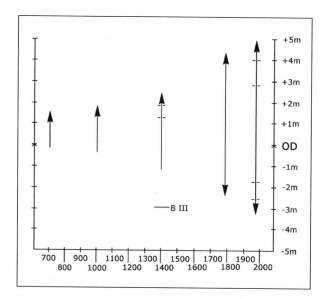

72 *Changing river levels: studying London's medieval harbourworks has facilitated a study of the Thames. The high-tide values for the eighth century, eleventh century and late fourteenth century are suggested, and compared with full tidal range for the early nineteenth century and for present day values. If true, data seems to show that the general trend is markedly upwards, and that the rate is accelerating. The line marked B III indicates the level at which the Blackfriars medieval wreck was found, which must have been well below the contemporary low tide. J. Stripe, LARF*

are possible, this could all be taken to imply a gradual but consistent rise in river level relative to the land from the seventh to the twelfth century.

Certainly there is strong evidence of a marked rise by or during the eleventh century, represented by silt deposits and erosion levels on a number of contemporary sites. The sea floods recorded in the Anglo-Saxon Chronicle for 1014 and 1099 may also be associated with this general trend, a consequence of a complex interaction of long-term climatic, isostatic and eustatic factors. However, another more local factor must also be taken into consideration: the construction of the London Bridge with its closely-set piles and piers. This major project would have impeded the flow of water, causing a regular but temporary increase in river levels relative to the land at every high tide, perhaps accentuating an already rising river level. On the Toppings Wharf site in Southwark, for example, a thirteenth-century flood eroded the site up to a level of at least 1.8m OD (Sheldon 1974). The level of the Thames relative to the land has continued to rise since the medieval period; the highest spring tides at the end of the eighteenth century seem to have reached a level of *c.*+4m OD, while just two centuries later, the figure was *c.*4.7m. If true, this is an alarming rate of increase when projected into the future. The archaeological study discussed above is therefore not just an 'ivory tower' academic exercise: by providing data on the long-term trends in river and sea level change over a 500 or 1,000 year period, waterfront archaeologists and geo-archaeologists can materially assist London's flood defence management strategy. They can use the past to predict the future, through the calculation of the long-term trajectory of London's rising river levels.

12

CHIEF OF THE REALM

Life in the late medieval harbour

In 1420, Henry V married Catherine, daughter of Charles VI of France, and brought her back to London in triumph. But just two years later, Henry died of dysentery while policing the southern parts of his enlarged realm. His son, Henry VI, succeeded to the throne of England and France, a magnificent title for a nine-month-old child. The period from 1421-3 is also noteworthy for the history of London's harbour. Every year each ward in the City was inspected and a medley of civic complaints was subsequently presented to the wardmote. By chance, the complete presentments for 1421 and 1423 survive and have been published (Thomas 1943). The following summary of the complaints received for the waterfront wards provides an evocative picture of the social context and something of the conditions in the early fifteenth-century harbour.

Our progress along the quayside from east to west would begin outside the Tower of London, in Tower ward, with all the complications that beset a cosmopolitan port (**73**). Here Allard Taillour, an alien, kept a hostelry 'colouring many strangers including Easterlings and other foreigners, to the great nuisance of his neighbours'. Some 20 years later, in January 1444, Lodewicus Deado, a merchant, and a group of Venetian mariners were convicted of breaking into the homes of John Pulter and John Abbey. The *London Chronicle* for 1440 records that two bargemen were sentenced to death beyond St Katherine's 'by hengen til the water hadde wasted them by ebbing and flowyd' for the murder of three Flemings and a child who had been aboard a ship heading for Flanders from London. A further insight into the make-up of the port is provided by the written returns collected from 1441-84 for the *Alien Subsidy*, a tax paid by foreigners living in London. The list for 1443 has been assessed by Sylvia Thrupp, and she notes 1,650 aliens, some having acquired property, and so charged 16d, the others simply renting, charged 6d. The most common label was 'Doche' a term that incorporated Dutch, Flemings and Germans, of whom the majority came from Holland or Brabant, the rest principally from Bruges or Cologne. There were also several Italians, many with exemptions, some French and then a miscellany including a Greek doctor, a Portugese sailor, some Icelanders, a Jew, two Danes and a Catalan armourer (Hollaender & Kellaway 1969, 247-272).

To return to Tower ward, in the heart of the early fifteenth-century harbour (Thomas 1943): the busy roadway of Thames Street was obstructed, since William Clauson and John Kempe, carter, kept carts standing in the street which hindered people night and day. His neighbours, Katherine French, Sybil Eddon, Katherine Clerk and Alice Moysant had all been charged with prostitution. However, a rather different impression of the area is provided by documentation concerning a property in nearby Water Lane in the parish of Allhallows. Here, we read of a lease from Thos Charleton and his wife Elizabeth to David Turbeville, vintner, of two tenements granted in 1425 for 30 years at an annual rent of a red rose for the first 11 years. The prosperity of the port is reflected in a splendid funerary brass in All Hallows-by-the-Tower that depicts one John Bacon, citizen and woolman, who died there in 1437. His feet are shown, appropriately enough, resting on a wool sack (**74**).

In Billingsgate ward, there were a number of tax evaders and other dubious characters. William Chaundeler of Greenwich was a freeman, but paid neither lot nor scot; neither did Nicholas Busche nor William Stafford. John Pette, Petigo and White of Gravesend neither paid taxes nor contributed to the watch. John Pette was a forestaller of salt and corn on the river, while Lambo the boatman, a foreigner who sold foodstuffs, was a rebel against the King's officers. John Nelham took advantage of the complex tax and tolls levied in the port, for he was accused of charging false customs, i.e. fraudulent taxes, such as 1/2d on a case of herrings, and illegally taking a share of wines, oysters, mussels and all manner of fish belonging to freemen. So too did Robert Gerveys, who took 'unlawful custom' of victuals from ships belonging to foreigners and freemen. It is worth noting that even Thomas Leicester, the official Deputy Searcher for the Port of London and William Sawce, the Searcher's Controller, had recently been imprisoned facing extortion charges. In March 1383, Matthew Passeleve was charged with owing John Hende and John Rote, former sheriffs of London, £64. He had rented the Billingsgate bailiwick from them but only paid half of the promised price. He claimed they took the wines and other goods forfeited as custom and that had discharged his debt, but the plaintiffs said that those were part of the initial agreement between the parties. A jury decided for the plaintiffs.

By 1407, coopers were obliged to mark their barrels and by 1420, they were also recording their individual marks in the Guildhall, so that the faulty barrels could be traced back to source. This increased regulation of the copper's trade was the result of a number of complaints between 1400 and 1413 concerning the capacity of barrels, leading to the adoption of new standards. Ale barrels were to hold 27 gallons, while a half barrel should be 14 gallons, for example. There was even a case of a Billingsgate man who made up 260 barrels and firkins of poor quality wood which held less than the agreed standard measure, by up to two gallons in some instances. All 260 vessels were taken to the Guildhall, certified as false, and then burnt.

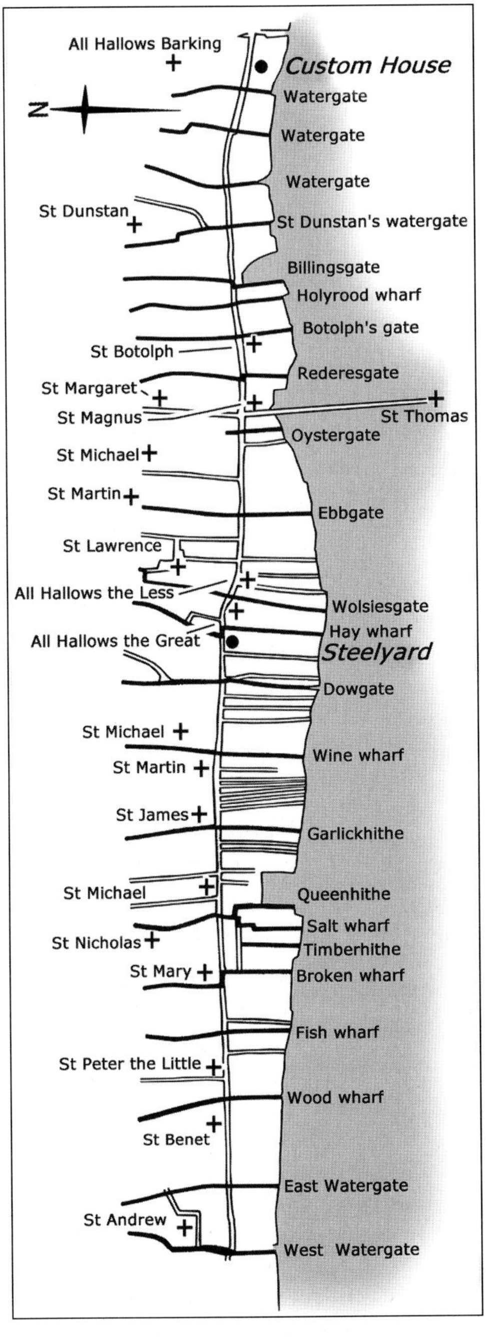
All Hallows Barking
Custom House
N
Watergate
Watergate
Watergate
St Dunstan
St Dunstan's watergate
Billingsgate
Holyrood wharf
Botolph's gate
St Botolph
Rederesgate
St Margaret
St Thomas
St Magnus
Oystergate
St Michael
St Martin
Ebbgate
St Lawrence
All Hallows the Less
Wolsiesgate
Hay wharf
All Hallows the Great
Steelyard
Dowgate
St Michael
Wine wharf
St Martin
St James
Garlickhithe
St Michael
Queenhithe
Salt wharf
St Nicholas
Timberhithe
St Mary
Broken wharf
Fish wharf
St Peter the Little
Wood wharf
St Benet
East Watergate
St Andrew
West Watergate

73 *London's late medieval harbour: schematic plan showing plethora of parish churches and waterfront lanes leading down to the Thames. NB: north to left.* J. Stripe, LARF

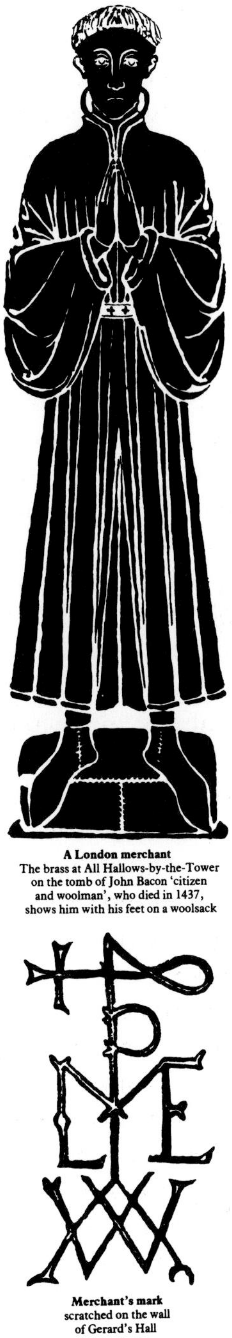
A London merchant
The brass at All Hallows-by-the-Tower
on the tomb of John Bacon 'citizen
and woolman', who died in 1437,
shows him with his feet on a woolsack
Merchant's mark
scratched on the wall
of Gerard's Hall

74 *A London merchant: funerary brass from All Hallows-by-the-Tower commemorating 'John Bacon, citizen and woolman' who died in 1437. His feet are resting on a woolsack, the source of his wealth.* Museum of London

The common stairs at Billingsgate also served as a terminal for the 'long ferry' to Gravesend. It is mentioned in the early fifteenth-century poem *London Lyckpenny*, a cautionary tale of the problems which beset penniless people visiting the city:

> Then hyed me to Billingsgate and one cried 'Hoo go we hence'
> I prayed a bargeman for God's sake that he would spare me my expense.
> 'Thou scapst not here' quoth he 'under two pence'.

In Bridge ward there was a plethora of inns to attract thirsty travellers arriving in London by boat or road. However, ale was not being sold in the correct measure by Robert Whadpole in *The Bell* or *The Swan*, or by John Cowper in *The Star*, Andrew Catour in *The Tabard*, John Botiller in *The Saracen's Head*, Roger Mutton in *The White Horse* and *The Katherine Wheel*, William Bateman at *The Hart*, Richard Bokenham in *The Horn*. The fishmongers' street market blocked the roadway in Fish Street Hill, Bridge Street and at the corner of St Magnus church with their tubs, barrels and boards, to the great nuisance of passers-by, horses and carts.

In Walbrook ward fishmongers, butchers and hucksters were a discomfort to all passing or dwelling there, because they threw entrails and offal onto the King's highway 'to the horribility of the whole ward'. The fish market in Bread Street ward near St Nicholas Cole Abbey was also a problem, since the boards for the stalls together with the barrels of fish jutted out too far into the roadway from Friday Street to Waley's shop, and then on both sides of the road as far as Thomas Russel's shop.

Easy access to the river was still an important factor in the everyday life of all Londoners, and thus the maintenance of the river stairs at the end of the common lanes was a major issue. The stairs at Cousin Lane were defective and the lane itself was blocked with refuse. So too were Ebbesgate, Wolseslane and Trin Lane, while Haywharf Lane was obstructed by fullers who washed their long rolls of cloth there. It was reported that the steps at Paul's wharf were blocked by so many boats moored there that it was impossible for servants to draw water. Harteshorne Lane had a large pothole in it, 'to the great nuisance and danger of people coming there' and the common stairs at Trig Lane were described as 'grievously broken'. Life on the river could also be a problem; two large river barges collided and sank in *c.*1400 just off the Trig Stairs. The remains were found during the rebuilding of the river wall in 1971 (Marsden 1996).

In Dowgate ward an important fifteenth-century waterfront feature was erected in Greenwich Lane; this was 'Whittington's Longhouse', a public latrine comprising two rows of no fewer then 64 seats, one set for male the other for female. The foundations of this large public facility were observed in 1959 during the excavations on the site of the Public Cleansing Depot (appropriately enough) close to the mouth of the Walbrook stream. A north-south section of masonry walling *c.*1m wide was traced for some 85m and almost certainly formed part of the gulley draining the latrine. The use of the great tidal river as a common sewer, and the need for Londoners to get access to the waterfront 'for their easement', remained an unpleasant but necessary fact of medieval life.

A number of common stairs were not reported as blocked or defective, and thus can be assumed to have been reasonably maintained. These include most of those east of the bridge, including Wool Quay and Billingsgate, the largest common landing places. In Queenhithe ward a syndicate of 'regraters' were operating. Ellen Steer, Katherine Lyle, Margaret Burg, Lucy Clerk, Janet Woodham and Katherine Wylde would rise early in the morning and wait up until late in the evening to catch boats bringing victuals, butter or cheese. They would then buy the produce privately on the boat before it landed, creating a dearth of such produce in the City. John Swayn and his wife forestalled a boatload of rushes approaching Queenhithe, taking 30 burden of rushes for which they paid the boatman 26d for the lot, rather than 3d per burden. When the boatman realised he had been short-changed he 'openly made much noysing and sclaundir'. Then there was John of Ely, who stood accused of not discharging his responsibilities for keeping an honest assay of the large trade in oysters. Some of the oyster ketches moored for two to three days with half their cargo unsold, but would then sail off only to return 'with a freshening of new oysters', i.e. with a few new ones spread over the top of the dangerously old ones. It would seem that John of Ely was allowing women to oversee the trade, an approach that was quite unacceptable in the fifteenth-century city. Also at Queenhithe, behind the Pye, was a privy place with 'a good shadowing for thieves': many strumpets and pimps had there covert there. The ward thought it should be closed up at night and only open during the day for a set time.

Dybleslane was a common lane that led down to the Thames, but needed a new river stair so that people who wished to wash or fetch water could do so more easily. The common stair at the end of the next lane was mischievously broken and perilous to people at high water or at night. As for the quayside itself, the boats which brought oysters, fish and so forth there, cast their ropes so high up the shore that men, women and children fell and hurt themselves, while at night old people were likely to fall into the Thames.

At Castle Baynard, the watergate opposite St Benet's church was so completely blocked in 1423 by boats and barges that it was impossible for the water to sluice out the rubbish which accumulated there. Part of this large accumulation of refuse was gleefully excavated by archaeologists in 1972 in the first major investigation of a medieval watergate (rather misleadingly called a 'dock' in the published reports). The three sides of the inlet, although all built at different dates by different hands, were all stone-faced by the early fifteenth century, and some still had the timber rubbing posts surviving, to protect the hulls of the moored river boats as the tide rose and fell. The fifteenth-century documentary records also state that on the adjacent wharf, the common latrine had so much firewood piled against it by John Talworth that it had become ruinous, with its walls and roof broken. That building extended out over the river, and was thus supported on piles. Unfortunately Edward Dene and William Hayneworthe tied their vessels to those posts, and they had become unsafe and liable to give way. Remarkably at least one of the posts was substantial enough to have survived and was recorded in 1972, although initially interpreted as a loading platform (Milne & Habley 1981, figs 12 & 14). Thus the archaeological team working on the first major medieval waterfront site in London in 1972-3 were able to record a typical slice of riverside life. They uncovered not only the substantial remains of the medieval townhouse of Baynard's Castle owned by the mother of the King of England, but also the adjoining common watergate, complete with its public latrine and associated detritus.

Corporate rebuilding

For the City in the fifteenth century, it could be argued that it was no longer powerful individuals running the port, but powerful companies and institutions. The formalisation of the City's trade and craftworkers into distinct guilds or companies can be traced back to at least the twelfth century (Page 1923, 101). The later medieval period saw their influence increase markedly, with their domination of the Court of Common Council from 1384, for example. The voice of the companies began to replace that of the ancient ward system for the control of taxation, in the regulation of entry into citizenship and in matters concerning the election and tenure of City officials (Keene 2001; Barron 2001). These organisations required places to meet and conduct their business, a need initially served by using premises owned by individual members or by renting. As their prosperity and influence increased in the fourteenth century, so too did their need to acquire more permanent accommodation. This was precisely the period when, following the pestilence, more land became available. It was also a time when the lords who had built substantial town houses, usually in the form of a large open hall set within a courtyard complex, were finding the demands of eating in the Great Hall increasingly unfashionable. The desire for greater privacy within the upper echelons of City society led directly to the design and construction of new types of multi-roomed, multi-storied buildings in which the great open hall was no longer a central requirement.

This was a clear break with a long-lived medieval concept, since the plan of the open hall saw the lord occupying the raised dais at one end, while his retinue occupied the space in the body of the hall around the shared open hearth. The building plan thus reflected both the hierarchy and the shared obligations of that society. Just as the aristocracy sought greater privacy in their domestic arrangements, so the City guilds were increasing in wealth and power by acting communally. They thus adopted the now abandoned great halls, either directly, or by design, by building a new hall to a similar pattern. The great hall therefore survived in London's townscape, no longer as a symbol of feudalism but as a symbol of free enterprise. It was the architectural expression of 'the enlargement of the idea of community by the principle of fellowship', a concept that was now replacing lordship, which had once been the central element of social union in medieval England (Unwin 1966, 16).

The powerful fishmongers had already had their own purpose-built hall by 1310, rebuilt in 1434. As for the others, a selection of examples makes the point. The Mercers acquired land for a new hall in mid-fourteenth century; the merchant tailors built their new hall at the same time; the vintners acquired a new site in c.1357, and a new hall in 1446; the skinners, in 1380. The process continued into the fifteenth century as the goldsmiths built their new hall in 1407; the drapers in 1425; the grocers in 1426, clothworkers (1432), salters (1454), ironmongers (1457), haberdashers (1478), and dyers (1482). Even the shipwrights built a hall in 1428, although this was in Ratcliffe, to the east of the City. Alongside this trend, the City itself was also expressing its corporate identity and civic purpose through a new building programme. We have already noted the new Custom House at Wool Quay (1380) to which can be added Blackwell Hall in 1396; the Stocks covered market building from 1406-11; the Guildhall itself, extensively rebuilt from 1411 and the purpose-built market building at Leadenhall (1420). By the fifteenth century there is thus documentary, architectural and topographical evidence that the companies ruled the port. Even the Lord Mayor took to the Thames: the *London Chronicle* records that the colourful tradition of travelling to Westminster by water for the inaugural procession was begun by John Norman in 1454.

The late medieval momentum for property amalgamation and redevelopment gathered pace on the harbour as in the body of the City. On the Baynard's Castle site in 1300, for example, the waterfront between the East Watergate and St Paul's Wharf was split into half a dozen tenements owned mainly by woodmongers. After the Black Death, the easternmost pair had been bought up for the Earl of Salisbury's town house, while the eastern properties were owned by St Martin le Grande, Woburn Abbey and St Mary Bishopsgate. Duke Humphrey acquired the Salisbury site, and developed it after a fire in 1420, with the building later known as Baynard's Castle. That structure was itself extended westwards, absorbing all the neighbouring properties following the royal confiscation of monastic holdings in the early sixteenth century (**75**). This general pattern had a pronounced effect on the riverfront itself, as a smaller number of waterfront property owners were represented by a rather more uniform frontage, with fewer indentations and fewer projecting private river stairs than had been the case in the thirteenth and fourteenth centuries. Between Trig Lane and Boss Alley, for example, the new

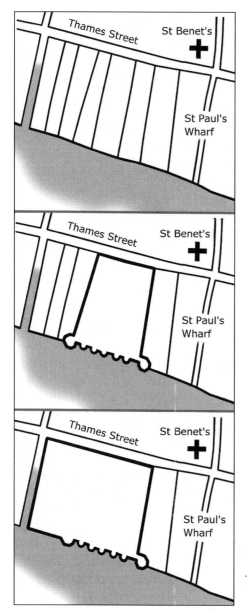

75 *Amalgamation of riverfront properties from the fourteenth/fifteenth centuries to the early sixteenth century: plans, showing the expansion of Baynard's Castle.* J. Stripe, LARF

mid-fifteenth-century river wall encompassed three earlier properties. A single central river stair now gave access to the foreshore where there had once been three narrow properties with three separate jetties. Even the narrow inlet to the east was now blocked up and became a lane, changing its name from Kingsgate to Boss Alley (**76**). Topographically, it seems that the town and its harbour were prospering in the century after the great pestilence: there was room to expand and resources to spend.

Traffic and trade in the late fifteenth century

Henry VI assumed power in 1437 but was unable to retain the realms that his charismatic father had won: Brittany was lost in 1449, Normandy in 1450 and, even more shocking for the London wine trade, even Gascony fell in 1453. By that date, of all the French domains, only Calais remained in English hands, a vital staging post in the English trade network. Such a political debacle did not enhance Henry's standing in some quarters. On the 22 May 1455, the first Battle of St Albans opened another unhappy, unsettled period in English history with the onset of civil war. To such internal concerns could be added the threat of the French; in 1457 the port of Sandwich was 'robbed and despoiled'; the reverberations were felt in London, where 'a great watch' was instituted. The guard on the gates was doubled every night, as the *London Chronicle* records. However, following the Battle of Mortimer Cross in 1461, London acclaimed a new king, the Yorkist Edward IV. He introduced new mercantile legislation onto the statute books in the 1460s, which was,

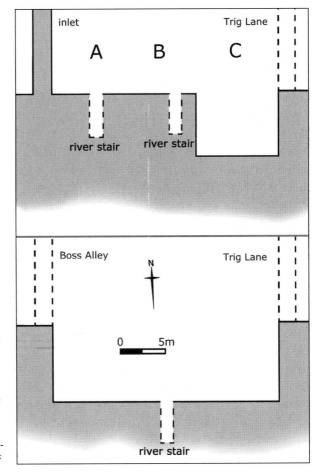

76 *The changing waterfront: schematic plans showing the gradual straightening of the irregular waterfront in the late medieval period, as riverside tenements are amalgamated, private river stairs are lost and inlets infilled. This example shows the Trig Lane area between the late fourteenth and mid-fifteenth centuries. J. Stripe, LARF*

remarkably, the first interest the crown had shown in such concerns since 1382. These included measures to prevent aliens exporting English wool, a revival of protectionist measures that shows how ineffective Richard II's *Navigation Act* had become. He also decreed that no corn should be imported until it exceeded a certain value, in a further effort to protect the price and sales of English stocks. It would seem that the London merchants who had helped him gain power now had his ear.

Hanseatic goods were seized in London in 1468, although their privileges were restored the following year when Henry VI regained the throne. The civil war was therefore far from over, as London discovered in 1471 when an army of Kentish rebels unsuccessfully attacked the bridge in an attempt to take the town. However, the Bridge was not the only building on London's waterfront to play a part in the Wars of the Roses. Following Edward IV's death in 1483, the Tower of London was the site of the alleged murder of the young princes, the uncrowned Edward V and his brother, while the crown was offered to the Duke of Gloucester, Richard III, when he was staying at the opposite end of the harbour in the mansion at Baynard's Castle.

Customs accounts

Three groups of customs officers were at work in late medieval London, compiling three separate sets of accounts. Each office was overseen by a controller, with two collectors, a searcher, a tronager (responsible for weighing) and their associated clerks and servants. There were also waiters, 'diverse other persons waiting and searching both by day and by night, by land and by water', who boarded vessels to inspect cargoes and impound uncustomed goods. By the end of the fifteenth century, there were some 42 officials directly involved in customs collection. They were remunerated by a series of fees, wages and rewards, the Crown providing fees for the more important staff, rent for the offices and up to £10 for the hire of boats. In addition, the searchers collected up to 6s for each bill of discharge made out for every ship leaving port, once they were satisfied that all goods had been accounted for. Each non-English passenger also had to pay the searchers 4d 'head money'. Even the collectors demanded a fee of 2d from the merchants for each set of custom papers prepared as invoices and receipts (the cockets).

The three accounts being compiled in the late fifteenth century were:
a) The wool custom, levied on wool, wool fells and hides whether exported by denizens or aliens. For example, a fixed rate was established in 1471, and raised some £10,000 per annum from 1471 to 1482.
b) Petty Custom and Cloth Custom; the former had been levied since 1303 on all goods imported or exported by alien merchants, while the latter was an additional rate charged on all cloth carried by both denizen and all alien

merchants, unless like the Hansa, they were exempt. Petty Custom only raised some £400 p.a., whereas cloth raised *c*.£4,500 p.a.

c) Tunnage and Poundage; the latter was an *ad valorem* duty charged on all goods bar wool and wine carried by deniens and most aliens, while Tunnage was the duty on wine imports; both charges had been levied since the 1340s. In the late fifteenth century, they could raise *c*.£4,500 p.a., twice as much as cloth, but only half as much as wool. The Tunnage listing for 1480-1 records 3,820 tuns of wine brought into London.

Imported pottery found in London can be used to construct a general picture of harbour traffic in this period (**78**). This may be compared with surviving exchequer customs accounts, such as those dealing with London's overseas trade in 1480-1 published by H.S. Cobb in 1990. This fascinating study provides a partial but evocative view of the port over a 12-month period from Michaelmas to Michaelmas, the medieval year. The accounts record the presence of all laden ships in the port, but not those 'in ballast', i.e. arriving or

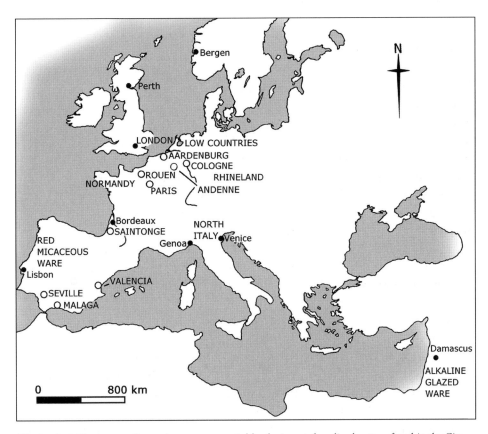

77 *London's European trading partners, as represented by the imported medieval pottery found in the City. The open circles indicate the sources of particular wares.* After Vince 1985, figure 36:
J. Stripe, LARF

departing without a cargo, and not those exempt from customs duty. Of all the 224 vessels recorded as arriving and leaving the port, some 40 per cent were English, over half of which were from London, with names like *Barbara, Le Bartilmewe, Blithe, Burnet, Christofer* (a popular choice), *Clement, Gabryell, Jesus, John, Julyan*, several *Kateryns, Leonard*, many *Marys, Martyn, Nicholas, Petyr Stokker, Rikmans, Thomas, Trinity Bole* and *Volantyn*. The rest of the English craft came from east coast ports such as Boston, Lynn or Yarmouth, or from south-western ports such as Weymouth, Fowey, Saltash or Dartmouth.

From study of the home ports registered for the alien vessels listed in the accounts, it seems that the London-Brabant trade dominated the port. This focused on four major international fairs, each one lasting for some six weeks. The season opened on Maundy Thursday with the Pask Mart at Bergen-op-Zoom, followed by Sinxten, the Whitsun Fair at nearby Antwerp. Then there was the Bamis Mart in August, also at Antwerp, the season closing with the Cold Mart in late October at Bergen-op-Zoom. Trade with the Low Countries accounted for some 60 per cent of the alien merchant vessels in London. In addition to those from Brabant, they came from Zeeland (Arnemuiden, Flushing, Middleburg, Reimerswaal) or were Flemish (Ostend, Sluys) or Dutch (Dordrecht, Gouda, Holland, Leek, Leiden and a convoy of at least five ships which arrived in December was from Purmerend). Cloth was the main export, but these ships brought in a range of items including over 900 books, as well as spectacles and spectacle cases for the literate Londoners.

Then there were the merchants of the Hanseatic League (**73**), operating from the Steelyard, at the mouth of the Walbrook near Dowgate. The treaty of Utrecht (1474) had ended a six-year conflict with the Hansa, for which they had won £10,000 compensation. That sum was to be paid off in tax exemptions and thus all their cargoes had to be costed, but no charges were levied. They had their own ship, *Maria*, which made no fewer than six round trips in 1480-1, returning in October, December, March, April, June and July. As for the other Hansa ports, vessels from Danzig or Hamburg arrived in London in October, November, April, May and August, with a convoy of three in July. Thus there was rarely a month in which there was not at least one Hansa vessel moored in the Thames. They traded in Baltic produce such as timber, fur, pitch, tar and stockfish, and exported cloth, pewter and candles.

Ships from the northern French ports of Calais, Le Conquet, Rouen, Harfleur, Caen, Guerande and Dieppe were also regular visitors throughout the year, including all the winter months. They imported wheat, apples, nuts, salt, millstones, fish, and woad in exchange for cloth, pewter, lead, brass, copper, pitch and candles. The wool fleets sailed out in December 1480 and again in July and September 1481, most bound for the staple port at Calais, but some sailed directly to Italy through the Straits of Marrock.

Genoese merchants made use of the ships from the Iberian peninsula. There were three Portugese vessels in London in November, one in February, and

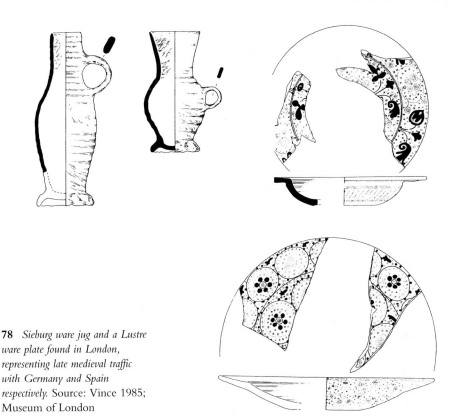

78 *Sieburg ware jug and a Lustre ware plate found in London, representing late medieval traffic with Germany and Spain respectively.* Source: Vince 1985; Museum of London

another three in March, hailing from Oporto, Viana and Sesio. These ships, with names such as *Sanctus Spiritus, Tres Magos, Maria de Lawe* and *St Saveour*, brought in 300,000 oranges, sugar and cork, and took away cloth, pewter, calfskins and tallow. There were also ships from the northern Spanish ports of Bilbao and San Sebastien, as well as from Cadiz, carrying woad, alum, grain, dates, raisins, paper, iron, oil and wine. This trade was clearly significant (**77**), as some 20 vessels are listed in the returns for 1480-1, a similar number to that representing the Hansa, for example. A small armada returned to Spain in November and December, with a cargo of 3,000 cloths, rabbit skins, salt meat, tallow, candles, pewter and beer.

London did not enjoy a monopoly of the Iberian trade. A port like Bristol, for example, recorded just over £3,000-worth of trade on the route in 1480. This was the same year that a Bristol vessel set sail westwards for the 'island of Brasylle', the fabled staging post en route to Asia. This was the first of several such expeditions from Bristol across the Atlantic, the most famous of which was John Cabot's voyage of 1497, with its landfall on the coast of North America, just five years after Colombus had discovered his New World.

To return to London in 1480, the trade with Venice was represented by just one vessel, less than 0.5 per cent of all the vessels in the port. However, the

159

size of this single galley and its remarkable cargo ensured its arrival was eagerly anticipated. A fleet of three Venetian galleys had arrived in Southampton in February 1480. They stayed there for three months then two left for Flanders and one went to London, arriving there in June with its £6,000's worth of cargo of silks, spices, wine, soap, glass, carpets and more. This was examined by custom officials on 14 June. Not only was it shipping goods for a wide range of merchants, but many of the crew also had a share of the imports. The commander, Bernard Bondymer himself, brought in material worth £267, considerably more than any other member of his large crew, who included Mononyon de Caudia (Navigator), and the confusingly named purser and assistant purser, Angelo de Nicholo and Nicholas de Angelo. Also listed in the customs accounts are the first and second mate, a steersman (*perviour*), a *palomber* (in charge of mooring) and the *portulat*, the stroke, or principal oarsman. There was also mention of nine crossbowmen and two gunners, a sure sign that piracy was still a problem on the high seas. Once unloaded, the galley then took on a new cargo of some 550 cloths, pewter, calfskins and tin, and was ready to leave some time after 18 September, three months later.

Not all London's trade was transported by river. A proportion of it was sent by road, as the customs officers noted. Pack horses went as far as Bristol and Plymouth with cloth for merchants in those ports, while a regular stream of carts trundled from London through Kingston, Guildford, Alton and Alresford to Southampton. Peter Jamys and William Sellam were responsible for almost 50 loads between them on this well-worn route, with John Rede sending 14, William Spigot 11 and Thomas Arnold 9, while Nicholas Parker and William Nash used the larger, slower wagons. These journeys were spread throughout the year, both summer and winter, which suggests that wheeled traffic could operate on the medieval roads in all seasons. This fleet of London carts carried an additional 3,500 cloths for Italian merchants that would later be exported to Italy from Southampton (Cobb 1990).

Ships, shipping and shipowners

The published *Plea and Memoranda Rolls* provide examples of the complexities of shipping and trade in the late fourteenth- and early fifteenth-century port. The majority of voyages and transactions presumably passed off relatively smoothly without recourse to law, and were consequently not recorded in the court rolls. However, the handful of cases summarised here throw light on questions of who actually owned or hired ships, how cargoes were bought and sold, the sometimes uneasy relationship of London to the increasingly large community of foreign merchants in their town, together with some cautionary tales of the perils of the high seas. It also shows that the waterman's trade was closely regulated, since action was taken in 1422 to prevent John Trevilias, a

79 *The excavation of late Medieval quayside buildings arranged along the western side of a narrow waterfront alley on St Botolph's Wharf. The view is from the river, looking north-east.* BIG 82 Museum of London

80 *A late medieval merchant's undercroft, with steps to the north-south lane leading down to the river, recorded at St Botolph's Wharf.* BIG 82 Museum of London

pewterer, from carrying cargoes or passengers by boat from London to Gravesend, 'openly or secretly'. He was 'not to derive any profit or advantage therefrom, unless licensed by the London court'. The journey to and from London and Gravesend, the 'long ferry,' was one of the more popular routes, since it connected with the direct road network to the Channel ports.

There were several instances of ships' masters pressing merchants for freightage, such as John Hauley in May 1387, who transported 86 tuns of red Bordeaux wine in his ship, the *Seynt Marie*, for Thomas Girdeler, who then did not pay Hauley for the transport. After bringing his case to court, Hauley received his money, and acknowledged the debt as paid on 22 October. William Prophet, a mariner of Westlenne, faced the same problem that December, charging William Jay with owing him £7 12s 6d for freighting 30 weys of salt on his ship *Seintemariebot*. He was awarded that sum, as well as 33s 4d for the debt being late. In September 1392, Thomas Lynne, master of the *Seinte Marie*, charged four Italians with not paying the delay fee owed to him if their merchandise was not loaded soon enough for him to meet their deadline. He too was awarded his fee.

In 1414, John Guy, master of *Le Trinity of Plymouth*, imported 16 casks of red Gascony wine from Menaldos of Bordeaux. This was stored in the cellar of William Reynold, the London vintner. It was agreed that he would pay £40 to Menaldos, even if the wine was not sold within seven weeks. The merchant Henry Wodeward shipped four casks of red wine and one pipe of red Gascony wine from Bordeaux to London in 1420, on his ship *George of Lynn*, for a cost of £4 10s. That sum had not been paid by Gerinus Darengos, a merchant who had lodged the wine in the cellar of the London vintner, John Neve.

Even the ownership of a vessel was not always straight forward. In June 1388, for example, we read that Roger Brymmor, a grocer, sold three fourths of the ownership of the ship *Le Andrew* to John Weneton, a fishmonger, and William Romesslie, a tailor. Another case concerned a ship valued at £40 that had been moored in the Thames near St Dunstan in the East which was taken by John Strecke, a chandler, to Sandwich. The vessel was apparently owned by Ralph Gresvale, an ironmonger, although Strecke claimed that it belonged to him and his partner Richard Martyn, and had been obtained in a suit he had against the former owner, one John Ryver. John Beterenden, a draper, who had his ship *Le Thomas of London* impounded in Bordeaux in 1417 by Edmund Arnold of Dartmouth, in settlement of a previous dispute.

Worse was to befall Alexander Ferrantyn's voyage to Bordeaux in 1426, where his ship the *St Anne of London* under her master John Starling, had been loaded with wine. On its return journey it was captured by Spaniards and taken to Sluys in Flanders. It was then sold to two Flemings before being bought back by John Waynflete. The venture had initially been insured for the sum of £250 by a consortium of 17 Florentine merchants in London but, citing the small print in the contract, they refused to pay up.

Marine insurance is mentioned again in May 1445, when Daniel Justinian, a merchant of Genoa, made a bond with Augustine de Loreto, that the latter would indemnify him in the delivery of 18 butts, 14 barrels, 2 casks and 5 hogsheads of Castile soap to Augustine Cassini. Another bond was made in 1426 between a group of Genoese merchants living in London with Sir Humphrey, Duke of Gloucester, High Chamberlain of England. It concerned a carrack with cargo, captured at sea near Sandwich that was to be held for a year before being disposed of if unclaimed.

The Hansa merchants living in London filed a complaint in 1435, regarding the fate of their cog *George of Prussia*, under its master Court Stole. It had been loaded in London for a voyage to Flanders, but had been driven off course by contrary winds onto the Downs. There it was captured by the (*Holy*) *Gost* of Newcastle on Tyne and another ship from Orwell of which Thomas Andrew was the master. The captured vessel was brought to the Thames, but the King ordered that it should be impounded until its fate could be determined. However, the cog was then taken by pirates who held it for eight days before it was rescued by the *Gost* and taken back into the Thames. There the cargo was sold and the ship fitted out for a voyage to Bordeaux. Then the king intervened again on behalf of the Hansa merchants and, in consideration of their compensation claim, had the vessel valued at £60 by 12 good and lawful men of the City who were 'experts on the art of duty on ships'. Merchants thus seemed resigned to the problems of piracy. Godfrey Wolleman, a merchant who had lost £300-worth of goods at sea to the King's enemies the previous year, nevertheless shipped 600 sacks of wool from London and Southampton round the Iberian peninsula and through the straits of Morocco into the Mediterranean in April 1447.

It was not only pirates that caused delays, so too did bureaucracy. Some foreign merchants tried to get around the laws governing sales in London by brokering deals in which goods were simply exchanged for others of similar value, rather than actually sold and therefore taxed. For example in 1429, James Gentille, a Jew and an alien, was involved in the exchange of £30-worth of woollen cloth for silks of the same value. Frederick de Nawfro, another alien, brokered a deal with Antonio de Maffeo and Thomas Loughton in which a sack of wool worth 100 marks was exchanged for woad, while Gerard Galganet, also an alien, oversaw the exchange of woollen cloth for barrels of sweet wine valued at £80. Francis Balbi, a merchant from Venice, was suspected of such a contravention of London's complex customs. He had bought 120 sacks of Cotswold wool from various places in England and from different foreign merchants in 1415. He brought it all to his galleys moored in the Thames, which were soon loaded ready to depart. The sheriffs, Thomas Aleyn and John Michell, then had the wool impounded, on the grounds that a foreign merchant had bought merchandise in the City from other foreign merchants and not from Londoners. This dispute delayed the departure of the entire fleet. The Venetian complained bitterly about his treatment, claiming that all his purchases had taken place outside London. He was given a fair hearing in the courts and won his case; the wool was freed from arrest.

Navigation still depended on the experience of seamen utilising such technological aids as were available. These included the 32-point compass to determine location and direction, sounding lines with leads to fathom the depth of water and the nature of the sea floor, and a sand glass to calculate time and therefore speed. There were also 'rutters', books that listed information on tides, coasts and harbour approaches to assist in the planning of routes. The earliest surviving English 'rutter', the so-called Lansdowne 285 document, dates to the reign of Edward IV and was compiled by one William Ebesham. Its five chapters describe the world of the late medieval English mariner. The first section gives sailing directions for the east and south coast, from Berwick-upon-Tweed to Land's End; the second the coasts of France, Portugal and Spain from St Malo to Gibraltar, with the route hugging the coast around the Bay of Biscay as far as the all important port of Bordeaux, described in more detail. The third chapter returns to British waters, describing the west coast from Land's End to Avonmouth, and the coast of Ireland. The fourth chapter lists soundings around Ushant, the Scillies and Beachy Head, while the final section summarises two non-coastwise routes from Finistere, one to the English Channel, the other to the Severn Estuary (Burwash 1947, 24-6).

However, horizons were clearly widening in this period. By 1415, the ships of east coast fishermen were working as far north as Iceland. In more southerly waters, English merchants were also sailing further, trading deep into the Mediterranean, in spite of Italian opposition. In 1446, for example, we hear that goods from Genoese merchants in London were seized and a fine of £6,000 was levied in compensation for an unprovoked attack on an English ship trading there. Such voyages became increasing common, and even more daring enterprises are recorded towards the close of the century. On 15 July 1480, a Bristol ship captained by John Jay, the younger, set off westwards on an expedition to the legendary 'Island of Brazil'. Although unsuccessful on this occasion, Bristol did become the port from which Englishmen first reached the New World, sailing under John Cabot in 1497. Merchants from London as well as Bristol supported some of Cabot's endeavours, and 20 years later a scientific expedition set out from London heading westwards for the Americas, led by one John Rastell. Unfortunately, his crew preferred the more immediate rewards of carrying cargoes to Bordeaux in preference to the glory of discovering a New World; they marooned Rastell in Ireland and sailed south to France. Four years later, in 1521, not even the King of England could persuade the London merchants to back a scheme to develop Cabot's 'New Island'. London's role at the beginning of this great age of discovery was thus a mixed one.

13

SHIPWRIGHTERY

It has been estimated that some 5,000 ships were built on the Thames between 1512 and 1915 (Banbury 1971, 17). It is much harder to suggest how many were built in the previous four centuries. What can be said is that London was a major medieval port and thus demanded thriving maritime service industries. In this chapter, a combination of archaeological and documentary evidence will be presented to suggest a model for the changing location of London's medieval shipyards, and to consider the organisation of the vessel building, breaking and repair industry. Although mentioned as a craft in the thirteenth century, and their apprentices in 1388, the earliest surviving set of ordinances of the London shipwrights date from *c*.1428, when it is recorded that 'an assembly of the brethern and sistern of the fraternity of St Simon and St Jude had been held in London by the craft of shipwrights time out of mind' (Ridge 1939, p xi). It is suggested here that London's shipbuilders were initially centred on the open foreshore in the Queenhithe/Vintry area in the tenth century, as discussed in chapter 4. They then moved downstream of the new bridge in the eleventh century as part of the port's reorganisation (**81**). There are incidental references to shipbuilders living – and therefore presumably working – in the two eastern-most waterfront parishes of St Dunstan's and All Hallows Barking in the thirteenth century. By the following century, they had extended their operations to sites in Southwark and eastwards into Ratcliffe and beyond. But it was not until 1600 that they formally left the increasing confines of the City itself, driven out by complaints over the noise and nuisance associated with their yards. There is thus a pronounced eastwards drift for shipbuilding on the Thames, as with much of the maritime industry of the port.

Shipbuilding in the late thirteenth century

One of the earliest explicit surviving documentary records of shipbuilding in London dates to 1295, when 50 shipwrights were put to work on war galleys in yards near the Tower (**82**). Since the crown had to pay for these ships, detailed accounts were compiled of the costs and time spent on the project. The craft discussed in the accounts were two warships, large-oared galleys, of

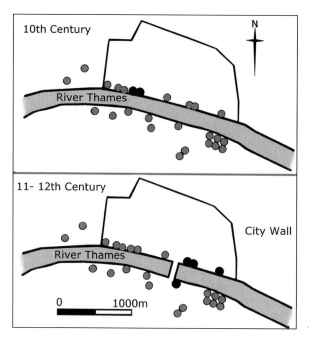

81 *London's shipyards relocated: the black circles indicate major medieval waterfront excavations on which ship timbers were recovered from tenth-century contexts (upper map) and from eleventh- to twelfth-century contexts (lower map). The changing distribution of vessel fragments suggests that London's ship repair and ship building yards were initially located in the western part of the harbour (near Queenhithe), but the building of the new bridge in c.1000 caused the shipyards to be relocated downstream.* J. Stripe, LARF

a type whose origins can be traced to the fleet depicted on the Bayeux Tapestry. It was a form that was still in demand in 1371, when the King ordered London to build two more 'each one 80 foot on the ground and 20 foot wide'. At least one was actually built – the 80-oar *Paul*.

Although the particular vessels discussed in the 1295 account were therefore warships, there is every reason to assume that the generalities of the contemporary practices described could be as readily applied to the building of merchant ships on the Thames. The account was written in medieval Latin and was translated and published in 1927 – it is that report which is summarised here (Johnson 1927). To begin with, the riverside plot where the vessels were to be built was enclosed by a fence built of 120 posts supporting the reused staves from 33 large wine barrels. A thatched shelter cum store house was then built within the enclosure, all of which cost £9 10s. The necessary timber to build the two ships was brought in by cart and river barge from woods in Wanstead (Essex), or Weybridge, Ham or Addington (Surrey); the cables from Faversham and from Sandwich (Kent). The smaller of the two vessels was built in 12 weeks from November 1294 to February 1295 at a cost of £225, while the larger one took 18 weeks to build and cost £355. There were 25 men working on the vessel in the first week, which then rose to 40 for all but the last month when it fell below 30 again. Andrew de Bayonne was hired as the master shipwright at 9d per day, which included Sundays and all holidays. His two assistants, William Turk and Robert de Winchelsea, were paid at the same rate, but only for a 6-day week. They were presumably responsible for the shaping and cutting of the timbers while teams of clenchers and holders fastened the long overlapping plank strakes together. There were a number of repeated names recorded amongst the 50 listed in the London account – Ballard, Hetfend, Smart, le Palmer, Stone and Tidy – which suggests strong family connections with the London shipyards (Friel 1995, 43)

Remains of a late thirteenth-century oared vessel, contemporary with the galleys just described, were uncovered in 1999 on a waterfront site in Southwark set, appropriately enough, opposite Galley Quay (**83**). Archaeologists recording a series of late medieval fishponds discovered that the lining of one of the ponds incorporated the reused hull planking of a clinker-built boat at least 9m long, and this has now been studied by Damian Goodburn. The timbers had been cut from trees felled between 1267 and 1276, and since there were three examples of oar-ports cut into the gunwale (the uppermost plank of vessel) set *c*.0.76m apart, it is clear that it had been propelled by oarsmen. Given the dimensions of the surviving oarports, the oars can only have been some 80 to 100mm in diameter, with a blade no more than 200mm across. The vessel seems to have been heavily and closely framed at 400mm centres, however, features that are not consistent with a warship built for speed. Perhaps it was an oared fishing boat, some of which required from 20 to 26 oars in this period.

Study of the wood selected for this vessel proved instructive. The uppermost strake (in which the oarports were cut) was beech, whereas the rest of the planking was the rather more common oak. However, comparison of the growth-ring pattern for the trees from which these planks were derived provided a surprise – the source appears to be Ireland, rather than more local woodland. This could imply that the ship was built in Ireland (like the famous eleventh-century longship excavated in the Roskilde Fjord in Denmark in 1963) or that Irish boards had been especially imported for the project. Whichever case proves to be correct, the point to stress is that the Irish boards were cut from ancient, tall, straight, slow-grown oak over 240 years old. Trees of that calibre, ideal for cleaving (as opposed to sawing) into shipboard were all too rare in England by the thirteenth century, as Goodburn's study of the contemporary timber water-front structures in London has so clearly shown (in Milne 1992, 106-130).

82 Medieval ship-building based on a scene from the Bayeux Tapestry. J. Stripe, LARF

83 *Part of a medieval boat, with its oarports clearly visible, discovered on a site in Southwark. The hull had been broken up and reused in the lining of a fourteenth-century fish pond.* MoLAS

Shipyards and shipbuilders

Tony Dyson's study of the documentary records has noted the absence of ship-wrights in any part of the port in the thirteenth and fourteenth centuries, with the significant exception of the two contiguous parishes of All Hallows Barking and St Dunstan-in-the-East (Dyson 1996, 215). He has shown that a pronounced concentration of shipbuilders lived here at the extreme eastern end of the London waterfront, where Galley Quay is situated. The names of specific shipbuilders and the location of their actual tenements are known in several instances. For example, William Talworth, John de Stokflete and Walter Sakyn, three neighbours from the parish of All Hallows, all worked together on the building of a *shoute* for the Bridgewardens in 1386 (Dyson 1996; Spencer 1996).

The archaeological evidence suggests that vessel building, breaking and repair activities were conducted on the open, undeveloped foreshore, but were gradually moved ever eastwards as embanking and encroachment on the City waterfront extended. This can be seen from the waterfront sites to the east of London Bridge, for example. The first substantial waterfront advances made over the foreshore to the south of the late Saxon embankments on the Billingsgate site were in the thirteenth century. Those revetments incorporated the remains of at least three vessels that had been broken up nearby. All had planking up to 200mm thick, and are consequently seen as river boats rather than seagoing ships, and the timber used for the planking had been cut from trees felled some time after 1180, according to the dendrochronological studies (Marsden 1996). This concentration of material suggests activities such as vessel breaking and repair had been conducted in the immediate area, while even more conclusive evidence for shipbuilding comes from the foreshore levels on the Custom House site just to the east. Here, a strip of unused iron roves was found (**84**), a diagnostic feature of shipbuilding in the age of clinker construc-tion (Tatton Brown 1974, 194), together with a rib from one vessel and a large proportion of another one, reused in a thirteenth-century riverfront revetment. That twelfth-century river boat had been some 10m long and 3.5m wide, had been built between 1160 and 1190, and had been much repaired. It seems to have been a century old before it was finally broken up and reused in the riverfront revetment (Marsden 1996). Such an age was rarely attained by the vernacular timber and thatch houses in the contemporary city. This particular section of the foreshore was gradually developed during the thirteenth and fourteenth centuries (**51**). Here, the encroachments were for the Custom House, Wool Wharf and its associated facilities.

The *Bridgewardens Accounts* for 1382-98 provide a window on commercial shipbuilding in medieval London at the end of that century. The records provide a terse but detailed listing of the costs and labour involved in the construction of at least three new boats and the repairs (frequently substantial) to several other vessels (Spencer 1996, 209-212). Hull planking (shipboard) cost from 1½d to 6d each, depending on the quality and length; framing elements (curved timber, stems; knees) were from 4d each; clenched nails were *c.*1s 6d per hundred, iron spikes *c.*9d per 100; wooden pegs (wrong nails) between 1s to 1s 6d per 100; timber for a mast could be 14d, the rope to bind it *c.*8d; canvas for the sail cost 4s 6d for 12 ells, rope for the sail, 7d. To waterproof the vessel would require large pots to melt pitch in at 6d each, half a last of pitch and bitumen at 15s, as well as 2 1/2d-worth of oil. An anchor weighing 38 pounds cost 6s 4d. At least two types of oar are mentioned, one at between 1s and 1s 6d, another type possibly twice the size at 2s 4d to 2s 9d. The size of the vessels being built and repaired is not mentioned, but two of the craft required 300 wooden pegs and one had 1,000 clench nails. Given that the late medieval wreck found off Trig Stairs in 1970 was some 14.7m long by 4.3m wide required *c.*300 wooden pegs and some 1,750 iron clenched nails, then it would seem that at least some of the bridgewarden's craft were proportionally smaller. However, it may well be that the lists only record those items recently purchased, ignoring material that had been stock-piled. For example, the accounts for the boat built in 1382 make no mention of any hull planking (Spencer 1996, 209).

Between 1428 and 1433, it is recorded that six London shipwrights were sworn in as masters of the mystery of 'shipwryghtis' (Friel 1995, 39). Clearly that figure is but a fraction of the total number of contemporary practising shipwrights, as London's late medieval shipyards were clearly expanding. An impression of that growth can be traced through the sporadic documentary references to work on ships for which the crown paid, since that same pattern also reflects the less well-documented development of the private mercantile shipyards and associated facilities that attracted and underpinned the royal interest. The largest fleet which ever left medieval England was fitted out on the south bank at Rotherhithe in 1340 (during the Hundred Years War), and certainly by 1356 maritime activities had extended as far as Ratcliffe, on the north bank for example (Friel 1995, 55). In 1401, 46 men were working on

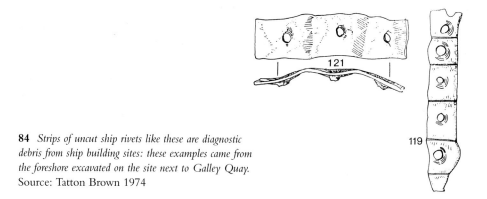

84 *Strips of uncut ship rivets like these are diagnostic debris from ship building sites: these examples came from the foreshore excavated on the site next to Galley Quay.* Source: Tatton Brown 1974

the balinger *Godegrace* there (Friel 1995, 55) and in 1415, the *Jesus Maria*, a very large galley apparently with 240 oars built in 1409-11, was brought to Ratcliffe and hulked, i.e. all reusable material stripped out of it (Friel 1995, 172). On the opposite bank of the Thames at Greenwich, Henry V's *Trinity Royal* was built from 1413-6 (Friel 1995, 43). In 1475, another large war fleet was fitted out on Thames, no doubt making use of all available yards. The vessels were being adapted to carry 1,500 men at arms and 15,000 archers (Broodbank 1921, 47). The *Great Harry* was built at Woolwich in 1488, a site that underwent major expansion, with 252 men conscripted to work there on the *Henry Grace a Dieu* and three other galleys by 1512 (Friel 1995, 41).

However, the expansion if the maritime service industries was not just eastwards. The poll tax returns for Southwark show that there were at least 18 boat and bargemen active on the southern shore in the fourteenth century (Carlin 1996, 269) and the archaeological evidence provides strong confirmation for maritime industry in the area. A significant concentration of vessel fragments has been found reused in the fourteenth- to sixteenth-century timber revetments erected during the process of encroachment, moat digging and drainage in the low-lying marshy area. From the Abbots Lane site alone there were fragments of at least nine late fourteenth-century vessels, the majority of which were represented by oak planking some 20-30mm thick, and were therefore from working river boats. All were constructed in the overlapping clinker plank tradition. Such a regular surfeit of broken up vessels strongly suggests boat building and repair conducted in the vicinity (**85 & 86**).

Consideration of all the approximately 30 vessels represented by the Southwark fragments provides a picture of the general nature of those clinker-built shallow draft vessels. There was no sign of the ancient logboat tradition, a type of vessel that was once such a common visitor to the Thames-side beach markets. The last archaeological example of such a dugout was found in the river at Kew and has been dated to the mid-thirteenth century (Marsden 1996, 222). Fragments from some of the rather larger contemporary seagoing ships have also been found in Southwark. An example for Gun and Shot Wharf comprised planking up to 0.36m wide and 60mm thick. Interestingly, the timber used for the planking was not from a local source, but was Baltic Oak which could suggest that this may have been a foreign vessel, especially as the seam-waterproofing used between the overlapping planks was moss (Marsden 1996).

London vessels generally used wool or cattle hair worked into a rough yarn for their luting (caulking) material, as an informative study by Michael Ryder has shown (in Marsden 1996, 200-207). The tenth-century Graveney boat used wool as its seam-waterproofing medium, presumably because it was available in large quantities. The twelfth-century Custom House boat, to be different, used principally cattle hair, a by-product of the leather industry, while the fourteenth-century river boat fragment found on the Trig Lane site and the fifteenth-century river barge found off Trig Stairs both used mainly goat hair, again providing incidental evidence for another major London industry dealing in goat skins (Grew & de Neergaard 1988, 44). Some of the wool used in other vessels was of the so-called 'hairy-medium'-type characteristic of medieval breeds, according to Ryder. Some had already been dyed and was clearly spinners' waste that had been 'dyed-in-the-wool'. Regardless of what fibre was used, most of the luting material was usually coated in a form of pitch or tar. As can be seen, the study of the vessel fragments can provide information on a range of issues quite apart from the obvious nautical ones, and range from timber supply to the types of wool being spun in London.

Among the studies that have yet to be developed is one into the metallurgy of the iron fastenings, a strangely neglected avenue of research. After all, the integrity of those clinker-built ships depended on the clenched nails not failing. If they rusted and disintegrated, corroded by seawater, then the ship would surely sink. It would therefore be of interest to know if the quality of iron used for ships' nails contained any particular rust inhibitor.

Navis

The London waterfront sites have therefore provided plenty of evidence for the range of vessel-types that the port would have accommodated, but with a pronounced bias towards smaller river craft, by far and away the most numerically common vessels. London itself provides less archaeological information on the larger craft, the *navis*. An idea of the size, form and capacity of later medieval shipping can be seen by studying the thirteenth-century wrecks being uncovered in St Peter Port harbour, Guernsey, the late fourteenth-century English merchantman found in the Cinque Port of Sandwich in Kent, the Hanseatic Cog built in 1380 and now on display in Bremerhaven, Germany, and the recent discovery of the late fifteenth-century ship from Newport in Wales. All were between 20 and 30m in length and between 3 to 4m in height above the keel, propelled not by oars but by a single square sail.

85 *Part of a moulded mast partner from a large Saxon sailing ship being recorded during a waterfront watching brief*

Maritime industries

Although the focus for shipbuilding was clearly shifting downstream by the fourteenth century, some of the ancillary maritime industries operated above the bridge. This is shown by, for example, the street name evidence which clearly identifies the area of the rope-makers by the term 'the Ropery' or the 'Street of the Corders'. This name was given to that part of what is now Upper Thames Street, running up to the eastern edge of the Walbrook mouth. Presumably before that stream was culverted and bridged over here, this part of the east-west waterfront street was effectively a dead end. It developed as a rope-walk, the area where great lengths of hemp could be laid out and turned into the long cables required by the port's shipping industry. Surviving documentary references go back as early as 1280 (*vicum regium cordariorum*), but the descriptions used for the two churches in this immediate area perhaps suggest that the rope-makers only arrived in force in the mid-thirteenth century. All-Hallows-the Great is at Hay Wharf in 1269, but by 1318 is 'in-the-cordery'.

The situation is similar for its little brother next door – in 1240, All Hallows-the-Less is suffixed by *super celarium* (upon-the-cellar) and it is not until 1349 that the associated term 'in-the-Roperie' first appears. Another explanation for these fourteenth-century suffixes is that a second area of rope-walks had been laid out, this time running north-south towards the Thames,

86 *The battered remains of a keel from a Saxon ship, reused in a riverfront revetment*

making full use of the extensive area of reclaimed land then available. Perhaps by that date, Thames Street itself was becoming too congested a highway to accommodate a rope-walk within it, causing the industry to divert off the main road. There are also other incidental references to ropers and corders around Queenhithe and Billingsgate at this time. Nevertheless, it remained a noticeable feature of Dowgate since the local administrative district was named *Ward of the Ropery* in 1408. Sometime after 1456, however, when Thames Street is last referred to as 'Roper Street', it seems that the rope-makers moved away, taking their ancient craft eastwards and out of the City.

From clinker to carvel (87 & 88)

In 1400, all the vessels being built in the Thames shipyards were broadly constructed in the clinker-built tradition, in which the hull planking comprised runs of overlapping planking held together by clenched nails. That technique can be traced back in England to the Saxons, since clench nails and roves have been found in fifth- and sixth-century Kentish graves and the remains of a seventh-century clinker-built ship was recorded at Sutton Hoo in Suffolk. By 1500, that situation was changing. During the fifteenth century, larger vessels were designed and built with decks, and had more than one mast.

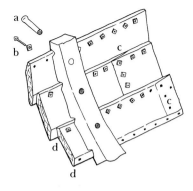

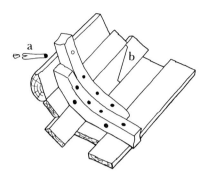

87 Diagram showing how ship hull planking is constructed in the ancient clinker-built tradition. After Milne et al. 1998

88 Diagram showing how ship hull planking is constructed in the carvel tradition. After Milne et al. 1998

Another major change towards the end of that century was in hull construction. The earliest surviving documentary record of an English vessel to be built in full carvel-style with its hull planking laid flush edge-to-edge is at Dunwich in Suffolk in 1465 (Friel 1995, 178). The new technology, requiring different skills, approaches and budgets, gradually replaced the clinker-building tradition, at least for larger vessels. For example, the warship, the *Royal Sovereign*, built in clinker fashion in 1487-8, was rebuilt in carvel style in 1510. The remains of this vessel (or of a ship of a similar size and date) were recorded during the building works on Woolwich power station in 1911. The 800-ton Great Galley launched at Greenwich in 1515 was probably the last clinker-built warship constructed in England. When it underwent major repairs in 1523, it was rebuilt in the new carvel style (Friel 1995, 175). Thus by the early sixteenth century, a new type of sailing ship had been developed, more robust, capacious, easier to manoeuvre, and potentially faster and cheaper to build than vessels of a similar tonnage constructed in clinker style. It was these carracks that took first Columbus and then other European adventurers across the Atlantic to open up the 'New World'. This was a new technology that profoundly changed not just the fortunes of the port of London, but also world history. By 1545, all the warships and merchant ships built on the Thames were carvel style. Indeed, when a flotilla of ageing German clinker-built ships was arrested in the Thames in that year, they were not considered suitable for use in the navy – the Lord High Admiral dismissed them as 'clenchers, both feeble, old and out of fashion' (Friel 1995, 179).

14

EPILOGUE

When does the 'medieval period' end? This is a question that still exercises the minds of historians and archaeologists, as they debate the origins of our modern world. Political historians have argued that it came with the advent of the Tudor dynasty in 1485, social or economic historians with the rediscovery of the New World by Christopher Columbus in 1492, or with the Reformation and the Dissolution of the Monasteries in 1520-40, while for nautical archaeologists the widespread adoption of new carvel-style ship-building technology and associated developments by the end of the fifteenth century is the key, as these facilitated the exploitation of the New World. For the port of London, all those dates and developments are of some significance and directly or indirectly were catalysts for substantial change in the harbour (**89**). The expanding world, the expanding economy, the expanding mind, all contributed to the eclipse of the inter-related elements which made up the 'medieval' port. Above all, the geography had changed. England was no longer on the northern edge of the Mediterranean world or the eastern edge of the Scandinavian world – it now found itself in a central position on the enlarged world map, looking east towards the old world, and west, if hesitantly, towards the new.

It must be remembered that the first European ships to reach the Americas were those sailing out from the Norse settlements in Iceland and Greenland, reaching the Labrador-Newfoundland coast. This was discovered initially by one Bjarni Herjolfsson in 986, and subsequently explored by Lief Eirikson in *c*.1000. Although permanent settlement was never achieved, there seems to have been sporadic contact, seeking furs and fish, as late as the fourteenth century. It was therefore not a completely New World that awaited the European Christopher Columbus a century or so later.

In 1527, Henry VIII had commissioned an English merchantman, built for the Bordeaux wine trade, for a voyage of discovery. She reached the North American coast, worked her way down to the Caribbean, and returned safely home again (Scammell 1981). But still the capital's gaze was elsewhere, for London merchants began to dominate the cloth trade with Antwerp as never before, often to the detriment of other English ports. Here was ready, tangible profit, so the risks of the American adventures were gladly left to the west coast ports As we saw in the previous chapter, the Merchant Adventurers Company

89 *The early Tudor port of London.* Artist's reconstruction by Chris Unwin

was established in 1486, through which English merchants exported directly to ports overseas. Less than a century later, London saw the rise of the French, Spanish, Barbary, Eastland, Levant and Muscovy Companies. A new commercial centre and meeting place for London's expanding merchant community, the Royal Exchange, was built by 1571, while closure of the Hanseatic Steelyard in 1597 ended a long chapter of alien domination of the port's trade.

The increased volume of shipping on the river led to letters patent being granted to Trinity House Deptford in 1514, an institution that now took over responsibility for pilotage in the Thames. By the mid-sixteenth century, they had become involved in many other river-related issues such as the provision of beacons, buoys, the supply of ballast, the conservation of the river and even the authorisation of Thames watermen. Continuing this theme, in 1555 an Act was passed that saw eight watermen elected to supervise the Thames from Greenwich to Windsor, to prevent accidents caused by the ignorance or incompetence of watermen. It also stipulated that the minimum dimensions for any vessel used for rowing or carrying passengers on the Thames must not be under '22 foote and a half in lengthe, and 4 foot and a half broade in the mydshippe', i.e. *c.*7m by 1.5m (*Statutes of the Realm 23*, 1919, 291).

Naval dockyards were established at Woolwich and Deptford and it was to Deptford that Sir Francis Drake returned from his circumnavigation of the globe in 1580. It was in these yards that new types of robust multi-masted, multi-decked ships were built. The *Mary Rose* is an example of the new design, in effect a merchant carrack design adapted for military duties. She was fitted out here on the Thames in 1512 and her armaments included bronze guns made in a London foundry. One of these has been recovered, and bears the proud and patriotic inscription, 'Robert and John Owyn brethren borne in the City of London the sonnes of an Inglish(man) made thys bastard (i.e. a non-standard weapon) AD 1537' (Rule 1982, 165). This product of the Tudor port can now be seen on display in Portsmouth, together with the impressive remains of the ship itself, having been salvaged from the sea in 1982.

The Reformation and the consequent Dissolution of the Monasteries also impacted upon the life of London's port in many ways. The political upheavals of the era saw the head of Sir Thomas More exhibited on London Bridge following his execution in 1535, while in 1554 the protestant rebels of the Wyatt Rebellion, a movement ostensibly against Mary's marriage to the Catholic King of Spain, battered unsuccessfully against the gatehouse at the southern end of the bridge, but could not break through. However, the reforming zeal of the new protestant order did see the suppression of the chantry chapels (many founded by merchants) in the waterfront churches. Attention also turned to the monastic properties. Not only were the 30 great monastic houses in London dissolved, split up and sold off, but sundry ecclesiastical holdings were also confiscated. For example, the waterfront house owned by the Archbishop of York was 'transferred' to the Crown in 1530 to become the nucleus of Whitehall Palace. Even the bridge's famous chapel of St Thomas, once a staging post on the Londoner's great pilgrimage to Canterbury, suffered. First its dedication was changed to Thomas the Apostle, following Henry VIII's denunciation of Thomas of Canterbury as a traitor in 1538, after which the chapel was defaced and despoiled. Two remarkable wooden statues, one of a monk, one of God the Father, were recovered from the Thames in the nineteenth century. They were presumably thrown into the river during this purge (Watson *et al.* 2001, 112). By 1553, the once beautiful fourteenth-century building had been converted into a house and grocer's shop. Ironically that was the same year that Mary Tudor's reign began, and Catholic traditions were re-established. It was in the church of St Nicholas Cole-Abbey that the Latin Mass was reintroduced on 23 August, in the same year that Henry VIII's Protestant flagship *Henri-Grace-a-Dieu* was destroyed by fire at Woolwich.

On the wider stage, Henry VIII's quarrel with the Pope had isolated protestant England from powerful Catholic states across the narrow Channel, leaving the port and country vulnerable to seaborne attack and possible invasion. The combined forces of France and Spain formed the principal threat from 1538 onwards, culminating in an attempted invasion in 1545. The threat was repulsed, although the Isle of Wight and Brighton suffered, but it lead to an expansion of the fleet, with Deptford growing to become the Navy's largest yard by 1550, with Woolwich also much enlarged in 1546.

Even the precinct of St Mary Graces, close by the Tower, was rudely trans-formed from a monastic house into major depot and victualling yard to hold stores for the new navy. Further downriver, the 1540s saw the construction of five artillery forts on the Thames to defend the reach where the estuary narrowed to a width of some 700m. Blockhouses were built at Tilbury and East Tilbury on the north bank, and at Gravesend, Milton and Higham on the southern shore. Although in the event these defences were not seriously tested, the war with Catholic Europe had profound consequences. For example, the fall of Calais in 1558 (the last English foothold in France) brought to an abrupt end a conflict between these two nations which has lasted for centuries and provided much of the political definition of the 'medieval' era. Two events that occurred just three years later also have signif-icance for the port, one iconic, the other economic. In June 1561, the mighty spire of St Paul's was struck by lightning and was burned down. This was the tallest building in medieval England, a landmark for London, a seamark for the Thames, the symbol of the port's piety. The same year, a decree was issued to promote the eating of fish, not just on Fridays, but also on Wednesdays. As befits the mid-sixteenth century, this move was not fuelled solely by religious fervour, but by the pragmatic need to revitalise and expand England's maritime industries. The London fishmongers warmly welcomed the initia-tive, whatever its motivation.

The sixteenth century is thus a catalogue of symbolic dates all arguably marking the end of the old order and the start of the new. Perhaps for the medieval port, the most convenient date to end our study is with the reform of the harbour in the early years of the reign of Elizabeth I. Thus we will conclude with a summary of the sixteenth-century surveys, the principal one of which followed the reform of the port in *c*.1559, instigated by William Paulet, Earl of Winchester. From this date onwards, cargoes could only be landed or loaded under the watchful eyes of customs officials in specified locations, the so-called 'legal quays' within the City of London (**90**). Before that date, although only Queenhithe, Dowgate and Billingsgate were the official 'legal' quays, many wharves were actually used, not just on the London waterfront but at Gravesend, Woolwich, Barking, Greenwich, Deptford, Blackwall, Limehouse, Ratcliffe, Wapping, St Katherine's and Southwark.

However, the new Act declared that 'all and singular quays wharves and other places within the City of London and the suburbs (the several keys wharves and stairs and places before limited and appointed only excepted) . . . shall be from henceforth no more used as landing or discharging places for merchandise but be utterly debarred and abolished from the same for ever . . .' (Dietz 1972, 160). The early sixteenth-century port was deemed to have grown too large for the officials to control, and thus was cut down to a more manageable size. This was a fulfilment of the age-old maxim, that a port will develop not where it is most convenient for ships to berth, but where it is most convenient for customs officials to collect taxes. For the next two centuries and more, the 'legal quays' in the pool of London were less than 600m in length, and it was to here that all shipborne trade was off-loaded, save for sea-coal from Newcastle, beer and corn

To that informative source will be added some comments from the City 'viewers' who inspected sundry building complaints in the town, including several down on the waterfront (Loengard 1989). That survey showed there had been the inevitable encroachment upon the common lanes leading down to the Thames – rights of public access to the river (as opposed to the loading and unloading of customable goods) were as important a feature of civic concern in the sixteenth century as in the thirteenth century. Issues debated included the case of a riverside lane leading down to the Thames near St Botolph Billingsgate and St Magnus – it should not be under 6ft 9in wide (no. 96). Boss Lane, in the parish of St Peter by Paul's Wharf, was only 4ft 8in wide in 1541, but a dyer had built a vat that projected 2ft into the lane – clearly that had to go (no. 157).

In the parish of St Andrews, Baynard Castle, a lane leading to a common stair was to be reinstated '9ft in wideness', and was to be 'common for all the king's subjects to go and resort to the stair and the water'. There should be a post set in the middle of the north end 'so that no manner of cart shall have recourse through the lane without nuisance and peril' (no. 150). In the case of one lane leading from St Martin Vintry to the Thames, 'that ought to continue to be common hereafter as it has been before', the authorities demanded that a new timber frame building erected in 1541 be withdrawn eastwards just one inch (no. 174). The year before, the authorities had been less demanding with a neighbouring alley that had been engulfed by a garden. On inspection, it was declared to be 'but narrow and a foul blind lane and did little good. It may be well spared and forborne, notwithstanding that it hath been of old time accustomed to be a common way' (no. 145).

Even in the sixteenth century, not all wharves were faced with stone. In 1535, we read that Marowes Quay required carpenters for work on the wharf and 'to amend the framework of the same towards the Thames' (Loengard 1989 no. 115). The same was true of the jetties and stairs that projected out into midstream. There had been a dispute in 1526 over a new river stair built at Sabbes Wharf, for example. The great timber frame extending 24ft southwards into the river was 8ft broad, and the stair itself descended some 19ft onto the foreshore at low tide. It was decided that the frame, bridge and stairs should be removed, as they were built on common ground 'to the great nuisance and hindrance . . . as well of the King's subjects as all manner of ships, crayers and boats repairing to this city' (no. 68). And the final responsibility for maintaining the waterfront still rested squarely on the shoulders of the landlord, not the City, as is shown with a case in the parish of All Hallows Barking in 1550, where a 25ft-length of the wharf was decaying, together with its house and stables. The lord of the house was requested to 'repair and amend them at their own proper costs and charges' (no. 285).

Our final snapshot of the port now considers the Legal Quays themselves, beginning at the eastern end of the City waterfront (Dietz 1972). The closest legal quay to the Tower itself was *Galley Quay*, no longer known for its ship-building but 'greatly occupied with all kinds of merchandise' and was provided with a crane and a jibbet. *Old Wool Quay* had only been used for wool and felt, but more recently for wood and other aspects of the coastal trade. Then there was *Custom House Quay*, with its eponymous new brick building. The surviving illustrations of this building conflict in the information they present (Jarvis 1976, 276), but the new complex may have incorporated a principal range of three storeys, perhaps with an open arcade at quay level, with subsidiary ranges to the east and west. It was here that the senior officials would be based, the collectors, the controllers, the head searcher, the surveyor and the tide-waiters. The latter were the team who actually boarded the ships to determine the nature of the cargo carried, as the tide swept the vessels into the port to anchor. The Petty Customs accounts compiled by those officials demonstrate the widely fluctuating nature of London's trade in the mid-sixteenth century. For example, the figures for the first five years following the reform are £30,951 in 1558/9; £36,982 in 1559/60; £27,605 in 1560/1; £25,250 in 1561/2; £18,146 in 1562/3. The records also show the continuing (if declining) importance of Antwerp both for the export of cloth and for the import of a range of spices, drugs, dyes and metalware, while wines from Spain and, of course, from Bordeaux, represented some 10 per cent of London's imports. There is thus a pronounced 'medieval' feel to the trade pattern represented in these Tudor documents.

As for the structure of Her Majesty's two main wharves at Old Wool Quay and at Custom House Quay, these had come in for criticism, since the former was an ageing timber structure badly in need of repair, while the latter, although faced in masonry, was now set back so far from the deep water channel at low tide that the lighters had difficulty berthing there (Dietz 1972, xiii). The sizes of the two wharves were measured up at 91ft (28m) and 107ft (33m) in length respectively. The latter was some 48ft 6in (15m) broad (north-south) and had two jibbets. It was 'greatly occupied with all kinds of merchandise both inwards and outwards'. It was to here that all 'fine wares' and haberdashery had to be brought by lighter. Indeed, during this period it was still standard practice to offload all cargoes carried on large vessel onto lighters in midstream, and then trans-ship the cargoes from the lighter to the wharf. The only exception to this labour-intensive system of double-handling was 'massy wares', material too heavy to handle in midstream. For those, the ship had to be brought alongside the quay and its cargo craned out.

Moving eastwards from the Custom House, *Greenberries Quay* was involved in the French trade, *Crown Quay* with the coastal traffic in corn and wood,

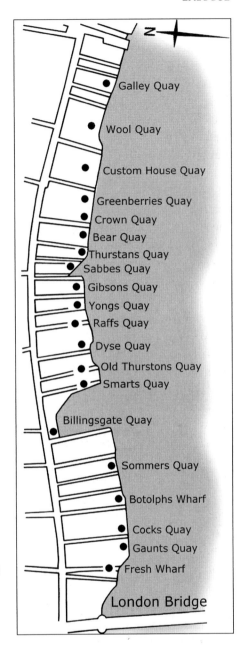

90 *London's 'Legal Quays': schematic plan showing the layout of the Tudor harbour between the Bridge and the Tower, following the sixteenth-century reform of the port.* NB: north to left. After Dietz 1972: J. Stripe, LARF

Bear Quay with the Portugese trade, while *Thurstans Quay* dealt with all manner of imports and exports. *Sabbes Quay* had a defective jibbet and dealt with 'pitche tar sope ashes and such like'; *Gibsons Quay* with lead, tin and other coastal trade; *Youngs Quay* accommodated Portugese cloth merchants, *Raffs Quay* 'all kinds of merchandise inward and outward'. *Dyse Quay* was another of those used for coastal traffic as was *Old Thurston's Quay*, but here they lay alongside Flemish traders.

The next set of wharves lay around the harbour at Billingsgate (**91**) and extended up to the Bridge itself, starting in the east with *Smart's Quay*, which dealt in fish, and *Sommers Quay*, mainly used by Flemish merchants. *Botolph's Wharf* was used by the Russia Company, who had warehouses for their wine there, as well as by coastal traffic. *Cocks Quay* was given over to foreign merchants who had storage facilities and lodgings there. Next, there was *Gaunts Quay*, where barrels of fish were landed without use of a crane and *Fresh Wharf*, used by eel and fish suppliers (Dietz 1972).

The assessments gathered for the Lay Subsidy tax in 1541 (Lang 1993) suggest that the more prosperous companies at that date were the drapers, gold-smiths, merchant tailors, fishmongers and vintners, with lesser contributions recorded from the brewers, grocers, coopers, clothworkers, dyers and wool-packers. The returns also show that the easternmost waterfront wards of Bridge, Tower and Billingsgate, nearly 20 years before the imposition of the Legal Quays, already accommodated the largest numbers of wealthy persons in the harbour, with 66, 54 and 36 valuations between £50 and £200. There were

91 *Billingsgate in the mid-sixteenth century: a section from Antonis Van der Wyngaerde's panorama of London.* The Ashmolean Museum, Oxford

92 *Three Cranes Wharf in the mid-sixteenth century: a section from Antonis Van der Wyngaerde's panorama of London.* The Ashmolean Museum, Oxford

two principal wharves above the Bridge in 1559. First there was the *Steelyard*, where the Hanseatic merchants still had their hall and wharf for their own exclusive use. Although it had been seized by Edward VI, its privileges had been restored when Mary Tudor came to the throne in 1553. The significance of the role they played in Tudor trade is shown by the large proportion of German stoneware in the total of all London's imported pottery from 1480 to 1600.

Just to the east of the *Steelyard* was *Three Cranes Wharf* in the vintry (**92**), the great wine wharf. Here there were 33 valuations of between 50 and £200 in 1541, a sign of some affluence. This is in sorry contrast to Queenhithe, once the very heart of the earlier medieval port, for it was no longer in the equation, not designated as a 'legal quay'. Indeed, there was not one 'hithe' mentioned anywhere in the reformed sixteenth-century harbour. Now the majority of names were those of the individual owners of the private quays; the process of privatisation was all but complete. Of all those quays, archaeology has shown that the Vintry probably has the oldest pedigree, one that was even older than its French name.

But this new Tudor port, although superimposed upon the site of Alfred's tenth-century new town, shared little else with that older harbour. In its fabric, its focus, its shipping, its coinage, its merchants, its merchandise, its philosophy, its language, its organisation and its religion, it inhabited a radically different world. In 1559, London built a new red brick Custom House and surveyed

the layout of its reformed legal quays, the same year that tobacco was introduced to Europe. The surprise is surely the modest extent of the proposed port
in the mid–sixteenth century. Had the good Queen known how much trade
would expand in future years, the document she then signed might have made
more generous provision for it. The total length of the new, improved Legal
Quay was less than the extent of London's waterfront embankments in the
heyday of the beach market.

FURTHER READING

Archer, I., Barron, C., & Harding, V., 1988, *Hugh Alley's Caveat: the markets of London in 1598*, London Topographical Society 137

Archibald, M., & Milne, G., 1995, 'Four early medieval coin dies from the London waterfront' *Numismatic Chronicle*, 163-200

Ashdown, M., 1930, *English and Norse Documents Relating to the Reign of Ethelred the Unready*

Ayre, J. & Wroe-Brown, R., 2002, *The London Millennium Bridge: excavations of the medieval and later waterfronts at Peter's Hill, City of London, and Bankside, Southwark*, MoLAS AS 6

Banbury, P., 1971, *Shipbuilders of the Thames and Medway*

Barron, C., 1995, 'Centre of conspicuous consumption: the aristocratic town house in London 1200-1550', *London J* 20:1, 1-16

Barron, C., 2001, 'The Government of London: the formative phase, 1300-1500', *London J 26:1*, 9-18

Bateson, 1902, 'A London municipal collection', *English Historical Review 17*, 430-511; 707-30

Biddle, M., Hudson, D. & Heighway, C., 1973, *The Future of London's Past*

Bill, J. & Clausen, L. (eds), 1999, *Maritime Topography and the Medieval Town*, National Museum of Denmark, Copenhagen, 4

Blackmore, L., 1999, 'Aspects of trade & exchange . . . Saxon and medieval pottery from London', *LAMAS* 50, 38-54

Blair, I. *et al.*, 2001, 'Two medieval Jewish ritual baths – mikva'ot – found in London', *LAMAS 52*, 127-137

Bluer, D., 1993, 'Excavations at Abbots Lane, Southwark', *LA 7:3*, 59-66

Bowsher, D. & Malcolm, G., 1999, 'Excavations at the Royal Opera House', *LAMAS 50*, 4-11

Brett-James, N., 1944, 'Pirates off Margate in 1315', *LAMAS 8.3*, 35-41

Broodbank, J., 1921, *History of the Port of London*

Brooke, C. & Keir, G., 1975, *London 800-1216: the shaping of a city*

Burwash, D., 1947 (1969), *English Merchant Shipping 1460-1540*

Campbell, B., *et al.*, 1993, *A medieval capital and its grain supply: agrarian production and distribution in the London Region c.1300,* Historical Geography Research Series 30

Carlin, M., 1996, *Medieval Southwark*

Chew, H. & Kellaway, W., 1973, *London Assize of Nuisance 1301-1431*, London Rec Society 10

Chew, H. & Weinbaum, M., 1970, *London Eyre of 1244*, London Record Society 6

Clark, J., 1995, *Medieval Finds from . . . London, 5: the medieval horse and its equipment*

Clayton, P. (ed.), 1999, 'Medieval London; recent archaeological research', *LAMAS 50*, 2-107

Cobb, H., 1990, *Overseas Trade of London: exchequer customs accounts 1480-1*, London Record Society 27

Colvin, H., 1963, *History of the Kings Works: 1*

Cowgill, J., de Neergaard, M. & Griffiths, N., 1987, *Medieval Finds From . . . London 1: Knives & Scabbards*

Cowie, R., 1992, 'The waterfront of Middle Saxon London', *Journal of the Society of Medieval Archaeology 36*, 164-8

Cowie, R. & Whythead, R., 1989, 'Lundenwic: archaeological evidence for mid-Saxon London', *Antiquity 63*, 706-18

Crowfoot, E., Pritchard, F. & Staniland, K., 1992, *Medieval Finds From . . . London 4: Textiles & Clothing*

Crumlin Pedersen, O. & Olsen, O., 2002, *The Skuldelev Ships: I*, Roskilde, Denmark

Dietz, B., 1972, *The Port of Trade of Early Elizabethan London*, London Record Society 8

Delgado, J. (ed.), 1997, *Encyclopaedia of Underwater and Maritime Archaeology*, British Museum

Douglas, D., 1969, *English Historical Documents, volume IV: 1327-1485*

Douglas, D., 1975, *English Historical Documents, volume III: 1189-1327*

Douglas, D. & Greenaway, G., 1981, *English Historical Documents, volume II: 1042-1189*

Drinkall, R. & Stevenson, J., 1996, 'Weighing it all up', *LA 8.1*, 3-9

Dulley, 1969, 'The early history of the Rye Fishing Industry', *Sussex Archaeological Collections 107*, 36-64

Dyson, T., 1978, 'Two Saxon Land Grants for Queenhithe', J. Bird *et al.* (eds), *Collectanea Londiniensia*, LAMAS SP 2, 200-215

Dyson, T., 1980, 'London and Southwark in the seventh century', *LAMAS 31*, 83-95

Dyson, T., 1981, 'The terms *Quay* and *Wharf* and the early medieval waterfront of London', in Milne & Hobley 1981, 37-3

Dyson, T., 1985, 'Early Harbour Regulations in London', in A. Herteig (ed.), *Waterfront Archaeology in North European Towns*, Bergen, Norway

Dyson, T., 1989, *Documents and Archaeology: the medieval waterfront*, Museum of London

Dyson, T., 1990, 'King Alfred and the restoration of London', *London J 15.2*, 99-110

Dyson, T., 1996, 'Three medieval London shipbuilders', in P. Marsden 1996, 214-5

Egan, G., 1991, 'Industry and economics on the medieval and later London waterfront', in G. Good *et al.* (eds), *Waterfront Archaeology*, CBA RR 74, 9-18

Egan, G., 1998, *Medieval Finds From . . . London 8: Household Objects*

Egan, G. & Pritchard, F., 1991, *Medieval Finds From . . . London 3: Dress Accessories*

Ekwall, E., 1954, *Street Names of the City of London*

Elkington, G., 1938, *The Coopers: company and craft*

Fenwick, V., 1978, *The Graveney Boat*, BAR 53

Freshwater, T., 1996, 'A lava quern workshop in late Saxon London', *LA 8.2*, 39-45

Friel, I., 1995, *The Good Ship: ships, shipbuilding and technology in England 1200-1520*

Gadd, D. & Dyson, T., 1981, 'Bridewell Palace', *Post-Medieval Archaeology* 15, 1-79

Galloway, J., 1999, 'Metropolitan market networks: London's economic hinterland in the later middle ages', *LAMAS 50*, 91-97

Garmonsway, G. (ed.), 1972, *The Anglo Saxon Chronicle*

Good, G. *et al.* (eds), 1991, *Waterfront Archaeology*, CBA RR 74

Goodburn, G., 1988, 'Recent Finds of Ancient Boats from London', *LA 5:16*, 423-8

Goodburn, G., 1991, 'New light on early ship- and boat-building in the London area', in G. Good *et al.* (eds), *Waterfront Archaeology*, CBA RR 74, 105-15

Goodburn, D., 1994, 'Anglo-Saxon boat finds from London: are they English?' in C. Westerdahl (ed.), *Crossroads in Ancient Shipbuilding*, Oxbow 40, 97-104

Goodburn, D., 1993, 'Fragments of tenth-century timber arcade from Vintners Place', *Journal of the Society of Medieval Archaeology 37*, 78-92

Grainger, I. & Hawkins, D., 1988, 'Excavations at the Royal Mint Site', *LA 5*, 429-36

Green, 1976, 'Excavations of the Abbey precinct, Westminster', *Journal British Archaeological Association 129*, 59-76

Grew, F. & de Neergaard, M., 1988, *Medieval Finds from . . . London 2: Shoes and Pattens*

Grimes, F., 1968, *The Archaeology of Roman and Medieval London*

Haddan, A. & Stubbs, W., 1871, *Councils and Ecclesiastical Documents relating to Great Britain and Ireland*

Harding, V. & Wright, L., 1995, *London Bridge: selected accounts and rentals 1381-1538*, London Record Society 31

Harvey, J., 1954, *English Medieval Architects: a bibliographical dictionary down to 1550*

Haynes, I. *et al.* (eds), 2000, *London Under Ground: the archaeology of a city*, Oxbow

Hertieg, A., 1959, 'The excavation of Bryggen in Bergen', *Journal of the Society of Medieval Archaeology 3*, 176-86

Hill, C., *et al.*, 1980, *Roman Riverside Wall and Monumental Archaeology in London,* LAMAS SP 3

Hodges, R. & Hobley, B., 1988, *The Rebirth of Towns in the West: AD 700-1050,* CBA RR 68

Hollaender, A. & Kellaway, W. (eds), 1969, *Studies in London History*

Home, G., 1927, *Medieval London*

Home, G., 1931, *Old London Bridge*

Horsman, V., Milne C. & G., 1988, *Aspects of Saxo-Norman London 1,* LAMAS SP 11

Hunting, P., 1988, *St Paul's Vista*

Hutchinson, G., 1994, *Medieval Ships and Shipping*

James, M., 1971, 'Gilbert Maghfeld, a London merchant of the fourteenth century', in *Studies in the Medieval Wine Trade,* Oxford, 196-217

Jarvis, R., 1976, 'The early Customs and Custom Houses in the Port of London', *LAMAS 27,* 271-9

Johnson, C., 1927, 'London Shipbuilding in AD 1295', *Antiquaries Journal 7,* 424-37

Keene, D., 2001, 'Roots and Branches of Power, 1000-1300', *London J 26.1,* 1-8

Kowaleski, M., 2000, 'The internal fish trade', in D. Starkey, C. Reid & N. Ashcroft (eds), *England's Sea Fisheries,* Chatham Publishing, London, 29-32

Laing, 1818, *The New Custom House, London*

Lang, R., 1993, *Two Tudor Subsidy Assessment Rolls for the City of London,* London Record Society, 29

Levison, W. (ed.), 1905, *Vitae Sancti Bonifatii Archiepiscopi Moguntini*

Locker, A., 1992, *Fish from Medieval Waterfront Sites,* unpublished archive report, MoLSS

Loengard, J., 1989, *London Viewers and their Certificates 1508-58,* London Record Society 26

London Museum, 1940, *Medieval Catalogue*

MacMichael, J., 1890, 'Baynard Castle and the excavations on its site', *Journal British Archaeological Association 46,* 173-85

Malcolm, G. & Bowsher, D., 2003, *Middle Saxon London: excavations at the Royal Opera House 1989-99,* MoLAS monograph 15

Marsden, P., 1994, *Ships of the Port of London: first to eleventh centuries AD,* EH AR 3

Marsden, P., 1996, *Ships of the Port of London: twelfth to seventeenth centuries AD* EH AR 5

Masters, B., 1972, *To God and the Bridge: the story of the City's Bridges*

McCann, B., 1993, *Fleet Valley Interim Report,* unpublished report, MoLAS

Miller, P. & Stephenson, 1999, *A fourteenth-century Pottery site in Kingston-upon-Thames,* MoLAS AS 1

Mills, P., 1996, 'The Battle of London 1066', *LA 8.3,* 59-62

Milne, G., 1990, 'King Alfred's Plan for London?', *LA 6:8,* 206-7

Milne, G., 1992, *Timber Building Techniques in London AD 900 to 1500,* LAMAS SP 15

Milne, G., 1985, *The Port of Roman London*

Milne, G., 1999 'Maritime Topography and Medieval London', in J Bill (ed) *Maritime Topography and the Medieval town,* National Museum of Denmark 4, 145-152, Copenhagen

Milne G, Battarbee R, *et al* 1983 'Roman Thames in mid-1st-century', *LAMAS* **34,** 19-30

Milne, G. & Goodburn, D., 1990, 'Early Medieval Port of London AD 700-1200', *Antiquity 64,* 629-36

Milne, G, & Hobley B, 1981 *Waterfront Archaeology in Britain & northern Europe,* CBA RR **41**

Milne, G., McKewan, C. & Goodburn, D., 1998, *Nautical Archaeology on the Foreshore,* Royal Commission on the Historical Monuments of England

Milne, G. & Milne, C., 1981, 'Medieval buildings at Trig Lane', *LA 4.2,* 31-7

Milne, G. & Milne, C., 1982, *Medieval Waterfront Development at Trig Lane,* LAMAS SP 8

Morris, J. (ed.), 1975a, *Domesday Book: 3 Surrey*

Morris, J. (ed.), 1975b, *Domesday Book: 11 Middlesex*

Museum of London, 1990, *Museum of London Department of Urban Archaeology annual review 1989*

Museum of London, 2000, *The Archaeology of Greater London: an assessment*

Nash, J., 1981, 'The foundations of London Bridge', *Canadian Geotechnical Journal 3,* 331-356

Norton, E., 1988, 'Moated manor house at Platform Wharf Rotherhithe', *LA 5.15,* 395-401

Olsen, O. et al. (eds), 1995, *Shipshape: essays for Ole Crumlin Pederson*, Roskilde, Denmark

Page, W., 1923, *London: its origins and early development*

Pearce, J., Vince, A. & Jenner, A., 1985, *London-Type Ware*, LAMAS SP 6

Pearce, J. & Vince, A., 1988, *Surrey White wares*, LAMAS SP 10

Pepper, G., 1992, 'An Archaeology of the Jewry in medieval London', *LA 7.1*, 3-6

Pritchard, F., 1984, 'Late Saxon Textiles from the City of London', *Journal of the Society of Medieval Archaeology 28*, 46-76

Proctor, J., 2000, 'Medieval and post-medieval waterfronts at Arundel House, Westminster', *LAMAS 51*, 45-79

RCHM, 1928, *Roman London*, Royal Commission on the Historical Monuments

Ridge, C., 1939, *Records of the Worshipful Company of Shipwrights*

Rigold, S., 1975, 'Structural Aspects of Timber Bridges', *Journal of the Society of Medieval Archaeology 19*, 48-91

Riley, T. (ed.), 1860, *Munimenta Gildhallae Londoniensis*, volume 2 part ii: *Liber Custumarum*

Riley, T. (ed.), 1861, *Liber Albus*

Riley, T. (ed.), 1868, *Memorials of London and London life in the thirteenth, fourteenth and fifteenth centuries*

Robertson, A. (ed.), 1925, *The Laws of the Kings of England from Edmund to Henry I*

Robertson, A. (ed.), 1939, *Anglo-Saxon Charters*

Rosser, G., 1989, *Medieval Westminster 1250-1400*, Oxford

Rule, M., 1982, *The Mary Rose*

Rutledge, T., 1994, 'A twelfth-century building on the London waterfront', *LA 7.7*, 178-83

Salisbury, C., 1991, 'Primitive fish weirs', in G. Good et al. (eds) *Waterfront Archaeology*, CBA RR 74, 88-101

Salzman, L., 1923, *English Industries of the Middle Ages*

Salzman, L., 1952, *Building in England down to 1540*

Scammell, G., 1981, *The World Encompassed*

Schofield, J., 1995, *Medieval London Houses*

Schofield, J., with Maloney, C. (eds), 1998, *Archaeology in the City of London, 1907-91: a guide to the records of excavations by the Museum of London*

Sharpe, R., 1876, *A short account of the worshipful company of shipwrights*

Sharpe, R., 1899-1912, *Calendar of Letter Books of the City of London, A to L*

Sharpe, R., 1913, *Calendar of Coroners Rolls of the City of London*

Sheldon, H., 1974, 'Excavations at Toppings..Wharf, Southwark' *LAMAS 25*, 1-116

Spencer, B, 1996 'Expenditure on ship building and repair...(and) on cargoes of stone by London Bridge, 1381-98', in P Marsden 1996, 209-213

Spencer, B., 1998, *Pilgrim souvenirs and secular badges*

Spurrell, F., 1885, 'Early sites and embankments on the margins of the Thames estuary' *Archaeological Journal*, 270-302

Steane, J. & Foreman, M., 1991, 'The archaeology of medieval fishing tackle', in G. Good et al. (eds), *Waterfront Archaeology*, CBA RR 74, 88-101

Steedman, K., Dyson, T. & Schofield, J., 1992, *Aspects of Saxo-Norman London 3: Bridgehead & Billingsgate,* LAMAS SP 14

Stevens, J. (ed.), 1970, *The Ecclesiastical History of the English Nation*

Strachan, D., 1997, *Dating of some inter-tidal fish-weirs in the Blackwater estuary*, Essex County Council

Tatton-Brown, T., 1974, 'Excavations at the Custom House', *LAMAS 25,* 117-219

Tatton-Brown, T., 1975, 'Excavations at the Custom House: 2', *LAMAS 26,* 103-70

Thomas, A., 1943, *Calendar of Plea and Memoranda rolls AD 1413-37*

Thomas, C., 2002, *The Archaeology of Medieval London*

Thompson, A., Westman, A. & Dyson, T. (eds), 1998, *Archaeology in Greater London 1965-90: a guide to records of excavations by the Museum of London*

Thorpe, B., 1841, *Florentii Wigorniensis Monachi Chronicon ex Chronicis*

Thrupp, S., 1948, *The Merchant Class of Medieval London, 1300-1500*

Thurley, S 1999 *Whitehall Palace: an architectural history of Royal apartments, 1240-1690*, HRP

Tite, W., 1848, *A descriptive catalogue of the antiquities found . . . at the New Royal Exchange, London*

Ulmschneider, K., 2000, 'Settlement, Economy and the 'productive' site: Middle Anglo-Saxon Lincolnshire AD 650-780', *Journal of the Society of Medieval Archaeology 44*, 53-80

Unger, R., 1980, *The Ship in the Medieval Economy 600-1600*

Unwin, G., 1966, (revised edition), *The Gilds and Companies of London*

Van Es, W. & Verwers, W., 1980, *Excavations at Dorestad I: the harbour* Rijksdienst voor het Oudheidkundig Bodemonderzoek no. 9, Amersfoort, Netherlands

Vince, A., 1985, 'Saxon and Medieval Pottery in London: a review', *Journal of the Society of Medieval Archaeology 29*, 25-93

Vince, A., 1990, *Saxon London: an archaeological Investigation*

Vince, A., 1991, *Aspects of Saxo-Norman London: 2 Finds & Environmental evidence*, LAMAS SP 12

Watson, B. & Dyson, T., 2001, *London Bridge: 2000 years of a river crossing*, MoLAS monograph 8

Weinbaum, M., 1976, *The London Eyre of 1276*, London Record Society 12

Wheatley, H. (ed.), 1956, *Stow's Survey of London*

Whitelock, D., 1955, *English Historical Documents, vol 1 c.500-1042*

Whitelock, D., 1972, *The Beginnings of English Society*

Williams, G., 1970, *Medieval London: from commune to capital*

Woodward-Smith, N. & Schofield, J., 1977, 'A late fifteenth-century account for a wharf at Vauxhall, London', *LAMAS 28*, 278-91

Wroe-Brown, R., 1999, 'The Saxon origins of Queenhithe', *LAMAS 50*, 12-16

ABBREVIATIONS

Archaeol J	*Archaeological Journal*
CBA RR	*Council for British Archaeology research report series*
BAR	*British Archaeological Reports*
EH AR	*English Heritage: archaeological report series*
HRP	*Historic Royal Palaces*
LA	*The London Archaeologist (quarterly journal)*
LAMAS	*Annual transactions of the London and Middlesex Archaeological Society*
LAMAS SP	*London and Middlesex Archaeological Society: Special Paper Series*
London J	*London Journal*
London Rec Soc	*London Record Society*
Med Arch	*Journal of the Society of Medieval Archaeology*
MoL	*Museum of London*
MoLAS mono	*Museum of London Archaeology Service: monograph series*
MoLAS AS	*Museum of London Archaeology Service: archaeological studies series*

INDEX

Antwerp, Belgium, 74, 130, 132, 158, 175, 180

Africa, 132

aliens, 9, 72, 75, 124, 125, 147, 156, 158, 163

America, 159, 164, 174, 175

Arundel House, 18, 21, 141

artefact studies, *see also* coins, pottery, 16, 28, 32, 35-6, 70, 86, 90, 95-6, 111-12, 129-31, 132, 170

Asia, 159

balance, 131

ballast, 157, 176

Bankside, 20, 26

barrels, 73, 148, 166

Baynard's Castle (Castle Baynard), 11, 14, 15, 23, 92, 116, 129, 142, 151-52, 153, 156

Bayonne, France, 118, 125, 133

Benfleet, Essex, 41

Bergen, Norway, 14, 70

Bergen-op-Zoom, Netherlands, 158

Bilbao, Spain, 133

Billingsgate, 15, 16, 20, 25, 42, 57-8, 64, 83, 97, 102, 116, 122, 126, 127, 133

Black Death, 10, 115, 117-8, 140, 153-4

Blackfriars wrecks, 12, 13, 23, 112, 150, 169

boats and barges, 37, 48, 60, 84-5, 88, 91, 100-3, 105-6, 114, 125-27, 150, 151-52, 156, 160, 162, 180

boat timbers, 14, 22, 23, 24, 25, 26, 27, 28, 49-50, 58-9, 167-8, 170, 171

Bosat, 75

Boss Alley, 141, 153-4, 179

Bordeaux, France, 118, 134, 162, 163, 164, 175, 180

Boston, Lincs, 9, 158

Boulogne, France, 115, 119

Bread Street, 150

Bremer Cog, 12-13, 171

Bridge ward, 102, 116, 127, 150, 182

Bridge Warden's Accounts, 168, 169

Bristol,   159, 160, 164

Broken Wharf,   122, 136

Bruges, Belgium, 130, 147

Bull Wharf, *see* Queenhithe

Calais, France, 34, 117, 132, 155, 158

Cinque Ports, *see also* Dover, Rye, Sandwich, Winchelsea, 63, 97, 105, 106, 118, 131

cloth, *see also* dyehouse, 74, 92, 93, 122, 133, 153, 156, 158, 159, 160, 180, 181, 182

coins and coinage, 16, 33, 34, 35, 36, 40, 41, 44, 50, 55, 62, 95, 131, 183

Covent Garden, 17, 18, 30

customs regulations and accounts, 8, 32, 43, 59-62, 72-5, 89, 97-100, 122-23, 129, 148, 159-60

Custom House, 10, 11, 14, 25, 153, 180, 183

Customs Officers, 7, 15, 30, 32, 73, 122-24, 148, 156

defences, 40-1, 47, 52-5, 62-4, 74, 88, 92, 116, 118-19, 120, 121, 155, 156, 178

dendrochronology, 16, 26, 37, 44, 45, 47, 56, 63, 64, 69-70, 76-81, 82, 168

Denmark, 10, 12, 47, 53-5, 62, 74, 147

Dorestad, Netherlands, 34, 35-6

Domesday Survey, 65-6

Dover, Kent, 63

Dowgate, 12, 17, 19, 20, 24, 127, 150, 158, 173, 178

dyes and dyehouse, 25, 92, 11, 133, 152, 179, 182

encroachment on Thames, chronology of, 11-12, 18-20, 90-1

embankments, 20, 21, 23, 24, 25, 35, 36, 37, 44-7, 57, 79

fatalities, 40, 64, 85, 87, 88, 100-102, 118, 125-7, 147

Faversham, Kent, 47, 97, 166

Fennings Wharf, excavations, *see also* London Bridge, 16, 26, 56

Flanders, 61, 131, 133, 158, 160

Flemings, 125, 131, 136, 147, 158, 162, 181, 182

Florence, Italy, 126, 130, 162

fish, 33, 39, 134, 148, 151, 153, 158, 182